DATE DUE			
DEC 17 85			
MAR 1 2 1986			
OCT 1 2 1988			
DEC 8 1992			
MAY 4 1996			
MAY 2 1 1997			

The Starr-Weiner Report

ON SEX & SEXUALITY IN THE MATURE YEARS

Bernard D. Starr, Ph.D. and Harris S. Goldstein, M.D.
Human Development and Behavior: Psychology in Nursing

Bernard D. Starr, Ph.D., editor
The Psychology of School Adjustment

Bernard D. Starr, Ph.D., Marcella Bakur Weiner, Ed.D., and Marilyn Rabetz
The Projective Assessment of Aging Method

Marcella Bakur Weiner, Ed.D., Albert J. Brok, Ph.D., and Alvin M. Snadowsky, Ph.D.
Working with the Aged

Title: **The Starr-Weiner Report**

ON SEX & SEXUALITY IN THE MATURE YEARS

Bernard D. Starr, PH.D.
& Marcella Bakur Weiner, ED.D.

STEIN AND DAY/*Publishers*/New York

First published in 1981
Copyright © 1981 by Bernard D. Starr, Ph.D., and
Marcella Bakur Weiner, Ed.D.
Designed by Louis A. Ditizio
Printed in the United States of America
STEIN AND DAY/*Publishers*
Scarborough House
Briarcliff Manor, N.Y. 10510

Library of Congress Cataloging in Publication Data

Starr, Bernard D.
    The Starr-Weiner report on sex and sexuality in the mature years.

    Bibliography: p.
    Includes index.
    1. Aged—United States—Sexual behavior.
I. Weiner, Marcella Bakur. II. Title.
III. Title: Sex and sexuality in the mature years.
HQ30.S72   306.7'0880565   80-51788
ISBN 0-8128-2750-3   AACR2

We dedicate this book to our children—Lorin and Jason Starr, and Larry and Steven Bakur—in the hope that they will inherit the legacy of a truly ageless society

Acknowledgments

Without the dedicated assistance of many people throughout the United States this book would have remained a vision rather than a reality. Some not only offered their personal generosity but persisted in the face of local opposition to a sex survey of older people.

We extend special appreciation to Rena Modell (San Jose, California), Josie Greene (Macon, Georgia), and Fran Parks (Chicago, Illinois), who initiated our contacts in their respective regions. Dr. Ken Dychtwald, founder of the Association for Humanistic Gerontology, was instrumental in putting us in contact with gerontologists nationwide who were of enormous help.

Judy Zacharia, Helen Metz, Mike Williams, John Etman and Lorin Starr were invaluable assistants in the data processing. We are grateful to Dr. Robert Buckhout, Director of the Center for Responsive Psychology at Brooklyn College of the City University of New York, for lending his expertise in overseeing the computer analysis of the data. Dr. Jeanne Teresi's critical evaluation of the manuscript provided welcome and comforting support. Will Weiner participated in almost every phase of the project. His unstinting availability as well as his clinical skills were most appreciated. We thank Jana Starr for her careful proofreading of the text and statistical tables.

We are also indebted to the following people who wholeheartedly gave of their time and energy: Beverly Aaltonen, Helen Ansley, Jan Arie, Barbara Arnold, Share Bane, Diane Bercovitz, Ruth Bograd, Marx Bowens, Jennie Byrer, Marion Corbett, Connie Crosby, John Duryea, Selma Einhorn, Virginia Lukens Elgin, Mary Francis, Dr. Marion Rudin Frank, Jerrie Folie, Leicha Gelman, Roslyn Gold, Jim

Grant, Lorraine Gruen, Rosamond Gumpert, Glynda Hall, Viola Haywood, Dr. Ruth Hersh, Ruth Hetzel, Florence Holmes, Jack Jensen, Andrew Katzanis, Jack Kessler, Dr. Martha Lang, Karen Lowenstein, Mary Jane Lyman, Ann MacConnacie, Sylvia Mendel, Pat Miller, Adele Murphy, Margaret Nicholson, Kai Pedersen, Joe Piros, Dr. Lenore Powell, Dr. Clara Pratt, Dr. Glenn Rothfeld, April Rubel, Philip Ruello, Adele Sachs, Dr. John Saunders, Marvin Schreiber, Emma Schultz, Kathy Sherman, Lynn Sofer, Helene Sokol, Mary Ellen Spencer, Marcy Stanley, Wilma Steckel, Steve Terner, Mary Tipsword, Dr. Hanno Weisbrod, Linda Williams, Dr. Barbara Witchel, Merrill Witten, Agnes Wohl, Ruth Wolfe, and Ruth Zimmer.

The older people themselves who participated in this survey deserve special acknowledgment. Their willingness to break through stereotypes and share private thoughts, feelings, and behaviors has revealed possibilities for human fulfillment not previously known and of enormous importance for young and old alike. They also taught us that, indeed, people at any age can be passionately committed to life.

Contents

The Starr-Weiner Report

ON **SEX &**
SEXUALITY
IN **THE MATURE**
YEARS

1

Sex and Aging: The Myth and the Reality

In the minds of most Americans, sex and older people usually don't go together. No one likes the thought of growing old, especially in a youth-worshipping culture like ours. Rather than thinking of gray hair and wrinkles as the signs of seasoning and grace that come from years of experiencing life, they are equated with decline and decay.

Imagine two older people sitting close to each other, holding hands and stroking each other's fingers until the disapproving looks of some people around them make them abruptly pull away from each other. Hands now in laps they gaze at each other intensely, obviously embarrassed. What both the couple and the observers are probably thinking is: "Act your age." Yet what does it mean to act your age?

Along with the belief that all old people are the same—old—comes the notion that they do not think about sex. Rarely is there talk about their actually engaging in sex or enjoying it. They are converted into neuter beings, objects. And as objects they are perceived as lifeless, devoid of all common human feelings. Or they are infantalized, made into something "cute," remarked about at social gatherings for the mere fact that they're still alive.

A young medical student at a lecture on sex and aging asked us: "But how can I tell an elderly male patient to be excited about his wife when I think how unexciting it must be to think of and see flabby breasts, an unshapely body, and an old face? I wonder how it will be in thirty years when I feel that way about my wife, and how she will feel about me?" We asked the student if it was possible that thirty years of marriage could itself be a turn-on. He said he had never thought along those lines. Another student in the same group admitted he did not know much about the sexual practices of older patients, adding that he would be embarrassed to inquire, since "old people don't like to talk

3

about something they don't do any more." Asked how he knew they no longer had sex, he shrugged and replied that he "just assumed so."

Dr. Alex Comfort couldn't have been nearer the mark when he caustically observed: "Older people weren't asked in surveys about their sexual activity because everyone knew they had none, and they were assumed to have none because nobody asked."

In television commercials older people are busy pushing vitamins, and drugs for constipation and arthritis, or we see them extolling the virtues of their retirement communities. The message is clear: Getting older means loss—loss of nutrients, loss of health, loss of one's long-standing style of living. Quite a different picture is painted of our younger people. They already have youth and vitality, so the ads tell us. All they need is the icing on the cake—the right mate, the flashy car, the appliances for easy living. Both these portrayals of young and old are equally stereotypes. They reflect our prejudices, our fears, and a good measure of our wishful thinking. They do not show a realistic picture of what life is about at any age, not just because of the picture they present but because of what they leave out.

Our personal and professional contacts over the years had begun to make us suspect that there was more going on sexually in the later years than met the eye. We knew that society did not quite accept the idea of sexuality for older people, so it occurred to us that many of the elderly were just not showing that side of their lives.

How could we turn this around? Wary of studies which use short-hand approaches to get at complex human psychology, we discarded the notion of designing research tools like true and false or multiple choice questionnaires. To allow respondents to report the inner experience of sex as well as behavior, we put together a 50-item open-ended questionnaire.

We were committed to finding the truth. But would older people even respond to our detailed questions?

There is the belief that older people are naturally suspicious; that they won't answer too many questions on any subject, least of all questions about the most intimate aspects of their lives. How would they react, then, to questions on masturbation, orgasm, fantasy, nudity, and sexual intercourse? We were reminded of the comment by a prominent psychoanalyst who, when writing about counseling older adults, declared firmly that "it is inappropriate to ask a 60-year-old married woman if she masturbates." Why this was inappropriate was not explained. But at the time we read the warning and did not question it; somehow, it seemed right. After all, how could you talk about masturbation to the generation that told their children they would go blind or crazy from the practice?

Yet as we listened carefully to the older men and women we encountered during our study, a very different picture emerged. Consider, for example, the elderly man from the Midwest who stood up at one of our community center lectures for people over 60 and said emotionally: "I was a widower for five years. Six months ago I remarried and everyone said to me, 'It's good that you married again because you need companionship.' Everyone tells me about companionship. It gets me mad. Sure I want companionship, but I also got married for sex. I always had an active sex life and still do, and I'm 82 years old."

"What is a good sexual experience?" we asked in our survey, and a 61-year-old woman from California responded: "To be really horny with a partner who is just as horny. To take plenty of time and when you can't stand it another minute, make it!" These comments hardly reflect the expected concerns of older people, yet we found such responses to be commonplace in our survey.

Clearly our society suffers from a split in its perceptions. Intellectually, we may assume that sexual behavior continues in some form throughout the mature years, but we seem unable to accept this on an emotional level. Our fear that our sexuality—alive and well in our 20s, 30s, and 40s—should suddenly atrophy and die as we move into the later decades, makes no more sense than the notion that our ability to enjoy food or smells or conversation will disappear. Many such functions do change as we age, but there is no reason to assume that the *potential* for sexual pleasure should fall off any more rapidly than other capacities; yet we persist in assuming that this is what happens. Just as the small child giggles at the very thought of his parents "doing it," an otherwise sophisticated adult is hard pressed to imagine his 70-year-old mother and father—or, worse, his mother and her gentleman friend—engaging in sex.

The responses we received from people all over the United States, from different religions and diverse educational and economic levels, raised questions about the very nature of aging. We began to realize that even the most favorable portrayals had been wrong. Most important, our findings raised questions about all the writings on sexuality from Kinsey onward. For example, it has been accepted as an indisputable fact that frequency of sexual intercourse declines markedly from early adulthood. Kinsey reported a frequency of 2.2 times per week for his 30-year-old group and .5 for his 60-year-olds. Yet our respondents aged 60–91 report average frequencies of 1.4 times a week. This figure is comparable to Kinsey's 40-year-olds. When asked how often they would like to have sexual relations, the frequencies our respondents mention are even higher. Since Kinsey's young adult subjects are the same generation as our older respondents, it appears that frequency of sexual activity does not decline all that sharply when the same generation is followed.

Other surprising findings of our survey are:

- a strong continuing interest in sex;
- the belief that sex is important for physical and mental well-being;
- the perception of most of the respondents that sex is as good now as when they were younger;
- that for a large number, both male and female, sex is *better* in the later years;
- orgasm is considered an essential part of the sexual experience;
- most of the women are orgasmic and always have been;
- the orgasm for many is stronger now than when younger;
- masturbation is an acceptable outlet for sexual needs;
- for a majority, living together without marriage is acceptable;
- an overwhelming number of respondents, including widows, widowers, divorcees and singles, are sexually active;
- most are satisfied with their sex lives;
- many vary their sexual practices to achieve satisfaction;
- for a surprising number of older people, oral sex is considered the most exciting sexual experience;
- respondents typically show little embarrassment or anxiety about sex;
- most enjoy nudity with their partners;

- the ideal or fantasized lover for most, particularly women, is close to their own age;
- most see their sex lives remaining pretty much the same as they grow even older.

We realized that these people could not all be lying, either to themselves or to us; nor were they suffering from memory loss. Freed of child-rearing and other midlife responsibilities, their lives—and particularly their sex lives—were opening up to new and exciting possibilities.

Unfortunately, this wasn't true for all the elderly we encountered. Some, who had cast themselves in society's mold of the older person, were living in a wasteland that senselessly denied them pleasure and fulfillment. And it was they, we felt, who could perhaps most benefit from what we were learning.

When older adults come out of the closet and begin to share their true feelings and experiences, as so many did for our survey, we will all be less likely to harbor these misconceptions or to be shocked at the forthright sexuality of people like the 74-year-old woman who told us: "The young people think they discovered sex. I've tried everything in my life and haven't heard of anything new."

Old age represents a big chunk of life, one of the biggest. Many people today live well into their 80s, which means that the years from 60 to 85 represent more than one-quarter of the life span. Eminent gerontologist Dr. Carl Eisdorfer tells us that cardiovascular research will soon stretch the life span to the ninth decade for those reaching the later years. This means that most of us can look forward to living one-third of our lives after passing our sixtieth birthday. In comparison, childhood lasts about eleven years, adolescence eight years (12–20) and early adulthood fifteen years (20–35).

The Plus Side

There are currently 21 million old people in the United States, and the figure is growing each year. By the year 2024 it is estimated that there will be 50 million older people. Contrary to the popular mythology that associates "old" with "sick," the overwhelming majority of elderly are healthy and live independently. Only 5 percent of all the elderly—including the very old and very sick—live in institutions or nursing homes. This means that at present 19 million, or 95 percent, are living and functioning in the community. Of these, 70 percent are home owners, a statistic which further demonstrates their independence.

Given the expected advances in medicine and health care, what can *you* look forward to? What is your maturity like now and what will it be like later?

Every period of life involves both losses and benefits. When you went from babyhood to childhood, you lost the dependency of infancy, the intense attention of parents and other adults, and the security of a nondemanding existence. But you gained some independence, a firmer sense of self, new skills to master your world, and a growing sense of confidence in relating to yourself and others. Other transitions have had, or will have, similar pains and losses: childhood to adolescence, adolescence to young adulthood, and subsequent stages of early and middle adulthood. In recognizing these losses, few of us would be inclined to overlook the gains. Who, for example, would want to stay an awkward adolescent forever? It is only when looking at the later years that our attention shifts to the negatives at the expense of the positives. We all have a stake in changing the image of older people because we will all be there someday. If some can achieve fulfillment and excitement, why not everyone?

The mature years are also potentially the most *conscious* part of life. As children, we are victims of the circumstances around us—our parents, our economic conditions, where we happen to live, who we come to know. As adults, we are still shaped by these often accidental circumstances. We then get trapped chasing our goals, without, usually, giving them thought. How many times have you looked back and said, "Why did I spend so many years doing that?" or "Why didn't I wake up sooner?" Most of us get on a track in our youth and just keep moving, too fast to make conscious decisions at critical junctions along the way. Then, suddenly, the mature years are staring at us. It is here that we must remind ourselves that there is still a big piece of life ahead.

We no longer have to be driven. Now we can be the drivers, fully conscious of our needs and our actions. We can look back, we can look forward, and we can look into ourselves. We can decide what we want and we can make things happen. With awareness comes personal power.

Cuddling for Life

Despite what society has conditioned us to believe, our data clearly show that the need to be touched, stroked, cuddled, and caressed is a lifelong one. Physical contact is a basic human need, and that need is as powerful in the 60s, 70s, and 80s as it is in infancy, childhood, and early adulthood.

When babies don't get enough fondling they look and act depressed. Their appearance is one of intense sadness; their eyes are glazed and unresponsive. Babies who are never touched and cuddled have been known to die from this kind of neglect. Animals, too, seem to need physical expressions of love. Baby monkeys who are not cuddled by their mothers become depressed and die, or, at best, behave abnormally. If the monkey were human, we would say he was neurotic. The "normal" monkey got the cuddling he needed.

Sex is a psychological as well as a physical need. We need sex as much for our state of mind as for the state of our body. Throughout life sex serves as a stage on which a host of emotions are played out. When we deny or move away from our sexuality we not only lose an important source of physical pleasure, we also cut off a whole range of feelings. We frequently use sex as an emotional outlet following anger or distance in a relationship, as the vehicle for reestablishing contact. The mutual touching and caressing are ways of welcoming the other person back. Similarly, sexual contact is a way of soothing and being soothed. When you've had a hard day you want to be held, rocked, stroked, made to feel special and lovable, like the baby at the mother's breast, truly cared for and adored.

All of these behaviors and emotions are a part of us when we are young *and* when we are old. The need to play out our angers, our fears, our frustrations, our joys—our need to master, to bargain, to manipulate, to dominate, to submit—is a deeply human one. It stays with us from birth to death.

Energy Dammed Up

Energy needs a place to go. When sexual energy is denied the outlet of behavior that can provide sexual release, it goes into other areas. This process, called displacement, may result in illness—diarrhea, ulcers, heartburn, arthritis, neuralgia, and many other complaints familiar to older people. This is not to say that there are not also physical causes associated with such illness. But it has long been recognized that the mind and body go together. When they fit, things go well. When there is a gap—for example, when the body wants to discharge energy and the mind refuses—there's a problem. If you remain unaware of the problem, you may become physically ill. The illness forces you to pay attention to your body without really listening to what the body is shouting.

Older people "acting their age" are afraid to listen to their bodies. Told by society that it is unbecoming to feel sexual, they are told the opposite about feeling ill. It is more than just acceptable to become sick as one gets older, it is expected. Many health professionals try to console the older person: "What do you expect? You're getting on in years." And so many of us, when we get older, fall sick and play the "patient," a safer role than the sexual one.

A middle-aged woman told us a story that demonstrates how the process of displacement can be reversed if a person's sexual energy finds a more appropriate outlet. Her 73-year-old widowed mother had numerous physical complaints. "If it wasn't her arthritis acting up, then it was her digestion, back, or aching legs. When one complaint stopped, another one started up. There was no relief." The daughter felt understandably burdened since her brother and sister lived farther away. One day, without any previous hints, her mother moved in with a man her own age. Almost immediately her complaints vanished.

Energy Redistributed

It has often been claimed that people who have been sexually active in their earlier years tend to remain active in later life. Probably so. But what has not been sufficiently recognized is that as our biological clocks change with age, it's not necessarily for the better or for the worse. And change is always dynamic; it signals a state of movement, a lifeforce at work. People who have been sexually responsive all their lives will in later years still be sexual. But they will be different. Maturity brings change. But how the change comes about and what it means to the person is still largely unexplored.

The reports of sexual athletics in popular literature imply that "more" is "better." But is it? If you eat less food and have fewer meals than you used to, is that better or worse? If you have respect for your body and are aware of nutrition you may eat less frequently but consume healthier, more enriched and less destructive foods. The love, energy, and pleasure of your culinary excursions may far surpass earlier binges on junk food. Similarly, with lovemaking it is the quality of the experiences, not the frequency, which is the measure of satisfaction. As a 72-year-old woman explained, speaking for many of our respondents, "your sex is so much more relaxed, I know my body better and we know each other better—sex is unhurried and the best in our lives."

The New Sexuality

Everyone is interested in sex. Sex, after all, is the lifeforce. That's why the thought of losing sex is so frightening for most people. This fear usually begins in the 40s (for some, even earlier), when we become aware of the signs of aging: the undeniable puckers near the mouth, the fine lines at the corners of the eyes, the gray hairs. It is then that we begin to question the worth of our bodies. In a recent study older people were asked to assign a dollar value to different body parts for the purpose of collecting on the loss of that part through an accident. A typical negative male attitude was reflected in the comment of one person, who said, laughing: "Now if you asked me about the worth of .my penis forty years ago, I would have said millions. Today, $1.98 and it's yours!"

In popular usage "sex" means a physical act or event. Alfred Kinsey described it more technically as the "sources" of physical arousal and the "outlets" for releasing the physical tension (orgasm). Most people

don't feel they have had a real sexual experience unless there is intercourse or orgasm. This narrow definition of sex has created problems
for many people, limiting their sexual experiences and dooming them
to fear and anxiety about the future. Usually, when younger people
worry about what sex will be like in the later years, it is the anticipation
of losing the physical powers of sex that generates much of the anxiety.

The vibrant responses we received to our survey suggest, among
other things, an entirely different concept of sexuality. Sexuality is a
quality of the person, an energy force that is expressed in every aspect
of the person's being. The way you talk and move, your vitality, your
ability to enjoy life, are all parts of your sexuality. The physical act of
sex—with its beginning, middle and (most of all) its end—is only one
way of expressing this sexuality.

Surely, sexual intercourse is a desired part of the sexual experience
for our respondents, and most achieve that goal regularly. But those
who overreact to the inevitable occasional failure can make a false
identification of failure with age. Failure to achieve an erection for the
male can occur at any age. After the age of 40 this may occur more
frequently, but as many respondents report, other stimulation can
compensate to maintain the erection. Some men, as our responses
indicate, regard the spontaneous, firm erection as a birthright. When it
fails to happen with the ease of the explosive years of adolescence some
men interpret their changed sexual response as a decline in their masculinity or worth as a person. Others who focus on pleasuring rather than
any one event experience no decline while achieving sexual gratification in a variety of ways throughout their lives. The flexibility of many
of our respondents explains why two-thirds of them report that sex is
the same or better in the later years.

A Step Forward

Many of our sexually active and sexually fulfilled respondents have
apparently arrived at a broader, deeper concept of sexuality on their
own. They talk about the pleasure of being unhurried in the sexual
experience, of not feeling they have to perform or reach a specific goal.
Some of the men who at times fail to have an erection find other ways
of satisfying their partners and themselves and don't let their "impotence" spoil their sharp enjoyment of sex. This heightened apprecia-

tion is also part of the reason why so many of our respondents told us that sex gets better in the later years. Interestingly, many women are remarkably undisturbed by even the lack of intercourse *per se*, if their partners continue to participate and share the mutual satisfaction of the sexual experience.

The Changing Woman

Two statistical realities of the later years are that there are more women than men, and that most of these women live alone. It is also true that older women have fewer options than older men for companionship, intimacy, and sexuality.

In the days when women accepted sex as the man's domain and themselves as passive and submissive partners, many of them repressed their sexual desires. It was, in fact, considered ladylike to do so. Today, most women—including many older women—recognize that they have at least as much passion and sexuality as men, and that they have choices. They don't have to accept the traditional male view of sex-as-performance, with its emphasis on how much and how often. In our survey we found that women are listening to their own needs and reaching for quality and variety. Speaking of the impact of the women's movement on her sex life, a 68-year-old woman reported to us: "Now I wake him up when I'm in the mood and afterward I even roll over and sometimes fall back asleep. He's been doing that for years!"

Up until age 60 the sexual responses of women change very little, and even after 60 the changes are surprisingly gradual. Why then do we characterize older women as sexless? And what happens to women when they cut off their sexual feelings? Where does this energy go?

Our data show that the sexual destiny of women is still tied to men. Women live longer than men and, in addition, many women marry older men who die leaving them widowed (3 out of 4 wives eventually become widows). Then, too, many men withdraw entirely from sexual activities because they fear they will be impotent or that they will have a heart attack during sexual relations. In any event, many women over the age of 60 find themselves without a partner and without regular sexual outlets. All our observations point to the fact that what is most crucial to the woman, and her only barrier to a more active sex life, is the availability of a man. Yet, on a more positive note, our data also indicate that changes are taking place. Women are becoming more open to masturbation as an acceptable outlet; many are also having heterosexual relations outside of marriage or are seeking other solutions to the problem of the uneven ratio.

Sex after 60: The Facts of Life

If you walk into any bookstore you will find shelves piled high with volumes on sex. But hardly any of these titles will address themselves to sex and older adults, and none of them will provide a factual account based on actual questioning of older adults.

Books like Dr. Isadore Rubin's *Sexual Life after Sixty* and Dr. Robert Butler and Myrna Lewis's *Love and Sex after Sixty* are supportive and encouraging about the prospects for sex in the later years, but since neither intended to investigate the sexual experiences of people over sixty, new data is not presented.

Starting with Kinsey, there have been a number of major works on sex that have made sparse reference to sex in the later years. Some have had more to say than others, and even where there is no comment at all something is still being said. Omission is a powerful statement.

Alfred Kinsey's two volumes, *Sexuality in the Human Male* (1948) and *Sexuality in the Human Female* (1953), contain the most extensive data ever published on sexual behavior, and most of what we know today about sex comes from these reports. Using detailed interviews or "histories," as he called them, with some 12,000 subjects, Kinsey and his associates established norms for different sources of sexual stimulation and sexual release. Although he included older people in his sample (his subjects ranged in age from 2 to 90), the emphasis was on 16-to-55-year-olds. In fact, Kinsey himself said that older groups were inadequately represented. For this reason he did not include his data on older subjects in many of his statistical analyses. In the two volumes, comprising 1,646 pages, older women are discussed on four pages and older men on three pages. In other places where Kinsey talks about "older" people, he actually means subjects between 50 and 60 years of age.

His discussion of subjects over 60 focuses almost exclusively on the frequency of sexual intercourse which, we are told, declines in the later years. Kinsey also reports that by age 70, one-fourth of the men in his sample were impotent. The possible causes of the impotence are not explored. Similarly, he offers no explanations or speculations about his observation that there was virtually no masturbation in his small sample of elderly men after age 70 (our results say otherwise). Did these older men lack interest? Were they incapable of sexual arousal? Was guilt or moral prohibition stopping them from masturbating? The descriptive "facts" do not give meaning to the data.

Perhaps Kinsey's greatest contribution, and one that has a bearing on sexuality in the later years, was his description of the different patterns of male and female sexual development. He clearly established the sexual superiority of the female. Males, he said, reach their peak early in adolescence and then show a steady decline throughout the life cycle. The rate of decline is fairly consistent at every age; thus it is not greater in the later years than earlier. Females reach their peak in the late 20s or 30s. They remain at that plateau through the 60s, after which they may show a slight decline in sexual response capability.

The implication of these different patterns was clear to Kinsey. Men and women of the same age are mismatched sexually. In the later years the discrepancy is greatest. As Kinsey stated:

> Many of the younger married females reported that they would be satisfied with lower coital rates than their husbands wanted. On the other hand, in the later years of marriage, many of the females had expressed the wish that they could have coitus more frequently than their husbands were desiring it.

Kinsey the biologist gave us mountains of descriptive information about sexual behavior, but he did not pose the important psychological questions. How is sex experienced? What is the meaning and importance of sex at different ages? How does sex feel at different times of our life? How important is orgasm as compared to other varieties of sexual experience? How does it feel to be sexually frustrated? How does masturbation feel, as opposed to other sexual acts? These and similar questions relate to the phenomenology of sex, or how it is experienced, rather than to the frequency and variety of performance, which can never tell the whole story.

Sex is a total human experience, not just a biological function, and

Kinsey's norms are presented as biological facts of life. Is it a natural function of aging that 30 percent of his male sample were inactive sexually by age 70? Or is this fact a function of depression, a Victorian attitude toward aging and sex, disengagement from life, or the result of other psychological and social forces? Our data show a much higher level of sexuality among older men comparable to Kinsey's younger groups. Has human biology changed over the last twenty-five years? Hardly. More likely reasons for the discrepancy between Kinsey's data and ours can be found in the changed attitudes toward sex (to which Kinsey made the greatest contribution).

The descriptive, biological approach to sex contributes to a distortion we mentioned earlier. That sexual intercourse is undertaken less frequently at 35 or 75 than at 25 does not mean that it is better or more meaningful at 25. It is possible to have many mechanical, unsatisfying sexual experiences. Frequency of orgasm or ejaculation is not the ultimate measure of good sex. We need to know about the phenomenology, the experience of sex at every age in order to arrive at a full understanding of sexuality. This is especially important when it comes to understanding sex in the later years, because so much emphasis has been placed on biological aging.

For example, the raw fact of less frequency of sexual intercourse could not tell you what this 69-year-old woman writes: "Sex is much more enjoyable and satisfying now. It used to be more frequent, and while pleasurable it has now become less frequent, *but* each time lasts longer and has much greater sensory impact during climax for both of us."

The Kinsey reports set the direction for much of the sex research of the 1950s and 60s. Kinsey had stated the facts. Now others would debate them and try to prove him right or wrong. On the heels of the Kinsey reports, Duke University began, in 1954, a longterm study of 250 people between the ages of 60 and 94. The only two areas of sex that were investigated in this primarily medical study of aging clearly showed Kinsey's influence: frequency of sexual intercourse and interest in sex, "interest" being more narrowly defined than in Kinsey's work as interest in sexual intercourse alone. On both scores their subjects showed a decline with age. "The decline of activity in the group was such that by the late 80s the frequency of intercourse approached zero." The fact that substantial numbers of their older subjects remained sexually active (38 percent at the beginning of the study) was underplayed against the observation of overall decline. The crucial question today, one that we will focus on in evaluating our survey, is not why some older people are active sexually but why others are not. We could find no differences between the two groups except that in our survey the sexually active and interested respondents were generally more turned on to life, while the others had pulled back. Certainly the Duke finding that older women are less interested in sex than older men is not true of our respondents. Our data clearly show older women to be equally if not *more* interested in sex than older men.

In the field of general sex research after Kinsey, sex became a wide-open subject. Questions even more probing and personal than those Kinsey had posed could now be asked: What positions do you prefer? How do you masturbate? What are your techniques of oral sex? Have you experienced anal intercourse?

In the tradition of Kinsey's biological emphasis, study after study appeared focusing on frequency and varieties of different sexual practices, and greater details and nuances of sexual behavior. In this race to the ultimate survey, older adults were left even further behind in the dust. They still weren't thought to be sexual, and their experience certainly didn't relate to the emerging swinging scene of experimentation. After all, revolutions have traditionally been for the young. But our beliefs about older people are so burdened by assumptions that we have not bothered to even inquire. When we did ask questions we found older people to be very much in tune with the sexual revolution. Our data show that older people are very much part of the times; as much as young people, they respond to shifting tides.

Any doubts or mysteries about physical responses during sexual activities or how they were experienced were put to rest by William Masters and Virginia Johnson. Kinsey had dared to ask the forbidden questions; Masters and Johnson would go a step further and observe sex, first with prostitutes, then with volunteers, and ultimately with people complaining of sexual problems. Just as Kinsey was meticulous in recording reported frequencies of orgasm, Masters and Johnson recorded all the nuances of bodily reactions. They would even interrupt their subjects during intercourse, masturbation, and other activities to take readings—blood flow, condition and appearance of the genitals, how the sensations were experienced. No more vague recollections from unreliable memories.

Masters and Johnson confirmed that the orgasm from masturbation is physiologically the same as the orgasm from intercourse, both following the same cycle of excitement, plateau, orgasm, and resolution. Also, Freud's distinction between the clitoral and vaginal orgasm was dealt the final blow; all female orgasms, Masters and Johnson told us, stem from the same source—the clitoris. Though they may be experienced in different locales, there is no such thing as a more mature orgasm.

In *Human Sexual Response* (1966) Masters and Johnson presented the details of physiological response during intercourse and masturbation from excitement to resolution. Their second volume, *Human Sexual Inadequacy* (1970), reports the application of what they had learned to the treatment of sexual problems, mainly impotence, premature ejaculation, and frigidity. The success of their sex therapy posed a challenge to existing therapies that explained sexual problems in terms of broader personality difficulties. Masters and Johnson were able to achieve success over relatively short therapeutic periods. For example, impotence and premature ejaculation they found could often be cured over a period of weeks and the success would be lasting.

Masters and Johnson make some definitive points about sex in the later years although they studied only thirty-one people over the age of 60 in *Human Sexual Response* (1966), twenty males and eleven females. First, their conclusion that impotence and premature ejaculation are mostly psychological in origin makes their therapy program as applicable to older men as to younger ones. Since these problems result in considerable sexual deprivation for many older men and women, it is encouraging to know that help is available and that the success rate is high. Their suggestion to older men on how to make possible more frequent sexual intercourse is also useful. Citing Eastern lovemaking techniques, they point out that it is not necessary for the man to ejaculate every time. Some men need rest periods of several days before they can have another erection. By holding back, the frequency of intercourse is more under the individual's control and can be better adapted to his partner's needs.

Another successful technique, recommended for helping women achieve orgasm during lovemaking and intercourse, applies equally well to older and younger women. It is well known that few women have any difficulty reaching orgasm through masturbation. By observing the woman during masturbation, the man can model his lovemaking techniques after the reliable way in which she brings herself to orgasm.

Masters and Johnson report one finding that our survey disputes. They say that hormonal changes in older women cause alterations in the vaginal wall making sexual intercourse painful. This "fact" about sex and aging is also widely reported elsewhere. Yet few of our female respondents report any pain or discomfort during sexual intercourse.

The eleven older women studied by Masters and Johnson hardly offer an adequate sample from which to draw far-reaching conclusions, and Masters and Johnson themselves acknowledge this point. Yet, it is understandable that writers hungry for facts about older people would jump on any tidbit and magnify its importance. On closer examination Masters and Johnson point out that three of the eleven women over age 60 produced vaginal lubrication similar to that of women in their twenties. Of even greater importance is their observation that these three women had "maintained active sexual connections once or twice a week throughout their mature years." Finally, Masters and Johnson's conclusion on the topic of age and female sexuality should be underlined: "In short, there is no time limit drawn by advancing years to female sexuality."

The Hite Report (1976), widely proclaimed the first and last word on the new female sexuality, starts with the premise that no one had ever surveyed women as to how they felt about sex. This no doubt is true. But it is equally true that no one had ever surveyed anyone, male or female, as to how they *felt* about sex; the emphasis had always been on statistical counts.

Shere Hite's 56-item open-ended questionnaire explores the feelings, attitudes, preferences, and experiences of women with regard to intercourse, masturbation, orgasm, homosexuality, etc. Hite asserts the sexual declaration of women's independence by emphasizing the ease with which women achieve orgasm through masturbation. An orgasm is an orgasm, says Hite, echoing the findings of Masters and

Johnson. An orgasm achieved through intercourse is not necessarily a better orgasm, she assures us, and offers countless quotes from female respondents that would seem to confirm her point. Other responses in *The Hite Report* show that women, every bit as much as men, want pleasure and orgasm in sex. Furthermore, women can orgasm (Hite coins the new usage—"orgasm" as a verb) whenever they choose. If intercourse doesn't work, the woman can climax through oral or manual stimulation, and release is as easy for the woman as the man. Although Kinsey had stated this nearly twenty years earlier, Hite makes the point more convincingly.

Hite's emphasis on sexual assertiveness for women—on the need for them to take responsibility for their own sexual satisfaction—has important implications for sex and aging.

First, older women outnumber older men. If we couple this with the fact that they have greater sexual response than men in their age group, we can easily see that women need flexibility and options in order to satisfy their sexual needs.

Of even greater interest is Hite's concept of liberated sexuality for women, not unlike our own concept of a new sexuality for both sexes. Sex, she says, may or may not include intercourse. Indeed, her data prove that the pressure to perform, even when orgasm does occur, can sometimes prevent a couple from having a gratifying emotional experience.

Hite's attitude toward sex in the later years is sharply positive. But although she includes a few quotes from respondents in their 70s (who indicate that sex is alive, well, and even more pleasurable than when they were younger), her chapter entitled "Older Women" is unfortunately not really about this age group at all. Her statistical sample of 1,066 women includes a mere 18 women over 60, with only 7 over 65. Since quotes in the chapter are primarily from women in their 40s and 50s, we must conclude that older in *The Hite Report* actually means middle-aged.

It should be obvious from this brief survey of the literature that the vast body of contemporary research on sexual behavior confirms the popular view that there is little sex in the later years. Even the passing references cast a negative image: you lose power and frequency, you lose interest, you dry up, you pull back, and you slip out of the mainstream of life. Positive indications and implications have been largely ignored in favor of negative ones. The positive evidence was there, but our "selective inattention" and—perhaps more importantly—a conspiracy of silence on the part of both young and old has helped maintain the stereotype.

Alfred Kinsey began interviewing subjects for his landmark studies on human sexuality in 1938, but it was not until ten years later that the first volume on male sexuality was published, and another five years before his important findings on female sexuality were made available to the general public. Considering the pace of social and technological change in our society, this kind of gap between research and results is no longer tenable. And nowhere is the time gap more glaring than in the field of aging. What we have found valid for older people today must be looked at now in order to understand what we may expect in the next ten years.

2

The Survey

"Why sex?" asked a young female physician when we told her about our survey. "Older people need so many things—more money, better housing, ways of combating cancer and heart disease. Why do research on sex?" Why indeed.

Surely life at any age has its problems. Cancer, housing, heart disease, and poverty are not solely the problems of the old. But if they are more prevalent among older people, that is only greater reason to emphasize the positives. Without an appreciation of the joys, fulfillments and pleasures, life deteriorates into morbid preoccupations at any age. Some balance between the positives and negatives must be struck if life is to be tenable.

"Why sex?" is an especially interesting question because we would not raise it about studies of sex among younger populations, who also by the way have a multitude of problems. It is only when we acknowledge the sexuality of older people that the question and our eyebrows are raised. Our "ageism" would like to confine older people to problems—sickness, complaints, depression and dependence. This is why so many professionals, the "gatekeepers" as we came to call them, would not let us in to do our survey.

The Gatekeepers

Before we even embarked on our survey, some authorities tried to discourage us. We were told that older people do not generally respond to questionnaires, especially on the subject of sex. Eric Pfeiffer, gerontologist and sex researcher, had reported that adults typically stop their parents from participating in sex research. Moreover, many administrators and other personnel at senior and community service centers were resistant to our survey, although their resistance often came in a disguised form. "Our seniors are depressed. Do you really think they will respond to your talk and questionnaire?" said the director of an affluent condominium-type senior residence. In this instance the director's curiosity overcame his skepticism and he permitted us to give our presentation. Much to his surprise the response was enthusiastic. We were not as fortunate at other senior centers and locations. An appointment to talk to two hundred older men in the Chicago area, for example, was cancelled after we sent the questionnaire to the director. "If their wives see the questionnaire, they will be angry," she told us, barely concealing her shock. In fact, no group we addressed became angry, and least of all women, for as our survey reveals, older women are as interested, if not *more* interested in sex than older men.

Another gatekeeper begged off because of "too many research requests." She suggested another center but added "don't mention my name," revealing her discomfort with the sexual content of our survey. Then there were the professionals who would open the gate only if we would remove the word "sex" from the title of our talk. In some instances there were endless delays; in others, it seemed that there was just no room in the season's schedule for our talk. Some directors assured us that they thought our work was vital and important, but that because of certain persons whom they were reluctant to identify they could not allow us to conduct our survey at their center. Invariably, however, they expressed eager interest in receiving the results of the survey. It is interesting how many well-intentioned people recognize a problem but fiercely resist seeing themselves as part of it or joining in the solution.

The "gatekeeping response" was also experienced by professional colleagues who volunteered to distribute questionnaires for us. A Philadelphia psychologist wrote to us: "All of the questionnaires you sent were distributed to direct service workers in older adult centers. Their feedback was interesting. Some felt the questions were absolutely astonishing—their people felt it was an invasion of privacy, etc. Others felt quite the opposite, that it started some wonderful discussions about topics never before discussed."

Apparently many who serve the elderly feel they must protect them as if they were children. Is it any wonder that older people keep their sexuality closeted? The condescending message they receive is that they are fragile, easily embarrassed, and certainly nonsexual. This is all the more ridiculous when we realize that these older adults have had sexual experiences all their lives. And even if some of them are not currently sexually active, given the openness of our times they are no more likely than any other group to shrink in shame from frankly sexual questions.

But then there was a more daring group of professionals who saw our survey as a chance to open rather than close the gates to a new outlook and a fresh approach. If it weren't for them this survey would not have been possible. Many of them invited us over the objections of other staff members. They were willing to take risks, for they recognized that the need to obtain facts about the sexuality of older people was long overdue.

The Response Rate

We were understandably pessimistic about the prospects of obtaining a large enough sample to draw significant conclusions from our survey. But as we began our actual data collection, our pessimism quickly vanished. Early on it became clear that our response rate would exceed that of studies done with young adult populations. For example, Shere Hite obtained only a 3 percent response rate. Only 3,000 out of approximately 100,000 women responded to her questionnaire. In our case, an average of 14 percent responded to our questionnaire, and in some of our groups the rate was as high as 30 percent. It was obvious that older people had something significant to say about sex, and the high response rate told us that the questions we asked were tapping a vital and hidden part of their lives. One of the reasons for our success was due to our personal approach. Instead of mailing questionnaires or handing them out to people with whom we had had no prior contact (a typical tactic in survey research), we established a personal connection with the people we were investigating by delivering a talk to assembled groups on "Love, Intimacy and Sex in the Later Years." The enthusiastic reaction of the older adults to the subject and to us was enough to compensate for the demands of a lengthy questionnaire.

Our talks were arranged through local councils on aging or other civic agencies, directors of senior centers, university professors who had contacts in the community, professional colleagues, or older people themselves who arranged programs for their community centers. We addressed groups as small as twenty and as large as three hundred, and many of our meetings included interested professionals who were helpful in arranging subsequent sessions. The talks were set up weeks or months in advance of our visits, and in most instances the group was made up of people who regularly attended programs at the centers. There was no reason to assume that the audience was any more especially interested in sex than they were in the other topics covered at the center. Since we often spoke just before or after lunch, we frequently found ourselves with a captive, though rarely indifferent, audience.

We talked about attitudes toward aging in our society and the negative stereotypes of older people, tracing early needs for love and physical contact, and stressing the continuing need for intimacy and sexuality in the later years. So little was known, we reminded our audiences, mostly because older people had never been asked about the subject. We wanted data, we told them, so that we could finally come up with a complete and realistic picture of older adults. Of course, we avoided giving information that might serve as cues for responding to our questions. At the end of the question-and-answer period we described the 50-item open-ended questionnaire and asked those who were interested to take one home, fill it out as completely as they could, and return it to us in the stamped self-addressed envelope we provided. We assured the respondents complete anonymity, reminding them not to include their names on the questionnaire.

The bulk of our data, totalling the 800 responses, were obtained in this manner. Those responses not so obtained were effected through colleagues in the field of aging, many of whom attended our presentations at community centers throughout the country and generously volunteered to distribute some questionnaires to older adults in their communities and centers.

Our 14 percent response rate is even more impressive when we consider the general educational level of the present generation of elderly. Born at the turn of the century, many of today's older people received little formal education at all. Education was deemed unnecessary for women, and men tended to enter the work world as soon as possible. It will be remembered that even children worked (it was not until the Fair Labor Standards Act of 1938 that child labor was curtailed).

Therefore, many of the elderly in our audiences simply were not able to fill out our detailed questionnaire even if they wanted to. We were often fooled by the articulateness that their natural intelligence had helped them acquire over a lifetime of experience. But many of them had never developed basic reading and writing skills. This point is best illustrated by one experience in a senior center in Brooklyn. We spoke to a group of working-class older adults who welcomed us enthusiastically. Before our talk a group of men paid a great compliment: "To hear you, we're not going to the track today." Not only was our discussion well received, but the question-answer period was the liveliest and most open we had encountered. Yet the response rate on our questionnaire was unusually low. The center director revealed that most of the seniors were foreign-born; they had started working at an early age and received little or no schooling. This kind of experience was repeated in senior centers all across the country where we encountered some of our liveliest audiences.

It is, therefore, not surprising that the educational level of our respondents is probably somewhat higher than the general population of older adults. Less than half, 46 percent, have a high-school education or less. Another 25 percent have some college education and 29 percent have a college degree or higher education (see Table 52). While most of our respondents are native-born (91 percent) it is impossible to estimate what our response rate would have been if not for the illiteracy problem. Of course, future generations of elderly will be better educated and, therefore, will not present this problem for research.

Who Are Older Adults?

In our survey, older adults refer to people over the age of 60. Much controversy abounds about who can be considered old now that people are living longer and working longer. Since 60 is an arbitrary cut-off point that is widely used in the aging literature, it is therefore the most practical designation for comparative purposes. We must keep in mind, however, that there are many differences within the over-60 age group. An individual in his early 60s may be quite different from an 85-year-old or even a 70-year-old. For this reason some writers have made the distinction between young-old and old-old, the latter referring to people over 75.

Consider, too, the concept of *psychological age,* of how you actually feel about your age. An especially active 76-year-old woman we encountered told us about some elderly people she had visited. "How old is elderly?" we inquired with some surprise. "Oh, about 80," she replied. Many older people reported to us that they didn't feel old and rarely thought about their age. On the other hand, even a 60-year-old may take on the demeanor of a desexed old person if she in fact conceives of herself as old.

The Respondents

The subjects for this survey are 800 adults between the ages of 60 and 91; 35 percent are male and 65 percent are female. They are from four regions of the country: the Northeast (47 percent), the West and Northwest (27 percent), the Midwest (13 percent), and the South and Southwest (13 percent). The locations in the four regions from which we obtained most of our data are: Northeast—New York City and the surrounding metropolitan areas of New Jersey (mainly Paterson and Clifton); South—Atlanta and Macon, Georgia; West—San Jose, Mountainview, Santa Clara, Palo Alto, Menlo Park, San Francisco, and Oakland, California; Midwest—Chicago, Illinois, and St. Louis, Missouri. Other cities from which we obtained significant numbers of responses are: Burlington, Vermont; Charlotte, North Carolina; Dallas, Texas; Denver, Colorado; Eugene and Portland, Oregon; Indianapolis, Indiana; Kansas City, Missouri; Los Angeles, California and surrounding areas; Richmond, Virginia; San Diego, California; Seattle, Washington; and Washington, D.C. (see Table 60).

Since our major interest was to obtain general data on the sexuality of older adults, we did not intend to examine the more refined issue of ethnicity. Nevertheless, many ethnic groups are represented in our sample. For example, some groups that we addressed in the South were predominantly Black. Also, we spoke at a number of Black and Hispanic senior centers in the New York City metropolitan area. Other groups throughout the country, although predominantly white, did include minority persons. However, most of the sample is white.

All of our subjects live in the community, in their own homes or apartments, in senior residences, or in a few instances (5 percent) with a relative. There are no institutional or nursing home cases in the sample. Most describe their health as "excellent" or "good" (72 percent) while 25 percent rate their health as "fair." Only 3 percent say "poor" (see Table 56).

Other characteristics of the sample are as follows:

1. Marital status (Table 55). Married – 48 percent; Widowed – 37 percent; Divorced – 11 percent; Single – 4 percent. Typical of this age group, more men (64 percent) than women (39 percent) are married but more women (46 percent) than men (20 percent) are widowed.
2. Religion (Table 53). Protestant – 48 percent; Catholic – 20 percent; Jewish – 26 percent; Other – 7 percent.
3. How Religious (Table 54). Very – 11 percent; Moderately – 41 percent; Somewhat – 24 percent; Not Religious – 24 percent.
4. Retirement (Table 59). Of those who had worked outside of the home, 71 percent are retired.

The Questionnaire

The questionnaire consists of 50 open-ended questions that require respondents to write in answers. We made every effort to ask questions that were not leading so that respondents would have to supply information from their own experience. For example, we asked "What in the sexual experience is most important to you?" rather than suggesting a practice and then asking for a degree of acceptance or activity. In some instances when it was important to have specific information we asked more direct questions like "Do you masturbate? How often?"

Open-ended questions yield more information than structured multiple-choice questions. Responses to open-ended questions are revealing and authentic because they are stated in the respondent's own words; multiple-choice questions force the respondent to pick one of a number of choices, none of which may reflect his or her true position. But at the same time the demanding nature of open-ended questions insures that there will be many omissions.

Most researchers would consider a project of 50 open-ended questions suicidal no matter what the age group. But our initial trials convinced us that a substantial number of older people were willing to fill out our questionnaire. We then were confronted with the choice of getting a large number of responses to a small number of questions or a smaller return from a wide-ranging questionnaire. We opted for the latter. What tipped us in that direction was the realization that nothing factual was known about sex and aging. In the absence of knowledge it is important to make the broadest possible inquiry. Until you have some facts it is not possible to narrow the focus to questions on the most important issues.

The 30 questions on our early pilot questionnaires avoided stepping on what we thought were sensitivities. But to cover ourselves we included one last question asking for comments or suggestions on what we might have left out. We were stunned by how many of the early respondents said things like, "How come you don't have any questions on affairs?" or "Why didn't you ask about oral sex?" Once again we found ourselves trapped by the very stereotypes we sought to break down. Our final 50-item questionnaire was revised to include the broadest possible range of questions that we would ask adults of any age, but with an emphasis on the special concerns and problems of older adults. With the feedback we got from early respondents the questionnaire grew from 30 items to its final form of 50 items.

Scoring the Responses

While open-ended questions which allow the respondent to express his own experience as fully as he chooses provide rich and interesting data, they also present scoring difficulties. For statistical analysis, responses must fit into categories. But how do you translate responses that are uniquely expressed? We went about this task by initially reviewing the responses of 50 of the questionnaires to develop primary scoring categories. Some questions posed no problem at all. For example, "Do you like sex?" (Question 5) lends itself easily to a dichotomous scoring of "yes" or "no." Other questions required additional categories to adequately cover most of the responses. "How do you think sex affects the health of older people?" (Question 7) is easily encompassed by three categories: "Positive," "Negative," and "No effect." In other instances, like "What makes you feel most excited during lovemaking?" (Question 16), a large number of categories was necessary to include all responses. When a few unusual or unique answers were given for a question, the category "Other" was introduced. We were striving to develop as many categories as were necessary to reflect the range of responses. As we proceeded with the early scoring, new categories evolved until we arrived at the final scoring system. When new categories were developed, the questionnaires already scored were reviewed and reliability of the scoring proved to be high.

Each questionnaire was scored on a separate scoring sheet and the data then entered into a computer for analysis. The analysis of the 47 questions that lend themselves to a statistical breakdown are reported in Tables 1–50 in the Appendix. The responses to the other questions (3, 8, 47) are evaluated qualitatively. For ease of reference the numbers of the tables correspond to the numbers of the questions. Descriptive characteristics of the 800 respondents appear in Tables 51–59.

Questionnaire

PLEASE FILL OUT THE INFORMATION REQUESTED BELOW. *Do NOT* FILL IN YOUR NAME. ALL RESPONSES ARE ANONYMOUS. THANK YOU FOR YOUR CONTRIBUTION TO SCIENTIFIC KNOWLEDGE.

Age _____ Sex (circle one) Male   Female
Place of birth _____
Where did you live before coming to this community? ____

Education (circle one):
Elementary School   Some high school   High school graduate
Some college   College graduate
Advanced degree
_____

Religious affiliation (circle one):
Catholic   Jewish   Protestant   Other
_____

How religious are you? (circle one):
Very religious   Moderately religious
Somewhat religious   Not religious
_____

Marital status (circle one):
Married   Divorced   Single   Widowed
_____

Physical health (circle one):
Excellent   Good   Fair   Poor
_____

Living arrangements (circle one):
Live alone   Live with spouse   Live with
children   Live with other relative
Live with friend
_____

Occupation (circle one): A profession
Own business   Office   Retail or sales
Factory   Homemaker   Other _____
_____

Retired? (circle one): Yes   No

1. What is a good sexual experience?
2. How does sex feel now compared with when you were younger?
3. What do you think is an ideal sex life for older people?
4. What in the sex act is most important to you?
5. Do you like sex? Explain.
6. How often would you like to have sexual relations if you could whenever you wanted to?
7. How do you think sex affects the health of older people?
8. What does it mean to be a sexy person?
9. How important is orgasm or climax in your sexual experiences?
10. How important is touching and cuddling in sex? Has this changed over the years?
11. What kind of pre-intercourse foreplay (touching, kissing, etc.) do you like best?

12. Do you get excited looking at sexy pictures, books, or movies? Explain.
13. What part should sex play when a couple gets married or remarried in later life? How does sex differ from an earlier marriage?
14. Many older people masturbate to relieve sexual tensions. What do you think about this?
15. Do you masturbate? How often?
16. What makes you feel most excited during lovemaking?
17. What about sex embarrasses you the most?
18. Some people say that intercourse is not the most important part of sex. How do you feel about this?
19. How has sex changed since the menopause (change of life)?
20. Do sexual experiences leave you satisfied? What do you do when you are not satisfied?
21. How often do you have sexual relations?
22. Does sexual intercourse give you any physical discomfort or pain? Explain.
23. How do you feel about older men and women without partners going to prostitutes to relieve sexual needs?
24. How long does the sex act usually last? How does this compare with when you were younger?
25. How does your partner know what you like in sex?
26. Describe the ideal lover of your fantasy—age, looks, type, etc.
27. Why do you think that some older people do not have sexual relations as often as they would like to?
28. Who do you think is more interested in sex, the older man or the older woman? How are they different?
29. How do you feel about older people who are not married having sexual relations or living together?
30. It is said that older people have more time on their hands. How does this affect sex?
31. In the later years there are more women than men. How can older women deal with this?
32. How can older people deal with their sexual feelings if they are not married or if they do not have partners?
33. What about sex do you like the least?
34. What do you think of while you are making love?
35. Who usually begins the lovemaking, you or your partner?

36. What happens when you are in the mood and your partner is not?
37. How often do you reach climax or orgasm when making love? How does this compare with when you were younger?
38. Do you talk about sex with your partner? What part of the sexual experience do you discuss?
39. How do you feel about being nude with your partner? Has this changed over the years?
40. It is said that older men have difficulty getting an erection. Is this true in your experience? Explain.
41. How and what were you taught about sex as a child? How and what did you teach your children?
42. Homosexuality seems much more open these days. How do you feel about it?
43. What can a couple do when the man is unable to have an erection?
44. How do you feel about older men having younger lovers? How do you feel about older women having younger lovers?
45. Does sex change after retirement? How?
46. Would you like to try new sexual experiences that you have heard about, read about, or thought about? Explain.
47. When in your life was sex best? Why?
48. How do you think your sexual feelings, attitudes and behavior will change as you get older? Explain.
49. Looking over your sex life, past and present, what would you want to change? Explain.
50. Is there anything about sex and older people that was not covered in this questionnaire? Please feel free to add or comment.

3

Interest in Sex

What do older people think about? Their grandchildren, pension plans, moving to a retirement community, the latest bargains at the supermarket? These subjects seem safely appropriate. But sex? That's a bit far-fetched. Yet consider the realities. If you are 20, 30, 40, or even 50, chances are that sex is on your mind quite a lot. You certainly don't lack for stimulation: even the most innocent-seeming PG-rated movies have a liberal sprinkling of bare breasts and frank lovemaking scenes. This stimulation doesn't disappear in the later years. Why then should the sexual thoughts? Yet we persist in thinking that this vital drive has somehow fallen off the edge of the older person's psychological life space.

Our data strongly suggest that not only are older people indeed interested in sex, they also think about it, desire it, and engage in it when they can, with the same average frequency that Kinsey reported for his 40-year-olds. Moreover, their ways of expressing interest are not much different from those of younger adults. Even though many people in their 40s and 50s grew up before the new sexual freedoms created a near-mandate to be sexual as an affirmation of self, they have gotten the message and have already changed. We have every reason to believe that older people have responded to the same sexual revolution.

And why wouldn't they? They watch the same movies, view the same television shows, read the same books and magazines. They even have an advantage over younger people: they have more time on their hands, more time to pay attention to the natural drives and urges that have been present all their lives. Without the intrusion of external pressures—jobs, appointments, demands from those around them—

they can slip into contact with other parts of themselves, their fantasies and feelings.

As one 72-year-old widow said: "I was reading this new, sexy book and realized I had drifted off into daydreams when the book fell onto my foot. Since I had the rest of the day free, I let myself drift and then—masturbated."

Many of the respondents consider sex a crucial part of their lives, providing a general sense of well-being and a good feeling about themselves. For example, in answer to question 5, "Do you like sex? Explain," most of the respondents indicate a strong interest in sex; 97 percent say "Yes." This resounding "yes" was true for each decade of respondents—97 percent of the 60-69 year olds, 97 percent of the 70-79 year olds and 93 percent of the 80-91 year olds (Table 5A):

> (Female, divorced, age 61) "Yes. When I'm being sexually active I feel alive and desirable and I look better."
> (Male, married, age 65) "Yes. Doesn't everyone?"
> (Female, divorced, age 79) "Yes. Feeling of deep response and communication with my partner. Gives me a zest for life."
> (Female, married, age 70) "Yes. The orgasm for myself but knowing I can produce it for my husband."
> (Male, married, age 68) "Yes. Like everything about it."
> (Female, widow, age 67) "Yes. Still need sex and enjoy it."
> (Female, widow, age 78) "Yes. It makes me feel good and improves my disposition."
> (Female, divorced, age 65) "Yes. What's to explain? It's a vital and integral part of life."
> (Male, single, age 67) "Yes. Successful sex acts give one a feeling of satisfaction, relaxation, exhilaration and joy."
> (Male, widower, age 81) "It's the most thrilling experience in life if you love the girl."
> (Female, widow, age 74) "I like sex tremendously with my sweetheart."
> (Female, divorced, age 63) "I feel exhilarated and loved after a good experience."
> (Female, divorced, age 64) "It makes me feel a complete female."
> (Male, widowed, age 74) "Yes. It is one of the supreme pleasures of living."

(Female, married, age 72) "Yes. I believe it relieves pressures of life. I feel much better physically and mentally when enjoying a good sex life."

(Female, married, age 65) "Yes. It is a natural way to ease the loneliness inherent in being an individual. It feels good and now I learned it's good for easing arthritis."

(Male, married, age 80) "Yes. I like sex because it is a feeling you do not forget."

(Female, widow, age 64) "It makes me feel more certain of myself and more at peace with myself."

(Male, married, age 63) "I have throughout my life been thrilled by the feel of the female body and still feel the same."

(Female, married, age 63) "Yes. Why not? Am I different now from when I was younger? Only my outer shell has changed."

(Male, married, age 69) "Yes. Sex is one of the pleasures of life. It is also one way in which men and women overcome loneliness and frustration. There's the added pleasure as we grow older, we can still enjoy sex and thus are still to be counted as total men and women."

(Female, widow, age 81) "Yes. I feel very wonderful and fulfilled."

(Female, widow, age 78) "Yes. I love to be near someone."

(Female, widow, age 70) "Yes. Married to same man for almost 50 years and enjoyed it always."

(Male, married, age 67) "Very much. I love the fondling, touching, nakedness and all the methods of achieving the end result."

(Female, widow, age 68) "Yes. It supplies a physical need, warmth and closeness to another person, a helper, a protector, a confidante, a friend and a lover all rolled into one."

(Female, married, age 64) "Yes, with all my heart. I don't know how to explain except it is beautiful to me."

(Female, widow, age 73) "Yes. Being loved, touched, wanted fills a need."

(Female, widow, age 66) "Yes. I like the feeling of being attractive, loved and wanted."

(Female, married, age 66) "Yes—it makes me feel young."

(Male, married, age 66) "Still satisfying, warm, exhilarating."

(Female, widow, age 71) "Yes. Because I feel I'm a beautiful woman and desired."

(Female, widow, age 68)"Yes! It makes me happy, my hormones seem to flow, I have a stimulation for life."
(Female, married, age 63) "Yes—and it helps to mitigate our sense of aloneness."
(Male, married, age 83) "Yes. It's pleasure."
(Female, widow, age 67) "Yes. It makes me feel young and desirable—same as I felt years ago."
(Female, widow, age 73) "Yes. It's not only a biological experience, but in a way mystical—to feel one with another person, with the world."
(Male, married, age 75) "To me sex can be beautiful if there is no guilt involved by either one; if they let themselves go."

Sex makes these older people feel "beautiful," "desirable," "exhilarated," even "mystical." For some who have bought the youth cult, it accomplishes the ultimate—it makes them "feel young"; and like younger people, they can place great value on themselves as sexual beings not only because sex is such a potent biological force but because of social conditioning. We now take it for granted that to be alive and potent is to be sexual, and older people are as aware of this idea as any other age group. In the words of one 67-year-old widower, "Sex is a necessary part of being a well-rounded, healthy adult."

People are interested in sex for a variety of reasons. Some of the elderly, who are understandably more concerned with the state of their health than are the young, believe that sex can improve the working of the body: "I believe it helps me sleep better and is good for helping urination and the prostate gland," writes one 75-year-old married man. More than 80 percent of the respondents think that sex has a positive effect on health (see Table 7). Psychological health also stands to benefit.

"It's very relaxing and relieves tension," says a 70-year-old widow. "It's life's most exquisite moment and drives every problem and care away," comments a married woman, age 60. "If you don't use it, it's lost. Don't let it rust," warns another married woman, age 66.

But as beneficial as sex may be for physical well-being, more than biology is at stake here. Being "turned on" or excited can determine the nature of our sexual experiences, regardless of how well our bodies function. Many of the people who responded positively when we asked if they liked sex considered it most important as part of a relationship:

> (Female, widow, age 78) "It's a beautiful feeling with the right person."
> (Male, married, age 65) "Yes. It fulfills faith and trust. And to a great extent is the personal expression of approval."
> (Male, married, age 68) "Very much so. Because my new spouse and I have the same interest in each other, it helps the enjoyment together."
> (Female, married, age 60) "Yes. When I feel OK about myself and my mate, there is lots of warmth and touching between us, I especially like sex."
> (Female, widow, age 83) "Yes. I've never forgotten my marital experiences."
> (Male, married, age 63) "Definitely. It is a means of confirming or continuing physical attraction for each other."
> (Female, married, age 73) "Yes. Because it is part of our love for each other—it is the fulfillment."
> (Male, married, age 68) "Yes, very much. It is the only private experience containing the elements of sharing."
> (Male, married, age 88) "I love my wife and sexual relations."

Fulfillment in love, faith and trust, approval and warmth—these are not very different from the needs and desires of people of every other age.

While the majority of our respondents say that they like sex, want it, and have by no means lost their "interest in sex," some stand out for the powerful needs they express:

> (Female, married, age 73) "Yes, I think it is one of our strongest emotions. Very important to our self-image."
> (Female, married, age 66) "Yes. I have a strong sex drive. In recent years my husband has an erection problem."
> (Male, married, age 69) "Yes. It's important to me. Like eating, going to the theater, etc. A part of my life."

(Female, widow, age 72) "Why not? I am only 72 and will like it till I die."

(Male, widower, age 74) "Yes. It is one of the supreme pleasures of living."

(Male, widower, age 73) "Yes, I need sex. I could not live without it."

(Male, widower, age 68) "Yes, I think it's the most pleasant experience I can have."

(Male, single, age 70) "I like it so much that I would rather die in the act of sex than any other way."

(Male, married, age 62) "Obsessed by it. Daily preoccupation. Always gazing at women on the streets."

(Female, widow, age 76) "Very much. I can't do without it."

(Male, single, age 66) "Yes. You reach a high where you're on a cloud oblivious to everything around you. You finally explode reaching a feeling of perfect contentment and relaxation."

(Female, divorced, age 64) "Very much and I need it."

(Male, divorced, age 74) "Yes. The most enjoyable thing in life."

(Male, divorced, age 60) "Yes. It's fun. A social act and satisfies a natural appetite. Its denial is painful."

(Male, married, age 64) "Absolutely. I love it because it is the culmination of everything I feel emotionally."

(Male, married, age 85) "Oh boy! I literally eat it—well, only when I get hungry for it."

If sex continues to be an important need, even a powerful one for some, does it feel the same as in previous decades? Even experts who insist that sex can continue throughout the life cycle often tarnish their optimism with comments like, "Although the intensity diminishes," or "The need may not be as strong," or "The urgency is gone." We, therefore, posed Question 2, "How does sex feel now compared with when you were younger?" to explore how our respondents rate the actual experience of sex.

For a minority of respondents (26 percent) there is a decline in sexual response and feelings (see Table 2). This is especially true for men who report erection problems and withdraw from sexual activity, having come to the false conclusion that without a reliable erection you can't have any sexual activity. It is, therefore, not surprising that more men (36 percent) than women (19 percent) say that sex does not feel as good now. Typical of this group are statements like "I've been impotent for five years so for me sex is nothing now" (male, married, age 71); or the 91-year-old widower who said, "Not a fraction of the pleasure now." Other respondents experience a loss in their sex lives because one or both of the partners withdraw from sexual activity. Curtailment of sex for these people sometimes stems from anxieties about sexual performance, or just the loss of sexual desire. Boredom may also be a factor. But as sex therapist Dr. Helen Kaplan has established with convincing clinical data, the loss of sexual desire often begins in middle age and has a psychological rather than a physiological basis; age in these cases is not the determinant of sexual decline or loss.

But contrary to the fears and apprehensions of young and middle-aged adults about the status of sex in the later years, a significant 75 percent of our respondents said that sex is the same or better now compared with when they were younger (Table 2). Quite remarkably, 36 percent of the sample say that sex is better (41 percent of the females and 27 percent of the males). The responses, though brief, are convincing:

(Male, married, age 75) "Still feels the same."

(Female, married, age 78) "Just the same."

(Female, widow, age 61) "Just the same plus no worries."

(Female, widow, age 69) "To me it feels the same as when younger if you have the right partner."

(Male, married, age 74) "Much fuller in satisfying my urges and desires."

(Male, widower, age 81) "Just the same."

(Female, married, age 73) "Not much different, less inhibitions and a feeling of accomplishment in giving pleasure."

(Female, widow, age 83) "If you reach a climax the reaction is the same. One needs more physical stamina and time takes its toll on your body."

(Male, married, age 69) "It still feels good. I enjoy it, I look forward to it."

(Female, married, age 66) "Not in force as frequently but sex drive just as strong."

(Female, widow, age 77) "I am a widow for seven years—married for over fifty years, and our sex life suffered no changes."
(Female, married, age 73) "Not much different. Less inhibitions and a feeling of accomplishment and giving pleasure."
(Male, married, age 63) "Fully satisfying."
(Male, married, age 73) "It feels great now as it did before."
(Female, married, age 72) "It feels great and makes me feel younger."
(Male, married, age 66) "Just as strong a feeling of well-being."
(Male, widower, age 82) "Very good."
(Female, widow, age 82) "Feels fine. Just doesn't last as long."
(Male, married, age 80) "Same."
(Female, widow, age 78) "The same as before."
(Male, married, age 72) "The same, but not as often."
(Female, married, age 63) "No difference. Same reaction, same satisfaction."
(Female, married, age 60) "Still great."
(Male, married, age 66) "Just as much a thrill as ever."

Over and over again the respondents report having sexual experiences that are just as gratifying as when they were younger. The key for some is in "having the right partner"; for others it is the loss of inhibitions and a greater understanding of sex. But perhaps the most impressive blow to the stereotype of sex in the later years is that so many feel that sex can be "great" or "just as much a thrill as ever." Even more surprising are the many respondents who find sex "even better and more satisfying," to use the words of one 75-year-old widow. Here is what others had to say:

(Male, single, age 70) "Getting better as I get older."
(Female, married, age 66) "Better. You know so much more."
(Male, married, age 73) "Better, more understanding and awareness."
(Female, married, age 66) "It is better. I am not at all inhibited anymore."
(Female, widow, age 63) "Better now because I really understand it."
(Male, married, age 74) "Much fuller in satisfying my urges and desires."
(Female, married, age 68) "Now it is necessary to stimulate my

clitoris during coitus to reach orgasm. However climax is much more intense and prolonged; contractions much stronger."

(Female, divorced, age 81) "I was cold in my very early life but became more proficient as I grew older."

(Female, married, age 60) "Much better because we are both more tolerant and understanding."

(Female, widow, age 64) "More complete."

(Female, married, age 61) "It is better now."

(Female, widow, age 67) "Better. You have no worries about getting pregnant or raising a family or trying to make ends meet for the rest of the family."

(Male, widower, age 68) "It seems that I appreciate it more now."

(Male, married, age 83) "Better."

(Female, married, age 60) "More carefree, no need to worry about being pregnant."

(Female, widow, age 66) "Has more meaning and it is more gratifying."

(Female, widow, age 73) "It was a hurried, worrisome experience in youth—fearful of being pregnant. Later, more enjoyable."

(Female, widow, age 68) "Much better. I am not concerned with my monthly period and being caught. I have no worries about children. Financial status is better and so is sex."

(Male, married, age 63) "Passion is not as intense but pleasure lasts longer. Probably better."

(Female, widow, age 70) "I am more relaxed than when I was young."

(Female, married, age 81) "Better as we have more time for bed-talk and are more relaxed."

(Male, widower, age 79) "Just as good, but more pleasant."

(Female, married, age 62) "I have a better understanding of my partner's needs and so am more cooperative and as a result seem to enjoy sex more."

(Female, widow, age 60) "Much better now. Less inhibited, more willing to do what pleases partner."

(Female, widow, age 64) "More comfortable. Freer. And more eagerly anticipate."

(Female, widow, age 71) "Sex is more enjoyable now, more time, more relaxed, no artificial protection. Can let myself go."

(Female, widow, age 68) "100 percent improvement."

(Male, married, age 76) "It is no longer a catch-as-catch-can experience but one to be thoroughly enjoyed."

(Female, married, age 62) "Better. Freer. Less hang-ups, no pregnancy hang-ups. We dictate the time rather than time being dictated to us."

(Male, married, age 68) "Always new and more profound."

(Female, married, age 65) "I've always enjoyed it but each time usually seems more perfect than the last, more satisfying."

Far from sitting on the sidelines or giving up their sexual selves, these older adults have achieved higher levels of sexual fulfillment. Their comments give power to the belief that the human mind is the most potent sex organ. Sex is better for these respondents because of greater understanding, increased self-awareness, loss of worries, and greater appreciation and meaning of the sexual experience—all states of mind that can enhance and even transcend biology.

What part should sex play when a couple gets married or remarried in later life? How does it differ from an earlier marriage? While companionship, love, caring and sharing are stressed, so is sex. In answer to this question (#13), some give personal accounts that sex is better in the later marriage than in the earlier one. For others it is the novelty that provides renewal of sexual enthusiasm. For still others, it is the responsiveness of the new partner:

(Female, married, age 63) "Same as always if not better since you have more time. Earlier marriage chance a child may walk in or hear."

(Male, married, age 68) "An important part on its own level. Should not be compared to any previous experience."

(Male, married, age 76) "It is just as important in a later marriage and should not be the basis for comparison."

(Female, widow, age 74) "In earlier marriage family responsibilities interfere with pleasurable sex. Interruptions by children crying—demanding. In later marriage attention can be given to pleasure your partner."

(Male, married, age 72) "A big part. The same as before."

(Male, married, age 62) "A good song title, 'The second time around.' I believe I would be as active as possible in the second marriage."

(Male, married, age 63) "I find that sex play is the icing on the cake. This is my second marriage and I find it as gratifying, if not more so, than the first."

(Female, widow, age 60) "I think sex is important at any time in your life. What difference does it make if you are young or old. If the desire is there, then sex should be an important part of the marriage."

(Female, divorced, age 62) "Sex is more important for women when they get older."

(Male, married, age 64) "Sex should play an important part and should be more satisfying than ever due to accumulated experience."

(Female, married, age 69) "There has to be some sex or they will not have a happy marriage. You really learn from experience of a first marriage."

(Male, married, age 61) "A very important part—earlier marriage usually contemplate children—later, sex is fun and emotional nutrition."

(Male, married, age 74) "a) An essential desire being satisfied. b) Approximately the same—except the second mate is sexier."

(Female, widow, age 63) "Since I view sex as a natural function I feel it should play an important part in later years—if physically possible."

(Male, married, age 61) "It is important and shouldn't differ from an earlier marriage."

(Male, widower, age 70) "a) 98 percent. b) Doesn't."

(Male, married, age 63) "The same, no matter when you get married."

(Female, widow, age 68) "Sex is an important part of marriage at any time—and would not be very different in later life."

(Male, divorced, age 69) "Don't be afraid of oral sex and be forward in one's desires."

(Male, married, age 65) "Sex plays a part in parts of married life at all ages."

(Female, married, age 70) "It should be the greatest! Sex should be better. One should have lost all their inhibitions—also they should keep in mind that it is later than you think—and you can't take it with you."

(Female, divorced, age 68) "I think it should be better—learning from earlier experiences."

(Male, widower, age 68) "To have fulfillment of their sexual desires."

(Female, widow, age 68) "Sex in later life can and should be a statement about the worth and value of the partner. In earlier life, is often casual gratification."

(Male, married, age 75) "A vital part. For me, marriage could end in disaster without sex."

Perhaps a good index of interest in sex is the frequency of sexual relations (Table 21). For all our subjects who reported frequency of sexual relations, almost 80 percent were currently sexually active while 20 percent were not. Among those who are sexually active, 50 percent report frequency of sexual intercourse to be once a week or more. Of the sexually active respondents 13 percent report twice-a-week sexual relations and 12 percent report three times a week or more. Twenty-nine percent have sexual relations three times a month or less. Some of our respondents did not report a precise frequency but merely indicated that they had sexual relations "when in the mood" (6 percent). This category is difficult to translate into a frequency but it is our impression that it reflects a relatively high frequency of sexual relations (judged by their responses to other questions), probably greater than twice a week. Using those categories that do reflect a precise frequency of sexual relations in Table 21, we estimate average frequency for the group to be about 1.4 times per week. This figure would, no doubt, be even greater if those who indicated "when in the mood" spelled out a frequency more clearly. Similarly, our category of "three times a week or more" includes those who clearly do have sexual relations more than three times a week. In fact, 18 of our respondents reported sexual relations five times a week or more, 9 of these having sex daily.

To Question 6, "How often would you like to have sexual relations if you could whenever you wanted to?," even stronger interest is indicated. Whereas Table 21 showed that 21 percent of those who answered the question were sexually inactive, Table 6 clearly demonstrates that the inactivity is based upon circumstances, not lack of desire or interest. A mere 7 respondents, less than 1 percent of our sample of 800, say they would not like to have sexual relations. An overwhelming 99 percent desire sexual relations with varying frequencies if they could whenever they wanted to. These figures unequivocally challenge the belief that older people are beyond sex. Among the sexually inactive respondents (Table 6A) only 5 subjects, or 4 percent, do not desire sexual relations; 96 percent do, with 57 percent of these respondents desiring sexual relations more than once a week; 18 percent opt for twice a week and 12 percent three times a week or more. Nineteen percent of the sexually inactive women would like to have sexual relations "when in the mood." One exuberant 70-year-old widow perhaps best reflected the spirit of our respondents when she expressed her desired frequency: "Morning, noon and night."

More women than men lack the opportunity for sexual relations because of the simple fact that there are more widows than widowers. This is borne out by the statistic that 8 out of every 10 older men are married, as opposed to 6 out of 10 older women. In 1976, according to figures compiled by the United States Senate Special Committee on Aging, 5.1 million women over the age of 65 lived alone. The sexual plight of older women is glaringly obvious in our statistic on sexual activity/inactivity. Whereas older women, as we have seen, are as interested in sex as older men, 30 percent of the female respondents are currently not active sexually compared to only 7 percent of the men (Table 21). Comments from our inactive female respondents emphasize the dilemma of the older woman without a partner who just does not have the opportunity to translate desire into behavior. "I like it, but where are the men?" writes a 72-year-old widow. "Yes, I would like it if I had a man," comments another, aged 67. "I'm ready and willing, but there just aren't any suitable men around," says another 79-year-old widow. Again, in answer to Question 27, "Why do you think that some older people do not have sexual relations as often as they would like to?" many factors are hypothesized—poor health, impotence, loss of desire, and the acceptance of the myths about older people and sex—but the largest group (28 percent) say it is the lack of a partner.

Whether one feels that sexual relations should be engaged in spontaneously, that is, "when the mood strikes" or one, two, or more times per month, per week or per day, the preferences reflect positive interest in sex. The approaches may vary based possibly upon individual life styles and the male/female sex differences alluded to, but interest in sex seems constant for our respondents.

There is widespread belief that frequency of sexual relations declines sharply with age. After age 60 the decline with each successive decade is assumed to be even greater. Our data certainly does not bear this out. Table 21 A dramatically illustrates this point. Using those categories in which a specific frequency of sexual relations is given, we arrive at an average frequency of 1.5 times per week for the 60–69 year old group, 1.4 times per week for the 70–79 year old group and 1.2 times per week for the over-80 group.

Furthermore, when desire for sex is used as the index of interest, older respondents are hardly distinguishable from younger adults. Our data provides some striking evidence for the conclusion that older people who remain sexually active do not differ significantly in the frequency of sexual relations compared with when they were younger.

One of the common errors that we make in interpreting research data that covers many age groups is to assume that the data on the older group will reflect the younger group many years later. For example, if Kinsey found that the 30-year-old women in his sample had sexual intercourse on the average of 2.2 times per week and his 60-year-olds 0.6 times per week, we are inclined to conclude falsely that within a thirty-year period sexual intercourse declines from 2.2 times per week to 0.6 times per week. Kinsey's 60-year-olds, however, are not the 30-year-olds thirty years later. Both groups come from different generations with different training and different developmental influences. If you want to know more accurately what Kinsey's 30-year-olds will be like at age 60, you have to wait thirty years to question them—or you can look at the data on our subjects who are generally the same generation as Kinsey's original 30-year-olds. Using a similar line of logic, if data on young adults today show a high frequency of sexual activity compared to a relatively low rate of sexual activity among older people today, we cannot conclude that these young people will decline to the level of today's older people when they reach the older age.

With this in mind, it is interesting to note that the 40-year-old married women in Kinsey's report engaged in intercourse on an average of 1.4 times per week; the rate for 40-year-old married men was 2.0 a week. These frequencies are not much different from those reported by our subjects, who are the same generation thirty to forty years later.

This data would suggest that frequency has hardly declined when a partner is available. It only appears that sexual activity decreases significantly when we erroneously compare older people with younger people in the same moment of time. These conclusions compel us to revise our thinking about sexuality over the lifespan. When a partner is available, the rate of sexual behavior may in fact remain fairly constant throughout one's life.

Question 32 asks "How can older people deal with their sexual feelings if they are not married or do not have partners?" A partner fulfills many needs besides sexual ones—support and intellectual stimulation, to name just two. But if older people have little or no interest in sex, then not having a partner should have no bearing on sex. If there is a strong interest in sex, then the alternate solutions suggested for dealing with sexual feelings when a partner is not available will reflect that interest.

Again our results are decidedly positive. For example, many of the respondents suggest masturbation as an alternative (26 percent). Others stress the need to find a partner (26 percent). A small number can even entertain maverick solutions such as sharing partners, communal living and lesbianism (4 percent). Not only do these solutions indicate interest in sex, but they also reflect the recognition of sexual needs in the later years and the need for alternative outlets when a partner is not available.

Very few of the responses show a rejection of sexual needs. Some do suggest other nonsexual outlets—"join organizations, keep active, develop other interests"—but what we are seeing here is the "cold shower" effect. What they are often saying is that you must find *some* way to cool off your sexual needs if you don't have a partner. For others there may be more pervasive denial of sexuality because, after all, it is difficult to acknowledge a need when you can't find an acceptable way of expressing it.

All our data strongly suggest, however, that the question we must really ask is not whether there is interest in sex in the later years— obviously there is—but rather what the nature of that interest is: Like all living things, we change as we grow older. But not all change is negative. In sex, we hear most about decline. Experts begrudgingly acknowledge that, yes, sexual intercourse is possible throughout the

life cycle, but that the intensity of the experience is reduced and perhaps
for some the frequency.

It is true that older men do not get erections as easily as they did
when they were young and that they must wait a longer time between
erections. But, as we have seen, these natural changes in physical
functioning do not have to hamper older people from engaging in
satisfying, even ecstatic sex, nor should it stop them from actively
seeking out sexual experiences.

When we devised Question 12, "Do you get excited looking at sexy
pictures, books or movies? Explain," we thought that we were tread-
ing on dangerous turf. Such "pornographic interests" would surely be
alien to this generation of elderly. Yet, most freely acknowledged that
these stimuli aroused them.

Sixty-two percent say "yes." While more men (75 percent) than
women (55 percent) acknowledge arousal from pictures, books, or
movies, the figures for both sexes are impressive and contradict the
stereotype of the nonerotic older person. In view of the Victorian
double standard, it seems remarkable that more than half our female
respondents answered in the affirmative. Among the sexually active,
75 percent of the men and 58 percent of the women said "yes" to Question 12. Among the sexually inactive, the figures are 84 percent for
men and 47 percent for women. So interest in sex remains fairly stable
whether or not there is current sexual activity.

Although some of the respondents were cautious or tentative on
Question 12 with answers like, "Well, only occasionally," or "Sometimes, if it is in good taste," a large number were straight forward.

> (Male, married, age 72) "Yes. Often read sexy books as an
> aphrodisiac."
> (Female, widow, age 74) "Many a time I've read sexy books and
> looked at sexy pictures."
> (Male, married, age 73) "Yes. It is as stimulating as smell or good
> cooking to a hungry person."
> (Male, married, age 75) "Do not get excited. But I enjoy reading sex
> books and view a movie once a month."
> (Female, married, age 69) "Yes of course—it's normal. I even like
> X-rated movies occasionally. Unless a person is narrow or limited in

knowledge, both moral and practical, he or she is titillated by erotic material . . ."

(Female, divorced, age 62) "Sexy pictures, yes. *Cosmopolitan* ads. The love scenes from *Gone with the Wind,* etc. But not explicit sex scenes."

(Male, married, age 75) "I certainly do, and think such reaction normal."

(Female, widow, age 78) "Yes—most of the time. I can sometimes just imagine it is me."

(Female, married, age 63) "Yes. They usually stimulate me—make me want physical contact."

(Male, widower, age 66) "Yes, I am human."

(Male, divorced, age 69) "Yes, I do. Partly, I think it's because I don't get as much sex as I'd like. Also it stimulates my fantasies about having other partners and other positions."

(Male, married, age 86) "Slight to strong erection when I fantasize with the action depicted."

(Female, divorced, age 65) "Doesn't everyone? They excite the mind and senses and heighten feelings."

(Female, widow, age 68) "Yes, I'm generally not concerned about sex—but following an exposure to stimulating visual experiences I feel excited."

(Male, single, age 66) "Yes. Erection and strong desire for sex."

(Female, widow, age 74) "Yes. Erotic art excites me."

(Male, married, age 67) "Yes. At times it starts sexual play."

(Male, married, age 67) "Some sexy pictures or movies do give me an erection."

(Female, married, age 71) "Yes. I love looking at male or female bodies at the beach in summer and at magazine centerfolds."

(Female, married, age 67) "Reading books about sex is exciting and gives one ideas."

(Female, married, age 67) "Yes. I get warm, moist, and desirous."

(Male, divorced, age 66) "Pictures, no. Books, no. Movies, yes."

(Male, widowed, age 74) "Yes. Puts my mind on sex when it would otherwise not be."

(Female, widow, age 66) "Sometimes. It is a reminder of my own sex life."

(Female, married, age 72) "I have noticed a heavy breathing and a very wet clitoris area."

(Male, married, age 82) "I get an erection looking at the nude pictures in the modern girlie magazines. I never bought any but got them out of an ashcan."

(Male, married, age 65) "Yes. Switches my mind and body to a sexy channel."

(Male, widowed, age 68) "Yes. So-called hard core, actual showing of the sexual parts and penetration."

(Female, married, age 77) "Yes. Maybe because I haven't had sexual relations for a long time."

(Female, widow, age 81) "Very excitable."

(Male, married, age 64) "Yes. It is erotic visual pleasure."

(Male, married, age 71) "At times it acts as a stimulant."

(Female, married, age 63) "Oh yes. Turns me on. I get a feeling in my vagina."

(Female, married, age 62) "Yes. Reading is usually more exciting and perhaps promises more than the actual act itself."

(Male, married, age 68) "Yes. I still do—then want to have sex with my partner."

(Male, married, age 69) "Somewhat. I imagine myself taking part."

(Female, married, age 67) "I find it stimulating as does my husband."

(Male, married, age 62) "Yes. I consider myself a voyeur."

(Male, divorced, age 74) "Yes—but not enough to be satisfied without a body."

(Female, widow, age 69) "Yes because of the power of suggestion and then there are our fantasies (Knight in Shining Armor, etc.)"

(Male, married, age 67) "Yes. It is much like foreplay to me."

Many times we were approached after our talks with statements like, "I want you to know that I'm 83 years old. My husband died two years ago. He was 85. We had sex right up until the end. We loved it and it was wonderful." And a 75-year-old woman confided: "Young people think they discovered sex. I've had three husbands and did everything in bed and will continue to do it." This is hardly what we had expected to hear from what appeared to be a typically grandmotherly-looking woman. But as we proceeded with our survey we wondered if there was such a thing as a typical grandmother.

There is, in truth, nothing really remarkable about these responses. Only the age of the respondents makes us take special notice. We expect an adolescent boy to think about dying while making love, but a 70-year-old man who would "rather die in the act of sex than any other way" reveals an erotic fantasy that is both surprising and encouraging in its frankness.

A further indication of our respondents' interest in sex is the answers we received to Question 3, "What do you think is an ideal sex life for older people?" Many gave enthusiastic responses showing that they have hardly lowered their expectations for active and fulfilling sexuality in their later years.

A widow of 70 expressed her notion of the ideal sex life as, "Each partner respecting each other's needs, responding sexually to them and trying to see that each reaches a climax, hopefully together, at the same time." Another, a married woman of 60, writes, "Sexual contact once or twice weekly. Daily caressing, kissing, touching." Some, like this married man of 60, can even project a forceful laissez-faire attitude usually associated with younger people: "*Equal* aggressiveness and no pressure from one to the other" (emphasis his).

As in their responses to many other questions, their concept suggests two people in a sharing, fulfilling, mutually giving relationship. "First you have to really like one another, respect one another, share the same interest and have the capacity of understanding one another, which all results in love," writes a 67-year-old widow. "Companionship, with an occasional hour together in the nude" is the ideal of a 79-year-old single woman. An 87-year-old divorced woman states, "With true lovers, if possible," while an 83-year-old married man comments: "To continue mutual sharing in sex."

The comments we have received certainly do not come from people on the sidelines of life. These men and women are telling us that they want and need sex; that it is obviously just as important for them as for young people. And it is not only the physical stimulation that is important. Sex is necessary for them to feel alive, to reaffirm their identity, and to communicate with a person they care about. It also generates a feeling of youthfulness and vitality, both physical and mental. And as one of the respondents said simply, "It's still thrilling—I love it and need it."

4

Masturbation

The people who responded to our survey belong to the generation that told their children in no uncertain terms that masturbation was an evil and harmful practice. This is what they had learned from their parents. In the early part of the century when our respondents were growing up, fear of sexuality reached a fever pitch. In 1914 one major publication warned parents that if their children were allowed to masturbate their impulses could get out of control and the youngsters could be "wrecked for life." Parents were advised to stop at almost nothing to keep their offsprings' hands off their sex organs. Metal gloves, chemicals applied to the hands, sleeves pinned to bars of the crib—all of these were recommended weapons in the battle against this pernicious, and obviously mighty, impulse.

Even in the 1930s, when our respondents were young parents of today's 40- and 50-year-olds, the attitudes toward autoeroticism were repressive. Insisting that he was enlightened on the subject, popular author Sherwood Eddy, writing on *Sex and Youth* in 1932, offered the reassurance that "epilepsy, insanity, tuberculosis and all the rest are never caused by masturbation." But rapidly switching gears, he went on to conclude:

> While on the one hand the evil effects of this habit of self-relief have been greatly exaggerated, and on the other hand the harmlessness of the practice has also been overemphasized, the weight of the best evidence would favor the view that there are such ill effects of the habit that it will be distinctly better for one to win and maintain complete control over this practice. . . . A man was made for bigger things than infantile fixations and morbid eroticism.

With this kind of "enlightenment," it is no wonder that generations grew up with the burden of guilt and shame firmly attached to their bodily pleasures.

But all this changed in the "swinging sixties" and "soaring seventies." As the *Redbook Report on Female Sexuality* humorously observed, "The activity once thought to cause warts is now recommended to do all but cure them." Today, it seems, masturbation is practically compulsory. Sex manuals are not considered up-to-date unless they include the obligatory exercises for individual and mutual masturbation. Feminist literature considers it essential for sexual development and a reliable means of achieving orgasm when partners are not available or are poor lovers. And it is now widely accepted that for many women masturbation is the best source of intense orgasm, an observation made by Masters and Johnson (among others) who actually regard the inability to have an orgasm through masturbation as a sexual disorder.

For males masturbation is today often recommended as a healthy outlet for the sexual needs of adolescents and young adults. It may be preferred by both men and women at times when sexual release is desired but the person is not in the mood for lovemaking. Other authorities suggest that a man masturbate when a partner is not available, on the theory that a man can lose potency if he does not experience sexual arousal and ejaculation with some regularity. Similarly, it has been suggested that high levels of female vaginal lubrication can be maintained by regularity of masturbation in the absence of sexual intercourse.

In *Liberating Masturbation,* Bette Dodson goes so far as to call masturbation "our primary sex life." This may be true since as children and adolescents most of us learn about our bodies and sexual responses through masturbation, which is often the only outlet for sexuality in those years. When we consider that for many older adults autoeroticism is also the only outlet, it is not an exaggeration to call it the most potentially important and frequently occurring form of sexual experience in the life cycle. Certainly it is the simplest—as one well-known sex therapist quipped, "You don't even have to brush your teeth."

Indeed, masturbation would seem to be one ideal outlet for sexuality during the later years, particularly for women. Females, as Kinsey and others have noted, show little decline in sexual responsiveness through the life cycle. Yet their sex lives and experiences are most often tied to men. And since men either die or withdraw from sex long before their partners (often because of real or feared impotence), many women are condemned to a no-sex existence. This is especially true if they feel masturbation and affairs are immoral, or if they have only limited opportunities to meet new men. Some of the saddest questionnaires we have received come from such women. Their responses overflow with exuberance, interest in sex, and indications of arousal from books, pictures, and their own fantasies, yet they have had no sex experiences at all since their husbands died (as long as thirteen years before). As one woman so powerfully brings the point home: "At age 69, without a husband, sex is as good as dead." For these women, and for many men who for one reason or another do not have a partner, why should masturbation not be one solution?

Nonetheless we didn't expect to find much masturbatory interest or activity among our respondents: first, because of the repressive era in which they were raised (could Portnoy's mother actually masturbate?); and second, because Kinsey had reported almost no masturbation in his older group. As he wrote in *Sexuality in the Human Male,* "Masturbation is the first major source of outlet to disappear from the [case] histories. A stray male is still involved at 75 years of age, but there is no complete masturbation to orgasm in any of the older histories." In his book on female sexuality, Kinsey didn't even bother to report on masturbation after age 60, despite the fact that he found an increasing interest in masturbation among women in each of the earlier decades.

We were, therefore, surprised at the frequency with which our respondents accepted, at least in principle, the practice of masturbation. Eighty-two percent responded positively to Question 14, "Many older people masturbate to relieve sexual tensions. What do you think about this?" A somewhat greater percentage of female respondents (85 percent) compared with male respondents (76 percent) accepted masturbation. However, when we asked "Do you masturbate? How often," their responses were not nearly as positive. Of those who accepted masturbation in principle, far fewer admitted doing it themselves. Less than half (44 percent males and 47 percent females) of those who responded to Question 15 said they masturbate (Table 15). This is a strikingly high incidence in the light of Kinsey's data, and the beliefs of the turn-of-the-century generation who were their parents. For example, ninety percent of the men and 87 percent of the women who answered Question 41, "How and what were you taught about sex as a child?" reported a negative experience (Table 41). Twenty-two percent acknowledge masturbation once a week or more, while another 20 percent boldly said they masturbate "when in the mood." Others indicate lower frequencies of masturbation (Table 15.5).

We were impressed that so many were willing to talk about and admit to masturbation, especially since, not knowing what their peers were doing and having virtually no guidelines about what was "normal," they might have been expected to react with guilt and shame. So we must regard the incidence of masturbation that our respondents reported as the expression of a powerful sexual need that transcends taboo and early training. Masturbation, incidentally, was not limited to people without partners; among those who report that they masturbate, 40 percent were married. Among the total married group who responded to Question 15. 39 percent masturbate compared with 47 percent of the widowed group (Table 15A). Not surprisingly, the divorced and single respondents show the highest incidence of masturbation. Sixty-three percent of the divorced and 76 percent of the singles report masturbation. As Table 15A also shows, males and females do not differ markedly within the married, widowed and divorced groups. But in the small sample of singles, 81 percent of females compared with 69 percent of males report masturbation. Also, our data show little abatement of masturbation from decade to decade (Table 15B). Masturbation is reported by 49 percent of the 60–69-year-olds, 42 percent of the 70–79-year-olds and 40 percent of the 80-and-over group.

Many saw masturbation as a positive, healthy, and necessary form of sexual release. Some were openly enthusiastic and outspoken in their endorsement of it and, as the following quotes show, many of the respondents had overcome the taboo of their generation and were once again responding with a resounding "yes!"

(Female, divorced, age 72) "It's about the only answer for singles. Yes, weekly plus."
(Male, married, age 83) "It is necessary at times for a partner if he or she is rejected."

(Female, widow, age 70) "I think it is perfectly acceptable. It's needed especially when there is no sexual partner available. If I am keyed up, feel optimistic, happy, I can masturbate several times a week. If depressed, lonely, longer periods of time elapse without masturbation."

(Female, single, age 65)"I only just developed a relationship six months ago—the first long-term relationship in my life. I sometimes masturbated before my present relationship, maybe once or twice a month—haven't felt like doing it lately."

(Female, married, age 73) "It's OK. Yes, once in a while, especially when I'm lonely."

(Female, widow, age 71) "There's no other way. Yes. Sometimes."

(Male, married, age 67) "I think it's OK. Yes. Fairly often."

(Female, widow, age 80) "If they feel they need it. I do not object to anything going on in privacy."

(Male, married, age 69) "I think it's an excellent chance to use your imagination."

(Female, married, age 65) "I think it's great. You only have to satisfy yourself."

(Female, married, age 60) "It's OK. I have done it many times when my husband climaxed and left me in want. Also when my husband was overseas. Yes. Not as often as I used to though. Only when my husband finishes sex before I do and it leaves me nervous and upset."

(Male, married, age 68) "Many do so and I feel that it keeps up physical feelings. Better than neglect. Yes. Biweekly."

(Male, widower, age 73) "I do it and don't see any harm in it. Yes. Sometimes twice a week."

(Male, single, age 61) "It's normal in both young and old. Yes. Twice a week."

(Female, widow, age 69) "Lots of older people who are alone. I think it relieves them. Yes. When I think of my husband because we were very much in love."

(Female, single, age 71) "I have practiced this from youth on and consider it something to become accomplished in. One should appreciate one's body most of all. Yes."

(Female, divorced, age 65) "Same as I did when younger. If you can't have a partner it's a way to achieve climax—better than nothing. Yes, when alone for too long a period of time."

(Female, divorced, age 61) "I think it's great. Yes—once a week."

(Male, married, age 71) "I believe it's the only choice in some cases. Not too often."

(Female, married, age 69) "Psychologists and psychiatrists today are almost of one mind that this is not at all wrong. In fact it is perfectly normal and probably commonly practiced."

(Female, divorced, age 62) "I don't know how many do. I think it's great. It solves the problem."

(Female, widow, age 78) "I don't know. But if it helps the individual, more power to them. Yes—maybe twice a month."

(Female, married, age 72) "It's better than going to a whore house."

(Female, widow, age 74) "Not bad at all—have at times used it to relieve tension. Once every three months or longer interval."

(Male, married, age 75) "I started masturbating at 12 and still do when I think it necessary. I have no guilt. Yes. When necessary."

(Female, divorced, age 69) "I cannot do without it. Yes—3–4 times a month."

(Male, widower, age 81) "I was taught it was a sin but I have changed my mind. I think in many cases it is a blessing. Yes, quite often."

(Female, widow, age 69) "Fine. Every time I feel like it."

(Male, divorced, age 65) "An absolute necessity, even if married. Yes—2–4 times a week."

(Female, widow, age 84) "I need it. About once a month."

(Female, widow, age 73) "I think if it satisfies you, go at it. Yes. Once a week—at least."

(Female, widow, age 72) "A good idea—it relieves tensions. Yes. Three or four times a month—usually after reading an exciting book or when I think of my husband and our love."

(Male, widowed, age 65) "Very good way to relieve oneself. Yes, twice a week."

(Male, married, age 66) "Approve of it 100%—especially for women because there is less availability of men as sex partners."

(Female, married, age 63) "Never to relieve tension. I do it because it makes me feel good."

(Male, widowed, age 62) "It beats tension but not sexual intercourse. Yes—rarely."

(Female, widow, age 67) "I do it quite often and it's OK."

(Female, married, age 71) "I approve. I do it intermittently after anything in the day has caused sexual arousal. But I do it in the bathtub, in privacy."

(Female, divorced, age 66) "Fine. At times it's a great nightcap. Better than alcohol for the body. Yes—maybe once a week."

(Female, divorced, age 63) "They do when young too. No difference. My husband did for the last 2 years of our 23, every night."

(Female, married, age 67) "I do masturbate. Maybe once in two weeks. Why not? It's my body."

(Male, divorced, age 66) "If it's the best you can do—do it! Yes, once a day when physically inactive; once every two to three days when active."

(Female, widow, age 81) "It's very satisfactory. Yes. When I need it."

(Female, widow, age 74) "Great. Younger people do it. Let's keep the juices flowing."

(Male, single, age 72) "People who say they don't are liars!"

While these respondents seem as open and free with the idea of masturbation as many young people, we must keep in mind that they represent only a part of our sample; others continue to be inhibited by Victorian attitudes, still unable to bridge the gap between acceptance of masturbation and the actual performance. Some who do masturbate feel guilty or ambivalent about it:

(Female, married, age 66) "I do it and I hate it. Yes. Very seldom."

(Male, widower, age 75) "Not a very good idea. It causes nervousness. Yes. Don't know how often."

(Female, widow, age 65) "I hope it's not wrong to do so. Yes. Sometimes not for years; sometimes after a date when the man makes advances and I refuse because I feel it's immoral and I feel nothing for the man. Then must release the desires he has stirred up in me."

(Male, separated, age 68) "Good for getting sex off the mind. Not for five or six months, then after seeing females in bikinis, etc., it overcomes me and I succumb."

(Female, widow, age 71) "Disgusting but have to do it sometimes to get relief. Yes. Once a week."

(Male, widower, age 67) "If sex isn't available with someone, we're bound to have the urge; and much as it may be that we try not to, I guess we all do. I do think it can be done too much for health. It varies. Sometimes I go for months at a time without and others every two weeks."

(Female, widow, age 71) "It's all right. About twice a year after having some alcohol."

(Female, single, age 65) "I think it makes me feel guilty so I think we should write some poems, sing, dance, etc., to sublimate the desire for this. Once several months ago; about twice in five years."

(Male, widower, age 78) "I approve? No, I don't masturbate. But occasionally I still have a wet dream."

Others like this 67-year-old widower rationalize masturbation by convincing themselves that it is necessary for health: "I think it is necessary to relieve tensions and clear the skin. Not having relief brings pimples, etc." Another 71-year-old married man said, "It's good to get the poison out."

It is also significant that many respondents mentioned masturbation without the prod of a direct question about it, particularly in answer to Question 20, "Do sexual experiences leave you satisfied? What do you do when you are not satisfied?" and Question 32, "How can older people deal with their sexual feelings if they are not married or if they do not have partners?" Again, since masturbation is not directly addressed by these questions, the fact that it is mentioned among the many possible solutions in 20 percent of the answers to Question 20 and in 26 percent of the answers to Question 32 underscores its importance for older people (Tables 20.5 and 32).

(Male, married, age 69) "Be less selective in one-night stands. Take some risks with affairs (women, lesbian relationships). Masturbate."

(Female, married, age 69) "I can't say about that. I never had any trouble getting a man when I wanted one or was attracted to one.... Either keep busy to keep their minds off sex or masturbate."

(Male, widower, age 73) "I suppose they will have to masturbate."

(Male, single, age 72) "Lots of ways. They have artificial things like vibrators."

(Male, married, age 65) "They will have to figure out for themselves on an individual basis as to their need and act accordingly. Also masturbate."

(Female, married, age 67) "If the need for sex is great, masturbate."

(Female, widow, age 66) "Rather than settle for anyone, masturbate."

(Male, divorced, age 69) "Most leave me very satisfied. On rare occasions when I'm not, I either masturbate or read or watch television to come down enough to sleep."

(Female, widow, age 71) "Hard work. Get involved in clubs, centers, etc. Masturbate for relief."

(Male, married, age 62) "Masturbate. Go to prostitutes."

(Female, widow, age 73) "If you don't have partners, then there is nobody to arouse you. Last resort—masturbation."

(Female, married, age 67) "Exercise, self-manipulation."

(Male, married, age 80) "If they think of sex strongly and no woman is around, go to the bathroom and relieve yourself. It takes a while but the feeling will come so you can relieve yourself."

(Female, widow, age 65) "Use artificial means."

(Male, married, age 75) "Yes, if I have an orgasm. If not, I usually masturbate."

(Female, married, age 66) "Yes, as a rule. At times I've had to masturbate."

(Female, married, age 61) "Usually masturbate or get up and read."

(Male, married, age 75) "I generally masturbate the next day."

(Female, widow, age 70) "They can masturbate or go out and look for partners wherever they want."

(Female, single, age 65) "Theoretically older women could have liaisons with younger men. Maybe ultra-sexually-active young men should form relationships with the extra supply of older women. Otherwise, older people can masturbate."

Again these respondents' attitude toward masturbation and the ease with which many of them do it is all the more surprising when we consider that so few in the sample felt they had received an enlightened sex education.

What about the fact that Kinsey reported virtually no masturbation in his male sample after age 70? We must bear in mind that Kinsey's

70-year-olds were born around 1870, whereas ours were born around 1909. Those born in 1909 in Kinsey's sample were in their mid-30s when he began interviewing, by which point in their lives 95.8 percent of the males and 60 percent of the females in his study had masturbated. It is, therefore, not surprising to find that many of our sample (who coincide with the mid-30s in Kinsey's sample) are still practicing it.

The discrepancy in our survey between those who accept the practice of masturbation and those who report actually masturbating is somewhat suspect. Kinsey's data suggest that the subjects in our survey have had masturbatory experience, at least when they were younger, in spite of being brought up under the taboo. Perhaps the guilt reemerges during the later years, when the need for alternate sexual outlets surfaces. Masturbation for many is still identified with childish behavior and reactivates old conflicts and feelings of shame. Perhaps for some who do not practice it there is the disengagement with much of life noted by gerontologists. This disengagement would extend to all sexual outlets where gratification or the giving oneself pleasure is denied as an intense involvement with life. For others who did not report masturbation, it is possible that this form of sexual release is considered "doing it alone." As such, the idea of masturbation may be avoided since it can evoke feelings of painful aloneness for those who are without partners, or an undesirable admission of a partner's inadequacy for those who have partners.

We suspect, too, that there is more masturbation among our respondents than they have reported. We cannot help recalling the comment of the 72-year-old single male, "People who say they don't are liars!" Half of those who endorsed masturbation left blank the questions of participation or frequency. Others used suspiciously guarded qualifiers that were not used in other responses: "only very seldom"; "not very often"; "only very occasionally"; "on very rare occasions"; "almost never."

Of all the sensitive topics that we probed in our study—nudity, orgasm, erection problems—only masturbation appeared to arouse pronounced guilt and defensiveness. "Yes, I do it," many of the older people seemed to be communicating, but "only because there's nothing better available." One 78-year-old widower even called older people who masturbate "nuts." Clearly, powerful taboos do not vanish easily.

The issue seems less one of allowing themselves pleasure than of who is to be the pleasure-giver. Our 78-year-old widower who said "nuts" to masturbation said he would try anything—but presumably he had in mind any*thing* with any*one*. And several women who called masturbation "revolting" went on to report, with no apparent sense of contradiction, that their most preferred form of sexual stimulation was having the clitoris stimulated manually or orally by their partner. The key word here, of course, is "partner."

It is unfortunate that the masturbation taboo still has a grip on so many older adults. One would hope that people who have had the toughness to survive into the later years would not be caught between their desires and irrational principles. Their dilemma is all the more poignant because, as we have seen, their sexual feelings are very much alive (the responses are peppered with words like "urges," "desires," "frustrations," "tensions"), yet they can't permit themselves this natural and convenient outlet.

Because of the limitations in sexual outlets for older people, masturbation surfaces as a crucial issue in their lives. Perhaps those who find it so difficult to allow themselves this form of pleasure are caught up in the same struggle they experienced at adolescence. In those days, confronted with an erect penis or moist vagina, they found that the hand was willing but the mind would intercede. Or, at least the mind would *try* to intercede; for the vast majority of adolescents the hand was usually quicker than the head. These dilemmas plagued older people when they were young, ironically engendering more preoccupation with sex than if society had not imposed its purifying restrictions. In those days our respondents had to follow the rules set down by their parents. But now that they have lived through and to some extent participated in the sexual revolution, it seems ludicrous that older men and women should cast their sights back to the repressive values of another generation, when so much more freedom and fulfillment should rightfully be theirs.

A lot rests on the older person's ability to change. Many younger people think of the old as rigid and inflexible, not capable of making significant shifts in attitudes and behavior. Yet many of our respondents suggest that they are willing and eager to embrace new forms of satisfaction. The very fact that so many endorse the practice of masturbation, even though others are inhibited about indulging in it themselves, indicates that they have begun to adjust to new times and new sexual mores.

5

The Female Orgasm and Love Experience

Women over 60 don't like or want to have orgasms. TRUE   FALSE

Women in their 60s, 70s, and 80s did not have orgasms
when they were young.   TRUE   FALSE

Women over 60 don't have regular orgasms in their
current sexual experiences.   TRUE   FALSE

Women over 60 have weak orgasms at best.   TRUE   FALSE

Women over 60 don't insist on orgasm in their sexual
experiences.   TRUE   FALSE

Women over 60 have trouble demanding orgasmic
fulfillment by their partner.   TRUE   FALSE

The answer to all of the above is FALSE. Who said that older women
weren't orgasmic? Even champions of female sexuality have made this
assumption. As recently as 1977 the authors of *The Redbook Report on
Female Sexuality* wrote: "Several decades ago, many women neither
expected orgasms nor sought them, and lots of wives never knew what
they were anyway." Our female respondents certainly told us
otherwise.

Not too long ago there was a prevailing view that men were sexual
and women were not. Men, supposedly, had orgasmic urgency. If they
got aroused, they needed immediate release—orgasm. For that reason
women were careful not to be "teases." Men were not to be aroused
unless the woman was prepared to "go all the way." After all, men
could get "blue balls," that painful condition that demanded they turn
to "bad girls" or prostitutes to ease their suffering. Every respectable

woman prior to the 1960s tolerantly accepted this. But who ever heard of "blue clit," even though there is actually a medical condition, called Taylor's syndrome, in which high levels of excitement in the female results in vasocongestion that can lead to pain, discomfort, and physical complications if orgasm does not occur. Somehow this condition has never gotten the publicity that the equivalent male syndrome received.

In retrospect, it all seems part of a grand chauvinistic fantasy. Women didn't really need sex. It was just their duty in the service of the male. Women were there to allow the male to discharge his tension in orgasm—to serve him in bed, as well as in the kitchen and living room. At least this was the male belief as dictated by society.

Women were also called "frigid" in those days. Men did not welcome this unhappy state, but at the same time it confirmed their idea of woman's nonsexual nature. Women were basically passive and receptive; men the active doers, needing women to achieve their goal—orgasm.

With man and woman existing in master/slave relationship, the world was secure in a prison of its own making. But slaves revolt. Revolutions create change. And a revolution was in the making. The goal was the liberation of the woman—in the marketplace, in the world of business, in the kitchen, and last, but never least, in the bedroom. Women were no longer "frigid." The prison bars of chastity and passivity had, miraculously, melted! Women were now talking about the inability to have multiple orgasms rather than the inability to have a single orgasm. Those special women with problems were now scientifically appraised as suffering from "orgasmic inadequacy," a term introduced by Masters and Johnson. Frigidity became as outmoded a concept as had the difference between the vaginal and clitoral orgasm—the long-standing smokescreen issue which Diane Keaton so humorously recalls in the Woody Allen movie *Manhattan* when she comments, "I finally had an orgasm and my doctor said it was the wrong kind!" Women no longer believed that the only valid orgasm was the one produced by the man's penis during intercourse. Hopefully, the comments of well-known sex therapists Graber and Graber can finally place a lid on the controversy of different kinds of orgasms: "In any case, it is an exercise in futility to compare orgasm. No orgasm is better, more right, or more mature than another. Each should simply be enjoyed for itself." Sexuality can now be seen as multidirectional. And women can choose which direction to take.

When the "orgasm is an orgasm" principle introduced by Kinsey, demonstrated by Masters and Johnson, and confirmed by Hite penetrated the mentality of women brainwashed by a "macho" society, the notion of frigidity quickly began to evaporate. The new word was out: almost any woman could have an orgasm—if not one way, with a partner, then another; and surely through masturbation. For the first time it became common currency that if a woman could not orgasm during intercourse it was likely to be either the man's inadequacy as a lover or the structural placement of the woman's clitoris. Recognition was given to the fact that, in many cases, the penis was not providing sufficient stimulation in the right places for the woman to orgasm or that the man was unable to maintain an erection long enough for the woman to climax. The mismatching was now on *both* sides. With this new consciousness-raising, women were freed to control their own orgasm and pleasure and they could now conceive of and achieve climax by hand, mouth, vibrator or other convenient object. The action could take place alone or with a partner—the choice was theirs.

Yet if in the past we had a blind spot about women having orgasms, we had—and still have—an even bigger blind spot about older women having them. It is strange that this myth has been perpetuated for so long when research by Kinsey and others since the 1940s suggests that older women are more orgasmic than younger women. Kinsey showed that after one year of marriage, his female sample achieved orgasm 63 percent of the time during sexual intercourse; after five years, 71 percent; after ten years, 77 percent; after fifteen years, 81 percent; and after twenty years, 85 percent. Carried to its logical conclusion, this decidedly upward trend gives us every reason to speculate that after thirty years of marriage there would be greater frequency of female orgasm and after forty years even more so. This assumption has compelling plausibility when coupled with Kinsey's finding that females maintain a high level of sexual response capability throughout the life cycle. He further recognized that when older women did show a decline, it was due to circumstances affecting their male partners—death, impotence, or the male's withdrawal from sex for any number of reasons. Yet these findings and their implications have been ignored in favor of sustaining our stereotypes and prejudices against the old.

Now the younger woman is pushed to be orgasmic. Moreover she demands it of herself and her lover. But what about the older woman? We still assume that she, even more so than the older man, "is over the hill." She has had it, we think, conveniently forgetting that, going backwards in time, we have always assumed that she never had it in the first place.

But contrary to popular belief, older women not only know about orgasms, they want them, they need them and, most of all, *they have them.* Our respondents certainly did. And their answers to Question 1, "What do you consider a good sexual experience?" leave no doubt on the matter. Sixty-nine percent of the females list orgasm first (Table 1). Only 17 percent of the females consider intercourse per se a good sexual experience—it is the orgasm that is most essential.

(Female, married, age 61) "When both partners achieve orgasm."
(Female, widow, age 70) "When both reach climax at same time."
(Female, divorced, age 66) "An orgasm with the man you love."
(Female, married, age 73) "Couple in love, man and woman, each desiring the other and climaxing at the same time."
(Female, married, age 66) "When it lasts long enough to have an orgasm."
(Female, widow, age 69) "A building-up to a mutual orgasm."
(Female, widow, age 81) "Climaxing together."
(Female, married, age 77) "Both having a climax."
(Female, divorced, age 74) "When both parties come to climax."
(Female, married, age 64) "Complete orgasm."
(Female, widow, age 65) "A warm loving physical fulfillment with orgasm."
(Female, married, age 70) "The fact that I am about to have a great big orgasm."
(Female, married, age 69) "A feeling of 'oneness' with my husband, tender foreplay and a climax together."

(Female, married, age 66) "A good relationship with complete orgasms for both."

(Female, divorced, age 65) "A mutual pleasure with affection, sexual excitement and orgasm/ejaculation."

(Female, married, age 70) "When both partners have an orgasm."

(Female, married, age 60) "A complete intercourse with orgasm."

(Female, widow, age 72) "When both experience the climax."

(Female, married, age 62) "When it occurs when both want it, in the proper atmosphere and setting, either quietly and traditionally or passionately and creatively and only if orgasm occurs."

(Female, married, age 67) "Foreplay to stimulate, delay of male entering to heighten desire for fulfillment, a long orgasm."

(Female, married, age 69) "An orgasm after much foreplay."

(Female, widow, age 63) "Touching, cuddling, kissing—the foreplay leading up to intercourse with a climax."

(Female, divorced, age 63) "Having sex with the person I like and respect. Excitement, music, warmth, sharing, caring, orgasm."

(Female, single, age 63) "Orgasm and affectionate lover."

(Female, divorced, age 64) "When two people can have an orgasm together, at the same moment."

(Female, widow, age 78) "Simultaneous climax."

(Female, married, age 64) "Responding to a desire for sexuality with a partner I love—being stimulated sexually—orgasm."

(Female, widow, age 72) "Both arriving at a climax."

(Female, widow, age 77) "It should be based on love, acceptance, comradeship, and mutual understanding. If there are no medical problems orgasms/erection will lead to good sexual experience."

(Female, widow, age 78) "Coming together."

(Female, widow, age 74) "Loving your partner and reaching satisfactory orgasm."

(Female, widow, age 82) "Coming together."

(Female, married, age 77) "Fondling before intercourse and then satisfactory orgasm."

(Female, divorced, age 61) "Mutual attraction—mutual consent—foreplay—arousement, coitus, ideally ending in orgasm."

(Female, widow, age 72) "A mutual orgasm."

(Female, married, age 62) "Sex act preceded by a pleasant time together—sense of humor, joking, laughing, talking, 'opening up,' good music, a shower together, bodily caressing, kissing, foreplay, a mutual orgasm."

While the feminist movement and the literature on sex therapy have played down the simultaneous orgasm, it is noteworthy that so many of our respondents (male and female) still look to it as the ideal.

Some elaborated further on the importance of the relationship as well as orgasm.

> (Female, widow, age 70) "When both parties have pleasure and climax. Preferably with strong affection and love."
>
> (Female, widow, age 73) "Unhurried sex, kissing and fondling before sex. My partner fondling my vagina, then inserting the penis, then orgasm."
>
> (Female, single, age 65) "With a partner with whom there is a long-term feeling of mutual respect, enjoyment, trust to spend time, cuddling, nude, gradually becoming more focused on genitals and ending with orgasm for both . . . me first."
>
> (Female, widow, age 67) "Includes affection, playfulness, foreplay, vaginal orgasm in concert with partner."
>
> (Female, widow, age 69) "To have an affair with a man you like and really enjoy it; to come to a climax together."
>
> (Female, widow, age 70) "A strong sense of being desired. Being highly stimulated by my partner, stroked where I am most responsive sexually and reaching an orgasm."
>
> (Female, widow, age 73) "When both partners are completely in agreement to having sex—in a relaxed environment. No children or others about. Taking time to fully enjoy our relationship. Orgasm."
>
> (Female, married, age 62) "When two people are compatible in their sexual needs, as playing, touching and loving and having an orgasm."
>
> (Female, widow, age 66) "Having orgasm with a partner that turns you on. Someone you care about."
>
> (Female, married, age 74) "When in harmony with mate and orgasm occurs."
>
> (Female, married, age 71) "The best includes love, tenderness, orgasm."

(Female, married, age 65) "Have loving touchings with talks and a climax and holding hands whenever you are together plus things in common."

(Female, divorced, age 79) "Mutual enjoyment of body, especially of genitals and, if possible, orgasm."

(Female, married, age 69) "Starting with foreplay without hurrying and enjoying the interaction of pleasing each other which stimulates both people to a full and successful climax, satisfactory to both."

(Female, married, age 72) "When both partners want it and orgasm is reached together is the best, but all is good, the loving and caressing."

(Female, married, age 65) "Have loving touchings with talks and a climax and holding hands whenever you are together plus things in common."

Our respondents clearly wanted their needs fulfilled. Orgasm was essential to the sexual experience, they said. Yet their desire was by no means purely narcissistic. Most often, the concern expressed was for two people; the focus was on mutuality, love, and caring. Unlike the joke in which the wife, responding to her husband's sexual offer, replies "Start without me," they needed and wanted the other person. Here are some other responses in which love and mutuality are considered primary in a good sexual experience:

(Female, married, age 79) "One in which both partners express their love for each other deeply and fully."

(Female, widow, age 68) "Love and caring between two people who want each other's needs to be expressed."

(Female, widow, age 66) "Able to communicate in a loving way— and act accordingly. Respect wishes of other partner."

(Female, married, age 64) "Both partners satisfying each other with mutual concern for each other."

(Female, married, age 62) "Making love with your beloved and pleasing both."

(Female, widow, age 65) "Relaxed. Good. Another person cares."

(Female, widow, age 63) "When each partner tries to please each other."

(Female, widow, age 83) "When husband and wife enjoy it together."

(Female, widow, age 74) "One that encompasses love, deep emotional experience, a oneness that is satisfying and gratifying."

(Female, widow, age 68) "An experience between two people who respect and care for one another—where relationships are satisfying and mutually enhancing—where both partners can fully embrace and love the other."

(Female, widow, age 68) "When you and your spouse truly love one another and are devoted to each other."

(Female, married, age 67) "Coupling with someone you care about."

(Female, married, age 67) "Having a man make you feel that you are very special to him and he wants you because he loves you. He should be made to feel the same."

(Female, married, age 70) "Any experience which makes one feel deeply loved by someone you really like very much or love."

(Female, widow, age 65) "When two people actually love each other."

(Female, widow, age 69) "Mutual enjoyment for both parties. Also mutual respect and never a casual one-night experience."

(Female, married, age 60) "Conveying feeling of love and caring together with a release of sexual tension."

(Female, married, age 67) "One in which both parties experience the enjoyment of closeness and a fulfillment that is both physical and emotional."

(Female, divorced, age 62) "A loving encounter with someone you care for."

(Female, widow, age 76) "A mutual satisfaction that includes a feeling of love and calm, fulfilled security."

(Female, divorced, age 62) "Being very much in love with the person—an ongoing relationship with empathy and tenderness between the partners."

To further explore what in the sexual experience was primary for our respondents, we posed Question 4: "What in the sexual act is most important to you?" Again, without using any leading language or suggestions in the question, it is striking that 40 percent of the female respondents spontaneously cited orgasm as the most important, a greater percentage than for any other category (Table 4).

Some were more strictly goal-oriented than others. They said:

(Female, married, age 69) "Reaching a climax."
(Female, divorced, age 65) "Mutual orgasms."
(Female, married, age 74) "Orgasm together."
(Female, married, age 64) "An orgasm."
(Female, single, age 72) "Climax."
(Female, widow, age 80) "Climax."
(Female, married, age 60) "Entrance and orgasm."
(Female, married, age 63) "When you come."
(Female, divorced, age 65) "The orgasm."
(Female, widow, age 65) "The actual act, not the foreplay, especially if both are ready. Why waste time?"
(Female, married, age 75) "Stroking and then orgasm."
(Female, widow, age 70) "The orgasm and the feeling of being one."
(Female, married, age 67) "The foreplay is very important—and next comes orgasm."
(Female, divorced, age 79) "Genital contact with heightened emotions. Orgasm. Touching—all over body."
(Female, married, age 60) "Feeling turned on and alive. Orgasm makes me feel good."
(Female, widow, age 64) "Foreplay and consequent orgasm."
(Female, widow, age 67) "The fondling that arouses the passion leading to orgasm."
(Female, married, age 70) "At this age clitoral climax or orgasm."
(Female, widow, age 69) "Orgasm, of course."
(Female, divorced, age 67) "Satisfying partner and reaching climax."
(Female, divorced, age 71) "Being able to have a climax."
(Female, married, age 62) "The foreplay, the innovative, imaginative procedures, the orgasm."
(Female, widow, age 67) "Climax is the most exciting feeling but the importance of foreplay and fun is almost equally important."
(Female, widow, age 80) "Orgasm."
(Female, married, age 66) "The finality of the act. I like to have a *good orgasm.*"

Even if orgasm is critical, again the partner is not neglected. An orgasm occurs, many women say, because two people are having a mutually stimulating love experience. Both emotional *and* physical pleasure were often stressed in their answers:

(Female, widow, age 67) "Love and orgasm."

(Female, married, age 65) "Tenderness and climax."

(Female, widow, age 66) "The lovingness of the two parties. Climax."

(Female, married, age 66) "Loving, touching, gentleness and finally the climax."

(Female, widow, age 70) "Mutual love, and then foreplay and orgasm."

(Female, married, age 63) "The care and thoughtfulness of each partner and the satisfaction of a climax."

(Female, widow, age 68) "The total life relationship—loving foreplay—mutual orgasm."

(Female, married, age 71) "The orgasm is probably the most important."

(Female, widow, age 83) "Preliminary affection. Touching. Communication. Both oral and physical sex. Patience to please and fulfill. Orgasm."

(Female, married, age 65) "Tenderness and climax."

(Female, widow, age 65) "The orgasm after tender touching and kissing."

(Female, married, age 62) "The expression of a loving relationship, the orgasm peak and later, release."

(Female, widow, age 83) "The warmth of contact with your partner and orgasm."

(Female, widow, age 82) "Relaxing afterwards in your lover's arms and feeling perfectly fulfilled."

(Female, married, age 68) "A bit of playfulness, affection, words of love and closeness—simultaneous climax is good too."

(Female, married, age 67) "Closeness, a few complimentary words of endearment and—wow—orgasm."

(Female, married, age 63) "Tenderness, warmth as well as orgasm."

(Female, married, age 62) "Touching and reaching climax, feeling you've shared love and given pleasure."

(Female, widow, age 69) "The deep feeling of belonging to each other after the climax."

(Female, married, age 71) "Earlier in life, the act itself, from anticipation to climax. Now I feel that the intimacy and tenderness involved in the coupling is most important for me—though there are times when I would settle simply for a good, hard fuck."

Some placed exclusive emphasis on the feeling during the sex act (19 percent "love" category):

(Female, widow, age 61) "If you love someone."
(Female, married, age 64) "Being with the one you love."
(Female, widow, age 66) "Kindness and consideration."
(Female, married, age 61) "Warmth and intimacy."
(Female, widow, age 69) "To make love and tell me nice things."
(Female, married, age 65) "Love."
(Female, widow, age 69) "The love-making."
(Female, divorced, age 63) "Preliminaries—closeness—affection—sharing."
(Female, married, age 60) "A feeling of being one with my husband and the warmth and love that is released."
(Female, widow, age 60) "One in which each partner is fulfilled."
(Female, widow, age 74) "The reciprocity of love."
(Female, single, age 71) "Understanding, sharing, good give-and-take. Free expression of needs together and effort to meet each other's needs."
(Female, married, age 64) "The fact that it is an expression of closeness to someone I have loved for 47 years."
(Female, married, age 67) "The feeling of closeness and the satisfaction when my body responds properly."
(Female, widow, age 71) "The feeling of communication with my partner."
(Female, widow, age 68) "My enjoyment and my partner's."
(Female, married, age 70) "Tenderness, understanding, appreciation of one's spouse without ever letting on that the spouse is aging, wrinkled, etc."
(Female, divorced, age 62) "Tenderness—a feeling of being loved—and foreplay—of course, touching and cuddling."
(Female, married, age 72) "The love and closeness I feel toward my husband."
(Female, married, age 64) "Being with the one you love."

(Female, widow, age 68) "Being caressed, kissed and loved."

(Female, married. age 81) "Closeness, intimacy."

(Female, widow, age 71) "Compatibility. Must like or *love* your partner."

(Female, widow, age 75) "Tenderness, appreciation, caring, faithfulness."

(Female, divorced, age 65) "The feeling of complete blending with another, yet staying individual."

(Female, divorced, age 74) "A strong arm under one's shoulders. A protective feeling for the night and an early morning coming together closely."

(Female, widow, age 73) "Love expressed in words, tenderness, caresses.

(Female, married, age 71) "Being in each other's arms, kissed and appreciated."

(Female, widow, age 66) "Holding, touching and knowing your partner loves you."

(Female, divorced, age 63) "Knowing I'm wanted, loved and desirable."

(Female, widow, age 73) "The feeling of being wanted."

(Female, married, age 64) "Comfort—touching, caressing, intimate sharing."

A number of respondents see orgasm as the "beginning and end." Their answers to Question 4 are most clearly summed up in the responses of a 72-year-old married woman and a 79-year-old divorced woman: "Going off!" "The finale!"

Many writers have given ample testimony to the fact that the female is superior to the male in both her capacity for and ability to sustain orgasm. Dr. Mary Jane Sherfey in *The Nature and Evolution of Female Sexuality* has stated: "The human female is sexually insatiable in the presence of the highest degree of sexual satiation." Such pioneers in the field as Kinsey, Masters and Johnson, and Hite have elaborated and offered empirical proof of this fact. Thus, Masters and Johnson speak of the female's capacity for "rapid return to orgasm immediately following an orgasmic experience" and of "maintaining an orgasmic experience for a relatively long period of time." Yet, in our culture, as

Masters and Johnson observe, the female orgasm has never achieved the primary status and attention given to the male's ejaculation. This is true even for younger women.

But what about the aging female, the woman in her 60s, 70s, and 80s? Again, though there are physiological changes—e.g., vaginal lubrication is produced by the younger woman within 15 to 30 seconds of initiation of sex play, but takes 1, 2, or even 4 to 5 minutes in the older woman—there is no objective evidence to suggest that there is any appreciable loss in sensation or feeling. The clitoris, in both the younger and older woman, continues to function as the main organ for sexual stimuli. That is, subjective levels of sexual tension initiated or elaborated by clitoral stimulation are no different for the older female as compared with the younger female. In fact, the woman of 80 has the same physical potential for orgasm as she did at 20! That the older woman is seeking discharge of tension through orgasmic release is also revealed in the observation of Masters and Johnson that women between the ages of 50 and 70 show increased patterns of masturbation after the onset of menopause. Women of all ages seek, need, and demand orgasm. The blunt responses to our questions dramatically affirm this.

Now that we have clearly established that older women want and value orgasm, the questions still to be answered are, do they in fact have orgasms, and if so, how often? The responses to Question 37, "How often do you reach climax or orgasm when making love? How does this compare with when you were younger?" convincingly show that older women are indeed orgasmic. Seventy-two percent of those women who responded to the question said they have an orgasm "always" or "most of the time." Another 27 percent say they have orgasm "sometimes." But the most dramatic evidence that orgasm is a reality in the sex lives of older women is the finding that *only* 1.5 percent—6 women in our entire sample—"never" have orgasm (Table 37). Even more startling is the analysis by age groups (Table 37A): 69 percent of the 60–69 year-olds are orgasmic "always" or "most of the time," as are 76 percent of the 70–79 year-olds and 68 percent of the over-80 group of women. This reported stability of rates of orgasm from age 60–91 confirms Masters and Johnson's conclusion that the female orgasmic response remains at a high level over the lifespan. If there were any lingering doubts about the older woman's orgasmic potential, one need look no further than our statistics for the "never" category, especially for the over-80 group. Not *one* female in the over-80 group who responded to Question 37 reported being non-orgasmic. The other groups reported similarly negligible levels. This supports Kinsey's observation of increased frequency of orgasm with each successive decade. Although Kinsey did not carry his investigation of this issue beyond age 60, the implication was there that older women would achieve high rates of orgasm. Now we have some concrete data.

How do our findings compare with rates of orgasm during lovemaking reported in other studies of younger women? In Shere Hite's sample, 88 percent say they are orgasmic. Similarly, the *Redbook* survey on female sexuality reports that 93 percent are orgasmic. In the more recent *Cosmopolitan* survey, the figure is 90 percent. These figures are somewhat lower than our 98.5 percent. Again, this confirms the fact that women who are orgasmic continue to be orgasmic, and for many, increasingly so. This is even clearer when we look at the figures on those who are non-orgasmic: Hite – 12 percent, *Redbook* – 7 percent, *Cosmopolitan* – 10 percent, Starr/Weiner – 1.5 percent.

Further evidence that the female orgasm becomes more predictable and reliable with increasing age are the figures on those who have orgasms "all of the time": 15 percent for the *Redbook* women, 20 percent for the *Cosmopolitan* women and 38 percent for the women in our sample (Hite does not report figures on "always").

While the three studies cited asked women about orgasm during sexual intercourse, our question inquired about orgasm during lovemaking. No doubt many or most of our respondents were referring to orgasm during intercourse, though this question needs further exploration. At the same time we must keep in mind Hite's observation that, whereas her question addressed orgasm during intercourse, many women considered the entire sexual experience as part of intercourse. She therefore cautions that orgasm during intercourse for many of her respondents does not necessarily mean *through* intercourse. Also, now that we have freed ourselves from the belief in primacy of orgasm through penile contact, it is the presence or absence of orgasm, by whatever means, that is the main issue.

Obviously, some of our respondents who are not currently sexually active are answering the question of the frequency of orgasm in terms of their most recent sexual experiences. For many, especially widows, the last experience may have been a number of months or even years earlier but during their later years nonetheless. Quite predictably, when we look at the data for the sexually active group, the reported frequency of orgasm is even greater (Table 37B).

Is orgasm a new phenomenon for our female respondents, a reflection and outgrowth of sexual consciousness-raising about the potential of women's sexual response that emerged from the feminist movement? Our data suggest otherwise. As part of Question 37, we asked our respondents to compare their current frequency of orgasm with when they were younger (Table 37.5). Eighty-six percent say that the frequency of orgasm is the same (66 percent) or better (20 percent). Only 14 percent say they achieve orgasm less often now. The message is clear—*these women are orgasmic and always have been*!

But is orgasm the most important part of the sexual experience for the older female? We sought to obtain direct clarification by asking Question 9: "How important is orgasm or climax in your sexual experiences?" The responses erased any doubt. Ninety-two percent of the female respondents say that orgasm is "very important" or "somewhat important" in their sexual experiences (Table 9). Of these, 63 percent are in the "very important" group:

(Female, widow, age 83) "The ultimate."
(Female, widow, age 70) "Orgasm is very important because without it I feel let down, disappointed, almost rejected. A sense of incompletion of myself."
(Female, divorced, age 66) "Quite important, but I did not know this until I reached my late 30s. I had three children *before* that."
(Female, widow, age 71) "I think it is important and I never had any trouble reaching it."
(Female, married, age 66) "I like the experience to culminate in that. I feel cheated if my husband doesn't work for that."
(Female, widow, age 66) "It eases all tensions."
(Female, married, age 66) "It relaxes me."
(Female, widow, age 89) "Feeling satisfied is very important. An orgasm does that."

(Female, widow, age 61) "Love it."

(Female, married, age 65) "An essential finality."

(Female, divorced, age 74) "Of utmost importance."

(Female, divorced, age 64) "The sex act is meaningless without it."

(Female, widow, age 79) "Complete satisfaction."

(Female, widow, age 81) "It's important to complete experience."

(Female, divorced, age 65) "On a scale of 1-10, and depending on the need of the moment, in the 6-10 area."

(Female, widow, age 66) "Very. It's a let-down when it doesn't happen."

(Female, widow, age 65) "I would feel the act to be incomplete without it and would leave me 'up in the air.' "

(Female, married, age 66) "I don't like sex without them—the absence of it leaves one frustrated."

(Female, widow, age 76) "A psychological feeling that spells satisfaction."

(Female, married, age 69) "Very important, being the end of the means. If it is not successful, it can be the most mentally depressing and bodily unhealthy experience any normal person can have happen to him or her."

(Female, divorced, age 66) "Very important. Relaxes your tension of love."

(Female, single, age 72) "If not, you are left nervous, irritable."

(Female, divorced, age 61) "Very important. I see no point in getting horny if you're not going to have an orgasm."

(Female, widow, age 63) "Very important, otherwise it is blah!"

(Female, married, age 70) "My God! What else is there?"

(Female, widow, age 73) "If you do not have an orgasm, it's time and energy wasted."

(Female, married, age 63) "It is very important—the earth is actually moved at times."

(Female, divorced, age 71) "What else?"

(Female, widow, age 68) "Makes it a perfect act."

(Female, divorced, age 88) "Very, very important."

(Female, married, age 63) "Very—it's a completion of the act."

(Female, widow, age 89) "It means everything."

(Female, married, age 64) "Most important. Women who never or

seldom have orgasm many times develop physical problems."
(Female, married, age 78) "It is it!"

As one married woman of 65 put it: "I like things finished."

Most of the answers were short, almost cryptic in nature, with the respondents underscoring the significance of their feelings by underlining, repeating or using exclamation points for emphasis:

(Female, divorced, age 73) *"Very important."*
(Female, widowed, age 76) "Very important!"
(Female, married, age 69) "Very, very important."
(Female, divorced, age 77) *"Very important!"* (Emphasis hers)
(Female, married, age 66) "All!"

Some, such as one 66-year-old widow, expressed the joy of discovering orgasm; "Never had one until I had been married three weeks. Found it wonderful." Others qualified their responses:

(Female, married, age 60) "Quite important, but it isn't everything."
(Female, widow, age 68) "I was always fortunate to have an orgasm but I don't think it should be built up to be so important as there are those who don't—and their 'peak' would be satisfying to them if they didn't think they had failed."
(Female, widow, age 66) "Orgasm is not always necessary. I never reached this stage when young and still felt satisfied as I loved my husband. Later, orgasm was reached."
(Female, widow, age 68) "It is important although it doesn't always happen. But if I can't, I'm happy if my partner can."

Of this group, there were those who expressed an attitude of "positive thinking"—patience, hope and a willingness to be flexible despite evident disappointment. As one 74-year-old woman put it, orgasm is "always to be desired, but not necessary. As you get older, you sometimes miss out on a climax." She did not elaborate, but the "missing out" was a clear statement of her underlying need and desire.

Surprisingly, only a small number revealed that they were "other-directed," expressing more concern for the man than for themselves:

(Female, married, age 60) "Most desirable, but not absolutely necessary. More important for and to my husband."

(Female, married, age 81) "I don't lose any sleep if I don't have a climax. I enjoy helping my husband have a climax. He looks so happy and peaceful afterward."

(Female, widow, age 64) "Not always important. Makes me feel good to see my loved one happy and contented."

(Female, widow, age 60) "Desirable but partner's climax is most important."

(Female, married, age 63) "Not necessary (for me)—so long as mate is satisfied most of time."

(Female, married, age 66) "I feel it is more important to a man than a woman."

This type of concern for the male's orgasm and the woman's denial or underplaying of her own need for orgasm recalls what was thought to be the popular stance of women up until recent times. Clearly the exuberant statements by the large majority of our female respondents show that they have never subscribed to the notion of "servicing" their male partners at the expense of their own needs. Orgasm, they say, is and always has been primary in their sexual experience.

Such a degree of orgasmic experience and desire among the respondents is startling in its variance from our stereotyped notions of grandma, chicken soup and the rocking chair. But do these older women who are reporting orgasms, both past and present, *really* have orgasms? Indeed, as some professionals have asked, do they even know what an orgasm is?

In considering the question "What is an orgasm?" Graber and Graber have written that many of the women they have treated for sexual problems (regardless of their age) do not actually know what an orgasm is and are unsure about having experienced them. The two therapists go on to add that many women who report having orgasms actually do not have them and, interestingly, that some who say they haven't had orgasms have in fact had them.

Physiologically, when orgasm occurs there is a contraction of a muscle known as the pubococcygeus muscle which brings the sides of the vagina together. According to Graber and Graber, some women who report orgasms are actually experiencing the pre-orgasmic sensations of warmth and tingling that occur before full orgasmic contraction.

But it is important to note that those experts who raise questions about the accuracy and honesty of women reporting orgasmic experiences are primarily therapists who treat women with orgasmic dysfunction. These investigators must, therefore, reserve at least a modicum of caution about generalizing their findings to normal populations of women. Of course, we have no conclusive proof that our respondents who report orgasm are actually orgasmic. By the same reasoning, doubts can be raised about all surveys of sexual experience—Kinsey, Hite, the *Redbook* survey, and many others. Only Masters and Johnson were able to verify orgasm by their method of direct observation of the sex act and the examination of the genitals during (by interruption of the act) and after sexual experiences; but their method is likely to be applied only to selected volunteers and patients, not to normal samples like ours.

In spite of the doubts, it must be noted that many of the descriptions provided by our respondents show that they make a clear distinction between satisfaction and nonsatisfaction, release and frustration, after a sexual experience. Also the numerous references to tension, irritability, nervousness, and other states of physical discomfort when they do not achieve release again suggests awareness of what is and what is not an orgasm. These women seem to know what they want, and it sounds convincingly like orgasm.

Masters and Johnson made it clear that the orgasmic response of older women is very similar to that of younger women in spite of some physiological changes that take place. Even some aspects of arousal remain identical. During the excitement phase (Masters and Johnson's four phases are excitement, plateau, orgasm and resolution), the external arousal of the nipple occurs in the same pattern for older women as for younger women. The engorgement of the areolae (the area around the nipple) in the plateau stage occurs in older women, but it is not as intense as in younger women. Far more important, though, is the fact that clitoral response remains the same at least well into the 70s.

While with advancing age there is a marked thinning and loss of elasticity of the vaginal wall, a shortening of the vaginal length and width, and a reduction of the vasocongestion of the outer third of the vagina, these changes have little impact on the orgasm *per se*.

Similarly, the frequently mentioned "fact" that intercourse inevitably results in pain and discomfort for older women because of reduced levels of vaginal lubrication is not borne out by our data. An overwhelming 84 percent of our female respondents report no such pain in response to Question 22, "Does sexual intercourse give you any physical discomfort or pain?" The few women who do report some discomfort during intercourse resort to lubricants, so that their sexual enjoyment is neither curtailed or diminished in intensity. The key to most older women not experiencing such pain may lie in the phrase "sexually active," for as Masters and Johnson astutely observe, continuous levels of sexual activity over the course of a woman's life make a significant difference in physiological response. Indeed, 3 out of the 11 women over age 60 in Masters and Johnson's study who had high levels of vaginal lubrication after the menopause had remained sexually active up to the time of the study; the other eight, who experienced a reduction in lubrication, had not.

Rather than age, it is desire, interest, and opportunity that seem to control the body's potential response. In particular, Masters and Johnson's data lend support to the popular adage "Use it or lose it."

Younger women assume that menopause signals the decline of sexuality. As authors Barbara and Gideon Seaman write in *Women and the Crisis in Sex Hormones,* "Today's woman . . . falls prey to such ludicrous fears as the end of her sexual desires and femininity." They go on to point out how our culture exaggerates the importance of menopausal changes, making the fears into self-fulfilling prophesies. Yet our survey confirms that sex and orgasm are alive and well in the later years and that orgasm can even be more intense.

We sought to obtain reflections from our sample on sex and the menopause with Question 19, "How has sex changed since the menopause (change of life)?"

For most respondents there was clearly no decline. Eighty-seven percent of the female respondents affirmed that sex after the menopause is "better" or "the same." Of this group, 42 percent feel that sex is "better" (Table 19). Individual comments are convincingly to the point:

(Female, widow, age 65) "No change."
(Female, widow, age 80) "None."
(Female, widow, age 76) "It hasn't."

(Female, widow, age 64) "Not much change, except I don't think about it as much as when younger."
(Female, widow, age 60) "Not at all."
(Female, married, age 66) "No. I'm still the same."
(Female, widow, age 78) "No difference."
(Female, widow, age 65) "Has not changed."
(Female, widow, age 76) "About the same."
(Female, married, age 69) "Not as passionate, or as often. In reading this answer, I realize it really isn't true. Sex hasn't really changed."
(Female, widow, age 74) "Still the same. Sexy."
(Female, single, age 71) "I began male-female (as opposed to masturbation) after menopause so it hasn't changed for me."
(Female, widow, age 68) "Scarcely changed at all except I've 'dared' to accept masturbation, which is more gratifying than many sex experiences with my marriage partner."
(Female, divorced, age 61) "No change—at first because I was still sexually active. Now I'm not often horny, mostly because there is no one to get horny about."
(Female, widow, age 77) "None whatsoever."
(Female, married, age 72) "None. I have the same desires."
(Female, widow, age 81) "None at all."
(Female, single, age 83) "Sex is just as good after menopause."
(Female, divorced, age 67) "No way."

(Female, divorced, age 60) "Why should it? One fear has certainly been discarded—pregnancy. If I continue to feel good about myself, I see no reason for menopause to make any difference . . . unless to enhance sex."
(Female, widow, age 75) "I think menopause is an old wives' tale. Never noticed when it happened."

With the fear of pregnancy gone, others were able to focus more fully on the total sexual experience:

(Female, widow, age 74) "It made no change for me. In fact, it was before the pill and did give you a sense of safety."
(Female, divorced, age 64) "More spontaneous and carefree."
(Female, married, age 69) "The absence of any possibility of preg-

nancy makes both of us far more relaxed and therefore more able to enjoy ourselves. Otherwise, no change."
(Female, married, age 67) "Better. No fear of pregnancy. No dangerous pills."
(Female, married, age 60) "I'm freer (no worry of pregnancy); not as hurried, no kids around, better knowledge and appreciation of partner. Some sensitivity, not as strong. But real enjoyment."
(Female, divorced, age 74) "Much more secure."
(Female, married, age 71) "More relaxed as I do not worry about reproduction."
(Female, widow, age 75) "At least I no longer have to worry about having any more babies."
(Female, married, age 67) "More relaxed and enjoyable without fears of pregnancy."
(Female, divorced, age 77) "No. That's a lot of hogwash. If anything it's better. You don't have to worry about children."
(Female, widow, age 78) "You do not have the problem of getting pregnant—therefore, with me, the change, if any, was for the better."
(Female, married, age 81) "For me it is more satisfying—as before the menopause at age 54, there was always the fear of getting pregnant."
(Female, widow, age 74) "I was freed from the need to 'be prepared.'"
(Female, married, age 67) "I like it better. I can have it whenever I want."
(Female, married, age 64) "No more need to watch the calendar. You can be more relaxed, more spontaneous."
(Female, married, age 72) "No concern about pregnancy, therefore an increase in pleasure."

And finally, these answers leave no doubt that the power of sexuality can live on well beyond the menopause.

(Female, divorced, age 69) "Whee! Freer."
(Female, married, age 65) "I feel better with sex."
(Female, divorced, age 72) "Improved."
(Female, married, age 72) "It is more pleasurable."
(Female, widow, age 71) "For the better."

(Female, widow, age 63) "More sexy."
(Female, married, age 70) "More enjoyable, more relaxing."
(Female, widow, age 68) "I had a hysterectomy before I was 50 and if anything, sex was more enjoyable afterward."
(Female, married, age 63) "It's better."
(Female, married, age 63) "Better, more relaxed."
(Female, widow, age 68) "Greater urge."
(Female, married, age 66) "More often."
(Female, married, age 62) "Much more freedom and desire."

But what happens, for example, when a woman who hasn't had sexual relations for many years remarries and then engages in frequent sexual relations? Do diminished physiological functions return to previous levels? Does lubrication increase? What part does novelty play? How much time need elapse between "no use" and "re-use"? Does age play any part at all?

To date, we have no data to clarify these and other provocative questions. Masters and Johnson have helped us raise the questions. Our sample provides some experiential answers. But there are still questions to be asked and answers to be given—if we consider the asking worthwhile.

6

Likes and Dislikes

If there were any lingering doubts about how open we have become sexually, one need look no further than a local newsstand. Even prominent popular magazines casually offer titillating suggestions for exploring nuances of sexual experience right along with recipes, decorating hints, and tips on fashion. Typical is an article in *Cosmopolitan* advising women to keep a chart of orgasms during the three phases of lovemaking—foreplay, intercourse, and afterplay. Experimenting with orgasms at different times during lovemaking, according to writers Patricia and Robert Travis, can break the rigid pattern of both men and women achieving orgasm only during intercourse and can lead to the discovery of new delicacies in sex. Another article in *Mademoiselle* by sex therapist Dr. Maj-Britt Rosenbaum advises women on the delights of the vibrator as an extension of their sexual pleasure. Perhaps even more convincing of the sexual revolution documented by Gay Talese is a recent finding by psychologists Cowart and Pollack that oral sex has replaced intercourse as the most frequent lovemaking technique, at least for the young people surveyed.

We take these new bits of information and advice in stride because our newly sexualized and technique-oriented society has mandated that we fully explore our sexuality and develop our own individual style. But we tend to reserve this knowledge and experience for the young, although if young people have body wisdom, why not older people? They too have delicate palates, perhaps far more refined over a lifetime of experiencing sex. What are their likes and dislikes?

As we saw in Chapter 5, The Female Orgasm and Love Experience, the women in our sample assigned great importance to orgasm in their sexual experiences. This emphasis on orgasm was also true for our male respondents. In response to Questions 1, "What do you consider a good sexual experience?" and 4, "What in the sex act is most important to you?" men also ranked orgasm first (71 percent and 50 percent respectively). Their actual responses punctuate the statistical data:

> (Male, widower, age 75) "One of adequate length climaxing in simultaneous orgasm."
> (Male, divorced, age 62) "A leisurely pace with soft music and both parties reaching climax."
> (Male, married, age 69) "When I have a chance to experience every possibility ultimately ending in orgasm."
> (Male, married, age 73) "Pleasurable release and emotional gratification shared with your partner."
> (Male, widowed, age 79) "Love with orgasm."
> (Male, married, age 73) "Two partners desiring each other equally and arriving together—orgasms."
> (Male, married, age 68) "When both experience climax together and both having the warmth of love that brings both closer together."
> (Male, divorced, age 74) "Male and female have an orgasm together."
> (Male, widower, age 90) "When you and your wife come at the same time."
> (Male, married, age 70) "Climax—achieving ejaculation."
> (Male, married, age 63) "Orgasm—but also enjoy foreplay."
> (Male, married, age 68) "When we both discharge."
> (Male, married, age 71) "Two people getting along and physically fit—and take enough time to perform the act and make sure each party is ready for the climax."
> (Male, married, age 74) "Satisfactory orgasm by both parties."
> (Male, married, age 65) "To come."
> (Male, widower, age 71) "The climax."
> (Male, divorced, age 60) "Intercourse lasting over half an hour with orgasm and good feelings afterwards."
> (Male, married, age 73) "A complete sexual union on both sides—to an orgasm."
> (Male, married, age 72) "Each one experiencing an exciting build up to a fulfilling climax."

Some respondents, male and female, reflect a powerful sexuality in stating their preferences, like this 72-year-old divorced woman: "Intercourse with a man who makes you feel desired and who is affectionate as well as passionate. I like kissing and having my breasts stimulated. I like to explore the man's body and penis." "When both are anxious for sex at the same time," writes an 85-year-old widow. A 75-year-old married man cites a wide range of activities: "Start out with kissing and caressing, playing with each others genitals, oral sex, then finish with vaginal sex." And not to be upstaged by the frankness of the younger generation, one 63-year-old married woman said simply: "A good fuck!" A 71-year-old widower responded by offering some good advice: "There is no bad sexual experience. Enjoy it!"

Likes and dislikes are translated into what is a turn-on or turn-off in lovemaking. To find out what is most pleasurable for our respondents, we asked Questions 16, "What makes you feel most excited during lovemaking?" and Question 11, "What kind of pre-intercourse foreplay (kissing, touching, etc.) do you like best?" Foreplay (49 percent) stands out as the focal point of excitement (Table 16). But in the arousal stage, most report being excited through some form of touching, kissing, and fondling—with touching most often mentioned (55 percent—Table 11). "Beholding and caressing her beautiful body" was the way a 73-year-old married man expressed it. A 68-year-old widow replied: "Touching, hugging, kissing." Others responded as follows:

(Female, widow, age 61) "Breast fondling and kissing and touching of all parts of my body with real feeling."
(Female, widow, age 75) "Tenderly touching my body all over."
(Female, widow, age 66) "Being close, having him caress me, especially my breasts."
(Male, married, age 62) "My wife, or any woman, being aggressive to the point of playing with any part of my body."
(Male, married, age 65) "Just being close and touching."
(Female, married, age 69) "Blowing on my neck or running his hands over body."
(Female, widow, age 76) "Being fondled and hearing words of love."
(Male, married, age 75) "Freedom to explore my partner's body and

her initiative and aggression in doing the same for me."
(Female, married, age 67) "Stroking and speaking softly."
(Female, single, age 65) "I love a whole body massage—best when my nipples are manipulated and sucked."
(Female, widow, age 74) "Kissing and touching."
(Female, widow, age 67) "Tonguing my clitoris and touching and kissing my nipples."
(Female, divorced, age 63) "Encouraging my partner's arousal by carefully handling and massaging his penis and balls. He is doing breast fondling, clitoris fondling."
(Female, widow, age 70) "A lot of kissing, tongues touching. My whole body stroked."
(Male, married, age 73) "Lips, breasts, cheeks, ears—feeling any place on partner's body."
(Female, widow, age 66) "Sweet talk. Kissing on the neck, scratching my back. Long mouth kisses."
(Male, divorced, age 60) "Nipple rubbing."
(Male, married, age 75) "Touching and kissing."
(Female, married, age 60) "Light touching all over my body and kissing all over."
(Female, widow, age 75) "Touching, kissing, reading sex books."
(Male, divorced, age 69) "Touching, kissing, stroking, licking, squeezing, oral sex, laughing, horse play, cuddling, rocking, quietly holding. Did I leave anything out?"
(Female, widow, age 68) "Kissing and I love his hands all over me."
(Male, married, age 75) "A great deal of touching by both parties and open mouth and tongue kissing, oral sex."
(Male, married, age 70) "Touching, kissing, sucking breasts, kissing and licking vagina."
(Female, widow, age 67) "Touching, kissing, and the feel of the body close to me."
(Female, married, age 65) "I love to be fondled and kissed all over, to have my breasts sucked and massaged, to be kissed on the genitals—sometimes I can reach an orgasm that way."
(Female, divorced, age 61) "Clitoral stimulation, manual and oral, hugging, kissing, sexy talk, massage."

Kissing is also a desired and enjoyable part of lovemaking. It was often included along with touching:

(Male, married, age 75) "Start is the kissing—later the penis stroking."
(Female, widow, age 63) "Kissing the man I care about and making love to him—also orally."
(Male, married, age 70) "Kissing—rousing nipples with kissing and sucking."
(Male, married, age 68) "Tongue kissing."
(Female, widow, age 60) "Mutual kissing all over body."
(Female, divorced, age 66) "Being in the nude and kissing."
(Male, widower, age 63) "Feeling, touching, kissing."
(Female, divorced, age 66) "Long and tender kisses."
(Male, married, age 62) "When I touch and am touched. When I kiss and am kissed. When I climax with my wife."
(Female, married, age 74) "When I know that I'm going to have an orgasm and my husband kisses me."

Some, primarily the females, expressed romantic concepts such as, "My partner's desire and love for me gently, and genuinely, and sincerely" (female, widow, 65); or "Kindness and lovingness" (female, widow, 66). For others it is body contact which is most exciting:

(Female, widow, age 67) "The feel of him."
(Female, married, age 66) "Coming together in body contact at the beginning and realizing the other person is in your body."
(Male, married, age 75) "Close squeeze standing up. Tummy-to-tummy and nose-to-nose."
(Male, widower, age 80) "Feeling the body."

Still others cite the direct stimulation of the genitals and (for women) breasts (18 percent—Table 11); and surprisingly a number say that oral sex is the peak experience (Table 16). Overall, in response to Questions 1, 4, 16, 18, 20, 43 and 46, 15 percent of the respondents make reference to oral sex. This is very impressive since none of the questions in our survey asks directly about oral sex.

(Female, widow, age 73) "His rubbing all parts of my vagina."

(Female, widow, age 70) "Breasts stroked, breasts kissed."

(Female, single, age 65) "His fingers stroking my inner labia. Also his penis rubbing against my vulva. My nipples manipulated and sucked."

(Male, married, age 72) "When my wife sucks my penis."

(Female, widow, age 67) "Playing with and tonguing my clitoris."

(Female, married, age 60) "Stimulation of clitoris by kissing or gentle touching."

(Female, widow, age 65) "Kissing of the breasts or sucking. Stimulation of the clitoris."

(Male, married, age 69) "Being sucked and watching my wife get excited when I do the same."

(Male, married, age 75) "Oral sex. I enjoy fellatio greatly."

(Female, married, age 62) "Having my husband lick my clitoris—cunnilingus."

(Male, married, age 68) "When she plays with my penis and caresses and kisses it."

(Male, widower, age 81) "Kissing and fondling her breasts."

(Female, divorced, age 65) "Clitoral stimulation—oral, manual, vibrator."

In these responses we see a range of preferences in arousal and lovemaking that is comprehensive and specific. Sex for these older adults is neither casual nor peripheral. Indeed, as we would suspect from many years of experience, they know what turns them on, and they seek it out. Contrary to Kinsey's finding of two minutes or less from entry to ejaculation, we found great variability even in the length of time for the sex act (Table 24). In fact, only 7 percent indicated the time to be two minutes or less. Comparisons with when younger (Table 24.5) indicate that this wide range of time for the sex act was always the case for our respondents. There is apparently no such thing as young people's or old people's lovemaking techniques. There are only lovemaking techniques.

Who touches the elderly? We touch babies and the young. We kiss them, cuddle them, and revel in the pleasure it gives them and us. We do it as parents, as relatives, and as friends. But we seldom think of giving long caresses to the elderly or touching them with more than just a momentary gesture. Yet touch is high on their list of priorities, certainly in lovemaking. More impressive is the fact that their responses are free of negative feelings about touching "sagging skin" or less than flawless bodies. The importance of touch and physical contact was further in evidence when we studied the responses to Question 10, "How important is touching and cuddling in sex? Has this changed over the years?"

> (Female, married, age 66) "Touching and cuddling gives me a wonderful feeling. No change over the years."
> (Male, married, age 60) "Very important. It's been increasing as I get older."
> (Female, married, age 73) "My husband and I touch and it is important. No change."
> (Female, widow, age 67) "I think it is the most important part of lovemaking. I have always felt that way."
> (Male, married, age 75) "No. It's still great as long as both parties still love each other."
> (Female, divorced, age 63) "Touching and cuddling give me warmth. It is as important as ever."
> (Male, married, age 70) "Extremely important. Yes, there is more as you get older."
> (Female, divorced, age 72) "Very important, even at a hundred."
> (Male, widower, age 72) "No change. I enjoy touching and cuddling even after intercourse."
> (Female, married, age 67) "I need to be touched and cuddled more now than when I was younger."
> (Female, widow, age 63) "Cuddling and touching is the best part of sex."
> (Male, divorced, age 67) "Most important, exceeding orgasm."
> (Female, married, age 65) "Very important. When we were younger we were always ready for the act; now we are satisfied to touch and cuddle, and we realize now how much our love has grown and gotten stronger."

Far from dismissing touching and cuddling, these older adults consider it essential to lovemaking. For some, touching can be "the best part of sex" and even "the most important exceeding orgasm." As one 66-year-old divorced man explained it, touching and cuddling are "better now because there is no rush to get to the other part of sex." One of our favorites was a widower of 76 who indicated that touching is number one, cuddling number two, "and then the act number three—and off we go!"

The variety of sexual preferences of our respondents is further reflected in the answers to Question 18, "Some people say that intercourse is not the most important part of sex. How do you feel about this?" While many (52 percent) consider intercourse important to a complete sexual experience, no doubt an experience that includes orgasm judging from their other responses, others (41 percent) prefer a variety of pleasuring, with or without intercourse.

What about sex, if anything, is disliked? We asked this in Question 33, "What about sex do you like the least?" The most common response is a simple but clear "nothing" (39 percent).

> (Male, divorced, age 61) "I like sex, period—nothing more, nothing less."
> (Male, widower, age 63) "Nothing."
> (Female, widow, age 71) "No special dislikes."
> (Female, married, age 73) "I like everything about sex."

Some add a reflective note:

> (Female, divorced, age 65) "The right partner produced no negative feelings."
> (Female, married, age 72) "Nothing. When I was young, I was afraid I'd conceive."

A married woman of 60 humorously turned the question around on us: "When it's over!"

The majority of respondents say they like sex from beginning to end. They revel in their experiences and, as with good food, enjoy them thoroughly. However, if most love the taste of lobster there are still some who disliked the cleaning-up afterward:

> (Female, widow, age 67) "Having to clean-up afterward."

(Male, married, age 62) "Having to get up and clean up."
(Female, married, age 62) "The messiness afterward."
(Male, divorced, age 60) "Cleaning up afterward."
(Female, widow, age 65) "The messy feeling afterward."
(Female, married, age 65) "His discharge in me. He doesn't want to use a prophylactic. He always used one when we were young and I was always nice and clean."
(Male, married, age 65) "The messy undersheet from the orgasm."
(Female, widow, age 65) "The messy condition."

Cleanliness in general seems to be a concern of many respondents as characterized by the comment of a 66-year-old widow: "Wouldn't want a person physically dirty and smelling. Baths are cheap." Others said:

(Female, single, age 72) "Smell."
(Male, divorced, age 66) "Can't find much about sex that I don't like if the woman and man keep clean."
(Female, married, age 64) "Smell."
(Female, divorced, age 63) "Sweaty bodies, dry breath."

For a generation that received virtually no positive or enlightened sex education (see Table 41) but rather was imbued with the dirtiness of sex it is encouraging that only 16 percent make reference to messiness. Despite their upbringing, most are able to keep their hangups in the background and are able to seek and enjoy sexual experiences.

Another group of respondents (18 percent) focused their dislikes on the selfish and inconsiderate lover:

(Female, divorced, age 74) "A 'quickie' or the reverse—so prolonged as to become tiresome."
(Male, married, age 63) "Sometimes being expected to perform when not in mood."
(Female, widow, age 68) "Being awakened from a sound sleep and expected to be ready."
(Male, widower, age 74) "A woman who thinks she is doing you a favor."
(Female, divorced, age 82) "The selfish partner who only satisfies himself."

(Female, divorced, age 63) "The impersonal, mechanical approach and performance."

(Female, married, age 60) "If my husband comes on too strong and too fast without lubricating me enough and without any foreplay. Also, if I've been angry at him and he insists."

(Male, divorced, age 74) "To be pressured."

(Female, widow, age 61) "Any feeling that it is 'expected' or obligatory. Being 'rushed.' Being left unsatisfied with a snoring partner."

(Female, widow, age 68) "The abrupt parting at the climax—almost a rejection by the male."

(Female, widow, age 72) "Just reach climax and stop all cuddling."

(Female, married, age 70) "Being awakened in the middle of the night or when I am trying to sleep."

Still others focused their dislike on lovemaking that was rigid and unspontaneous. "The stereotyped routine I get into with some women. I fall into it myself and they demand it. 'Don't touch my vulva, you haven't sucked my breasts yet,'" writes a 69-year-old divorced man. And a 66-year-old divorced woman responds: "Having it at a scheduled time. It should be spontaneous."

It is possible to participate in an experience, even be enthusiastic about it, but nevertheless feel embarrassed or uncomfortable about some aspects. We wondered what about sex was embarrassing for our respondents, so we posed Question 17. Most of the responses are emphatic in asserting that nothing about lovemaking is embarrassing (57 percent).

(Male, divorced, age 61) "Nothing about sex embarrasses me."

(Female, widow, age 87) "Was married thirty-seven years. No embarrassment."

(Male, married, age 73) "Nothing."

(Female, married, age 63) "No embarrassment."

(Female, married, age 66) "Having sex does not embarrass me at all."

Only a small number are embarrassed about nakedness (9 percent) with more women (11 percent) than men (4 percent) showing this concern. Some answers seemed almost apologetic:

(Female, divorced, age 66) "The act of undressing, I think. Or watching someone undress. Strangely enough, I do *not* think the male body is beautiful."

(Female, married, age 66) "Nakedness."

(Female, married, age 74) "Still today, after all these years, I cannot just strip and it must be in the dark. I have *never* walked around in front of him naked. I do *not* consider myself prudish. I just can't."

As we will see later in this chapter, however, these reactions to the naked body are not typical, and often stem from specific childhood upbringing.

Another small group finds talking about sex embarrassing. A 76-year-old married woman captured the feeling of this group when she wrote: "Public discussion about it. I have always felt it a private affair." It isn't surprising, in view of what we know about Victorian ethics, that it is largely the women who feel uncomfortable about public discussions of sex.

Men have a different source of embarrassment, namely the failure to have an erection. Even if it only happens on occasion, impotence or the fear of it is a major male preoccupation. It should be noted, however, that references to impotence came up only sporadically in responses to Question 17 but 15 percent of males cited erection problems as the greatest source of embarrassment.

(Male, widower, age 73) "Unsuccessful intercourse, that is no erection."

(Male, married, age 72) "When I fail to obtain an erection."

(Male, married, age 68) "When unable to finish the act."

(Male, widower, age 68) "If you don't get an erection when kissing and hugging."

(Male, widower, age 63) "When the erection doesn't take."

(Male, married, age 63) "When I can't get an erection to last long enough."

(Male, married, age 80) "Not to be able to be erect."

(Male, widower, age 74) "When unable to get erection fast enough and partner is waiting and all hot."

(Male, married, age 68) "When the erection of the penis goes down if the phone rings or there's a knock on the door. It sometimes takes a little more time for the penis to get erect again."

Some women expressed embarrassment over the man's plight. "It embarrasses me when I see his frustration when he does not get an erection," says a 66-year-old married woman. But only 1.3 percent of our females mention the male erection problem as a primary source of embarrassment.

Other areas of discomfort mentioned by a small number of respondents are reflected in these comments: "When you perform with someone you really don't care for" (male, widower, age 74); "Positions I am not willing to take" (female, widow, age 65); "Talking about or trying to analyze failures" (male, married, age 75).

Take away the identifying information about the respondents and you would be hard pressed to judge the ages of those writing the responses. The comments have a familiar ring. You've heard them before: you've read about them in books, magazines and conversations— but previously they only came out of the mouths of young people.

Nudity

Surprisingly, most older people in our sample are comfortable with their own bodies and those of their partners—in fact, nudity is still a very important aspect of the excitement of sex. This may seem paradoxical, in a society geared toward youth and its flawless appearance. As we grow older, especially as we approach the 30s, 40s, and 50s, we become keenly aware of the visible signs of aging. As the signs get more pronounced they lose their charm. The media reinforces our anxiety by overwhelming us with youthful images and tempting us with a vast array of weapons for the all-out battle to sustain a young appearance—creams, dyes, exercises, surgery, meditation, and others. An article in *Family Circle* (July 17, 1979) entitled "Aging: How to Fight It, Hide It, Cope with It" captures this combative attitude toward aging. The article goes on to describe "the tricks time plays" and "how to beat the clock." Implicit in this approach is the notion that aging is not a natural process to be accepted but a bad trick that needs to be undone. The world is made for the young, we are told. If you can't be young then you must try to look young. And if you can't fool yourself, you may be able to fool others.

While the publicly displayed parts of our body, face, and hair may give us away, at least the parts hidden under our clothes can be kept secret. Just as in the hair-dye advertisement—"Only her hairdresser knows for sure"—so in the case of the body, "Only your lover will know for sure."

Wrinkled tummy, flabby thighs, pot bellies. and sagging breasts can be covered over, pulled up, pushed in, or cut away. But during sex all is bared, at least to the touch.

If older people are ashamed or embarrassed about their aging bodies, these feelings should intensify during sexual relations as the years progress, especially for sexually active widows, widowers, and divorced men and women and singles who are involved in new relationships.

We devised Question 39, "How do you feel about being nude with your partner? Has this changed over the years?" to explore the issue of body image and aging. Do older people cover their bodies more to conceal the signs of aging? Do they feel increasingly uncomfortable in the nude with their partners? Do they like nudity? Buying the popular myth that young bodies are to display and old bodies are to hide, we expected to find a great deal of anxiety and defensiveness in response to this question.

As with many of the questions, our projections were wrong. The actual responses, in general, showed a positive attitude toward nudity; in fact, 81 percent of our sample (87 percent males and 77 percent females) express positive feelings about nudity.

> (Female, married, age 60) "I love it—hasn't changed a bit."
> (Male, married, age 74) "What we each enjoy most in our intimate relations."
> (Female, married, age 64) "Never bothered me and never will. He is the same. Bodies are nice to look at—always thought so."
> (Male, married, age 68) "We sleep nude—no problem. We are proud of our bodies and find no need to be ashamed."
> (Female, widow, age 79) "Both very free with nudity, even more so than in our youth."
> (Male, married, age 83) "I love to see her beautiful body—no change."

(Female, married, age 63) "Great. No change."

(Female, married, age 66) "Not ashamed of my body as it is very youthful, not withstanding my age."

(Female, married, age 66) "Sexy. No change."

(Male, married, age 70) "Great. Women are less prudish now about being in the nude."

(Female, widow, age 69) "I don't mind nudity. I am very well-shaped for my age."

(Female, married, age 73) "Nothing embarrassing. He helps me bathe and I help him."

(Female, widow, age 81) "It never bothered me."

(Female, married, age 79) "Being nude is natural."

(Male, married, age 63) "No problem. Desire it more."

(Male, married, age 69) "Strictly nude. No change."

(Female, married, age 70) "Feel fine. Not aware I'm nude."

(Female, widow, age 60) "Pleasant, enjoyable, very natural, seductive."

(Female, divorced, age 63) "I like being in the nude as much as possible."

(Male, married, age 75) "Always both of us were nude. Both of us like it nude."

(Female, widow, age 63) "I feel good about my body."

(Male, married, age 77) "Nudity is part of the marriage relationship. No change over the years."

(Female, married, age 69) "I do not feel the least bit embarrassed about it and never have."

(Female, married, age 63) "We were always nude since our first night thirty-five years ago."

(Male, married, age 70) "We are childless and spend most our time nude or semi-nude; plenty of privacy."

(Female, widow, age 65) "I think it's a beautiful feeling when two bodies meet skin to skin. It has not changed over the years. It seems the older you get the more you enjoy it."

These responses reflect no embarrassment or self-consciousness about the aging body. On the contrary, nudity can be "pleasant, natural, great," even "sexy." Where changes do not occur, it is possible that lovemaking over the years with a consistent partner is an affirmation of one's beauty, at least "in the eyes of the beholder." Involved in the relationship, the people pay little attention to minor details; as in good theater, the play is the thing and not the scratches on the seat. Therefore, one might conclude that nudity gets taken for granted after many years of marriage so that comfort derives solely from familiarity rather than true ease. But when we compared married and unmarried (widows, widowers, singles, divorced) on the question of nudity (many of the unmarried are involved in new sexual relationships) the findings showed little difference. Among the unmarried group 79 percent (84 percent males and 77 percent females) have positive feelings toward nudity while 83 percent of the married (89 percent males and 77 percent females) have positive feelings toward nudity.

What we continuously find is that present behavior is largely determined by past behavior. If nudity was desirable and comfortable in the early years, it continues to be welcome later on. The past influences the present and this is particularly evident among those who are uncomfortable with nudity:

(Male, married, age 74) "I'm not comfortable being nude. No change."
(Female, married, age 80) "Never nude."
(Female, widow, age 65) "I did like to see a nude man. I never let him see me in the nude."
(Female, single, age 63) "Never could. Not embarrassed, but since I had such a strict and rigid upbringing—rather had a thing about being nude."
(Female, widow, age 64) "I don't like it and never did. I'm safe. I have no partner."
(Female, married, age 74) "Don't like it even today, but I accept it as he likes it."
(Female, married, age 60) "I don't see the necessity. 'Nude' is not a turn-on. No, it has not changed. My body is not beautiful."
(Female, married, age 69) "I never enjoy being nude in front of my husband and never have."
(Male, single, age 67) "I am opposed to nudeness. I wear something. I do not know what others are doing but I was never nude."

These respondents never liked nudity. They were uncomfortable about it when young and have continued to be uncomfortable throughout their lives. Embarrassment and self-consciousness in these cases are not functions of age.

One 74-year-old divorced woman cautions about the possible dangers of nudity: "I do not believe in being in the nude. Too much of this is going on now-a-days and is partly responsible for rape, murder, crimes of all sorts." Her view, fortunately, is a negligible minority.

Even for those who have become self-conscious about their bodies, there is often no great intensity about these feelings. Sometimes there is almost casual acceptance. In a number of instances surgery such as mastectomy is the reason for the changed attitude:

(Female, widow, age 65) "I used to like being seen in a nude state. Now I am doubtful of my beauty."

(Female, married, age 62) "Somewhat less comfortable since my figure is not as good as it used to be."

(Male, widower, age 73) "Lights off now. I don't want her to see my body too good. I hide her glasses."

(Female, divorced, age 63) "It is fine except that my body is not so OK. Drooping breasts, stretched skin, flab. With my husband we were covered with sheets—his idea. I loved to see my men nude."

(Female, divorced, age 81) "When I was young and had a good figure, I liked getting nude before him. In my old age I don't like the looks of my body so I prefer not exhibiting it."

(Female, married, age 67) "Nudity is natural. I was comfortable until I had a mastectomy—my body doesn't look as lovely now."

When changes do occur, they are more likely to be in the direction of greater openness and acceptance:

(Female, married, age 66) "Feel much more at ease now."

(Female, widow, age 72) "Shy when younger and now I'm not."

(Female, widow, age 62) "I feel better now because I seem to have grown up more."

(Female, widow, age 75) "Somewhat embarrassed. Improved in later years."

(Male, married, age 66) "It doesn't upset either of us as much now as years ago."

(Female, widow, age 64) "OK. He was more modest than I at the

last. I was painfully shy at first, but overcame much of that shyness."
(Female, married, age 63) "OK. We sleep in the nude. In my first marriage I did not feel comfortable."
(Female, widow, age 65) "Yes, it has changed over the years. I am a different person now and being nude doesn't bother me."
(Female, married, age 66) "We will be married two years. At first he shocked me. He was shaving nude in the bathroom. But now I find it easy to be nude in front of him, too."
(Male, widower, age 64) "I think you are more relaxed the older you get."
(Female, married, age 62) "I grew up in an atmosphere of modesty. As I get older I'm less modest."
(Female, married, age 66) "Very comfortable, more than formerly."
(Female, widow, age 61) "Nothing like full body contact. Used to undress in the walk-in closet, but now enjoy even slow disrobing when the partner and occasion are right."

It is encouraging to note that older people do change. Personal growth has no age limit. If older people are not all that anxious about their bodies, what is the origin of the belief that they are preoccupied with physical decline? It may be that the characteristics attributed to older people, even by leading professional researchers and writers, have been projections.

We have pointed out a number of times that "older" frequently means between the ages of 40 and 60. Clearly this was true for Hite, and Masters and Johnson. In the Kinsey reports, "older" usually refers to subjects between 50 and 60. Similarly, when author Adele Nudel in *For the Woman over 50* advises older women not to be ashamed of their bodies, as she reports so many are, she backs up her counsel with examples of women between 50 and 60. It is the attention to middle-aged anxieties and preoccupations that has falsely led to the assumption that the same concerns are carried into the later years, intensified at that time. Our data indicates that crises of middle age (between the years of 40 and 60) dissolve into acceptance in the later years, and that older people can more easily focus on concerns beyond the bodily decline after age 60.

All the areas of likes and dislikes reported by our respondents are similar to those found in studies of younger adults. Even the concern for cleanliness and the distaste for the clean-up after sexual relations are cited by *The Redbook Report on Female Sexuality* as well as by Pietropinto and Simmenauer in *Beyond the Male Myth.* The importance of orgasm, extensive foreplay, and a caring, loving partner are universally emphasized by respondents of all ages in surveys of sexuality; just as the inconsiderate lover is a source of frustration and unhappiness for all age groups. Our data force us to conclude that what is remarkable about the likes and dislikes of our respondents is simply that they are *un*remarkable.

7

Sexual Experimentation and the Ideal Lover

There's an old joke in which one man says to a friend, "I know a thousand positions for making love." "That's incredible," the friend responds. "I know only one—the man on top of the woman." "That makes a thousand and one!" the first man replies. The joke holds up even more today because of the sexual revolution, which brought with it the age of sexual technique. Today there are numerous sex books on the market, with diagrams, photographs, and descriptions of a staggering variety of lovemaking techniques and positions. If the books don't do a good enough job, you can go to an X-rated film and see everything demonstrated in color on a wide screen.

Many couples now go through an almost obligatory period in which they run through the hundreds of positions that Dr. Alex Comfort describes in *The Joy of Sex* and *More Joy of Sex*. Things were quite different in the old days when "dirty books" meant novels with "erotic" descriptions, which are tame by today's standards. As one 64-year-old man pointed out, "In my day you skipped through novels, feeling guilty, looking for the hot parts. I remember almost coming from reading a description of a man slowly slipping his hand into a woman's lowcut dress. If they had *Playboy* when I was a teenager, I probably never would have come out of the bathroom and my brains would have been splattered all over the wall."

Sexual experimentation is assumed to be a natural part of the sex lives of the young. But what about older people? They have lived through the sexual revolution, know about the technique explosion and have equal access to the books, magazines and movies. Have their imaginations been sparked? Have they been tempted by the variety of possible sexual experiences that are now out in the open?

The answer is yes for 39 percent of our respondents, 51 percent of

109

the men and 32 percent of the women. The spectrum of responses we received in reply to Question 46, "Would you like to try any new sexual experiences that you have heard about, read about or thought about?" shows that older people are indeed open to sexual experimentation.

Eight percent of our respondents feel that they *have* tried "everything" and some, therefore, do not need further experimentation. We don't know exactly what "everything" means to them, but their receptivity to experimentation is apparent:

(Female, divorced, age 65) "Tried them all."

(Female, married, age 73) "I think we tried all the ways I ever heard of."

(Male, divorced, age 66) "I feel all sexual experiences out today have been tried by me."

(Female, widow, age 67) "I've tried most everything except anal intercourse, which I would never try."

(Male, married, age 63) "I read *Playboy* and have done most of the things that they have discussed."

(Female, widow, age 68) "My husband took me to the Circus in Cuba. I've experienced everything."

(Male, married, age 74) "I've read about every sexual variation and I have tried those we both decided to experiment with."

(Female, widow, age 70) "If it was any better than the way we did it I could not take it."

(Female, married, age 60) "Have tried everything except swinging, group and communal sex, homosexuality, sex with animals and anal sex. Do not desire any of those."

(Female, widow, age 74) "I was not inhibited and I think I tried whatever I heard or read about. Did not necessarily like everything."

(Male, married, age 72) "Have tried so-called new sexual experiences."

(Male, married, age 84) "I have tried everything and loved it."

(Female, married, age 64) "I think I have done everything."

(Female, married, age 63) "Think or hope I tried it all."

Some of our respondents are obviously open to new experiences but are reticent about them. For example, one 64-year-old widow said, "Possibly, but I might be hesitant to try very unusual experiences."

And another 67-year-old widow commented, "Perhaps some, but I was usually fulfilled in the traditional way." A 66-year-old married woman said, "I think about it, but not for practice."

In some instances one partner is more daring than the other. Since sex is a two-way venture, experimentation is limited in these cases by timidity or the unwillingness of their partners.

(Male, married, age 69) "I would like to try anything possible—groups, etc.—but don't have the courage or ability."
(Female, married, age 61) "I would, but my partner is not so game."
(Male, married, age 65) "Have, but wife not interested."
(Male, married, age 75) "Yes—I would like to pursue many different positions and oral sex. But they are not acceptable to my wife."
(Female, married, age 69) "I would but am too disciplined and am scared."
(Male, married, age 69) "Yes. But I would have to find a partner willing and interested in variety."
(Male, married, age 60) "Yes, but I have inhibitions and extra-curricular sex is not acceptable to me. Fantasy is unimpeachable."
(Male, married, age 69) "I would like to try a lot of things I have seen or heard about but don't have the nerve."
(Female, married, age 67) "I would. Convention holds me back."
(Male, married, age 69) "Yes. I have always had a desire to try sex anally but my wife has strong objections."
(Male, married, age 68) "Yes. But my wife is not amenable though I suggest them."

The 39 percent who are clearly drawn to exploring new sexual experiences express a variety of preferences and interests.

(Male, widower, age 77) "Yes, I would like to try all of them."
(Female, widow, age 69) "Yes—variety."
(Female, widow, age 76) "Yes, I would."
(Female, married, age 60) "I would not be averse to it with my spouse if you mean positions or techniques. I think oral sex is revolting."
(Male, married, age 70) "Yes. But I sure have tried everything."
(Female, divorced, age 61) "I've had most of them. I'm not interested in group sex, which is the only thing I know of that I haven't tried."

(Male, single, age 72) "Yes, I've tried, not always successfully, rear entry. Also in between the breasts, etc."

(Female, widow, age 61) "Yes, unless they are bizarre such as group sex."

(Male, married, age 73) "Yes, ménage à trois."

(Female, married, age 67) "Yes, I've read Dr. Comfort's book on fun and sex—don't recall the title exactly—and would like to try lots of those ideas."

(Male, married, age 69) "I like to experiment in all phases."

(Male, married, age 85) "Yes, if they work satisfactorily."

(Female, married, age 66) "I've tried them except for homosexual, and they haven't been necessary so far."

(Female, widow, age 70) "Yes, why not? Oral sex is not as bad as I thought it would be."

(Female, married, age 65) "Yes. Can't really explain, but would like to change the format of our lovemaking."

(Male, married, age 64) "Why not? I would like to try everything."

(Female, divorced, age 61) "Would love to see one man with two women, one of them me."

(Male, married, age 66) "Always interested in experimenting."

(Female, married, age 60) "We do. We own a new book on this subject and have tried anything that appears interesting."

(Female, divorced, age 71) "Indeed yes. I am curious about many things."

(Female, widow, age 68) "Yes—there are other means of stimulation and I'm open to experimentation."

(Female, married, age 67) "I would like to have sex other than in the bed. I'd like to try it on the floor, in a chair, or while taking a shower."

(Female, widow, age 74) "Of course. I'm curious by nature."

(Male, divorced, age 69) "Yes I would. A full homosexual experience with a loved and loving man is about the only sexual experience I haven't had."

(Female, widow, age 82) "Yes."

(Female, widow, age 70) "If I had a real good husband I believe I could stand on my own as well as he could."

(Female, widow, age 81) "Yes, if I had a husband."

(Female, single, age 71) "Yes. I think I should experience female-female but I'd have to locate a partner."

(Male, divorced, age 61) "Am constantly looking for new sexual experiences—one of the many joys of living and loving."

(Female, widow, age 64) "I've tried some new ones because each man is a new experience."

(Male, widower, age 73) "Yes, after I went to an adult movie with a woman we tried the things we saw them do and liked it."

(Female, divorced, age 71) "To add excitement, oral sex is good."

(Male, widower, age 67) "Yes, oral sex and different positions."

(Female, widow, age 71) "And how!"

(Female, married, age 66) "I've thought about group sex but haven't tried. Also about another woman but haven't tried."

(Male, married, age 69) "Yes, I would like to try but haven't got the nerve."

(Female, divorced, age 60) "Yes. If it makes the experience more pleasurable, why not?"

(Male, married, age 73) "Yes, do try to indulge in new sex positions in lovemaking."

(Female, married, age 60) "Always interested in learning about new positions."

(Female, widow, age 72) "With the right partner—yes."

(Male, married, age 67) "Always willing to learn new tricks."

(Female, widow, age 71) "Indeed, yes. I am curious about many things."

(Female, widow, age 89) "Yes. More excitement."

(Male, married, age 69) "Yes, to possibly improve otherwise unsatisfactory results."

(Female, widow, age 71) "Yes. Anytime."

(Female, married, age 63) "Yes. Just someone else would be a new experience—wouldn't it?"

(Female, married, age 62) "I don't know—but I might. If it's pleasure-giving, why not?"

(Male, widowed, age 65) "I'll try anything that has to do with good sex."

(Female, widow, age 67) "Yes, but I probably never will—group sex is the thing I'm curious about."

(Female, married, age 62) "Yes. There are lots of interesting books with erotic pictures conducive to excitement."

(Female, widow, age 67) "Yes, you might have missed a lot of fun."

(Male, married, age 66) "Yes. Would like to try swinging couples."

(Male, married, age 74) "I think by doing this it makes the sex act more enjoyable and doesn't get dull."

(Male, single, age 66) "Yes. Making love to two women at the same time."

(Female, single, age 69) "There are so many positions—why not? But I do not go for sadistic or masochistic behavior and a disregard for physical and emotional feelings."

(Male, married, age 64) "Absolutely. I have learned from books, erotic films, lectures, and articles by authoritative professionals. They all were beautiful and I derived great pleasure."

(Male, divorced, age 64) "Yes. From what I have discovered as I have grown older, I have expanded the horizons of my ignorance. I feel sure there are broad horizons and I eagerly search for them."

(Male, married, age 69) "We have tried all experiences and continue to do so."

(Male, married, age 60) "Yes, I like anything that thrills."

The comment of a 69-year-old widow reminds us of the limitation on the sex lives of a large number of older adults when she responded, "Yes, I would. But how can I?" It is difficult to estimate the number of older people like her who would like to try new sexual experiences, but in reality don't have the opportunity for sexual relations. But far from being rooted to traditional notions of acceptable sexual practices, our survey clearly shows that older people can be as adventurous as the young.

Sexual Fantasy and the Ideal Lover

We have already established that older people think about and are interested in sex. But what is the nature of their sexual fantasies? As we age, changes in our fantasies are so slow and subtle that we are hardly aware of them. Think about it. What were the age and characteristics of your fantasized lover when you were a teenager, compared with other times in your life and now? You will be quite surprised at the dramatic changes that have very likely taken place. Yet the concept of the "dirty old man" is that older men who are turned on sexually dwell on their past fantasies—nubile and busty young women. Similar notions apply to the "dirty old lady." But, contrary to the popular myth, most men and women fantasize ideal lovers close to their own age. In response to Question 26, "Describe the ideal lover of your fantasy, age, looks, type, etc.," of those who specified an age, most depicted an ideal lover within 15 years of their own age; in some instances it was as much as 5 to 10 years older than themselves.

As Table 26 shows, 32 percent of the respondents assign an age of 60 or greater to their ideal lover. More women (39 percent) than men (19 percent) give this designation; 13 percent of those who responded describe a middle-aged person (45–59). Here, men (12 percent) and women (14 percent) do not differ greatly. A large number of respondents (32 percent) did not specify an age (our "ageless" category), but simply described the qualities of the person—e.g., "compassionate," "mature," "sensitive," "considerate," "intelligent," "tender," "humorous," "fun-loving," "sophisticated," etc. Although we cannot be sure what age these respondents would associate with these qualities, we are reasonably confident that they are not likely to be references to very young ideal lovers.

When truly young ages (under 30) were given, the responses typically had a blunt and brusque quality—e.g. "young, sexy, 20's, hot in bed" (male, married, age 68). This interpretation is further supported by the fact that very few young ages were specified at all. Only 2 percent (4 percent males and 1 percent females) described ideal lovers between the ages of 20–29. A teen-ager was designated in a mere 0.4 percent of the responses (3 respondents, all male). Another 3 percent (2 percent males and 4 percent females) describe a popular figure, usually a movie or TV star, as the ideal lover without giving an age (our "celebrity" category)—e.g., "Johnny Carson," "Hal Linden," "Clark Gable," "Greer Garson," "Hedy Lamarr," "Ronald Colman," etc. Here too the images suggest a middle-aged or older person, surely not a teen-ager. Four percent of the respondents said "a young person." Again, we cannot be sure what "young" means to, let's say, a 70-year-old—it could very well mean 45 or 50. Similarly, what does middle-aged mean to a 60- or 70-year-old?

Nevertheless, taking the categories "20–29," "young person," and "teen-ager," we arrive at only 7 percent of the respondents who select the substantially younger ideal lover consistent with the popular mythology.

The individual responses describing an ideal lover compatible in age and interests are graphic and revealing:

(Female, widow, age 69) "Around 70, intelligent and alive."

(Female, widow, age 65) "I would like a man about 65, fairly good-looking and one who would be good and kind to me."

(Male, divorced, age 69) "55 years old, pretty, clean, shapely, warm and loving."

(Female, widow, age 74) "About my age and healthy, good-looking and neat. Nice, lovable, and kind to me and others."

(Female, divorced, age 81) "If I had a lover now I would like him to be somewhat my age. I'd feel embarrassed with a young man with my having such an aging body. I'd have to have real affection for him or not have a lover at all."

(Female, widow, age 73) "My age or near it. Healthy, vigorous, nice-looking, not too handsome, active."

(Female, married, age 66) "I like my man rugged, tan, an outdoor type, 60 or 65. Mind not always on sex. Talented in sports."

(Female, married, age 66) "Approximately my age, slim, athletic, gentle, low-key."

(Male, widowed, age 72) "Between 50–60, attractive (not necessarily beautiful), intelligent, good company."

(Male, married, age 70) "Tall, clean, not plump, age to 70, gray hair or white hair is fine. Neat clothing and cares about appearance."

(Female, widow, age 70) "Ten years younger than I am—Latin type—Scorpio if possible."

(Female, widow, age 67) "62 years old, tall, broad shoulders and not too much stomach—neat and also considerate of me and my feelings."

(Female, widow, age 73) "Reasonably attractive, my age, intelligent."

(Female, married, age 62) "50 to 65, tall and blond, gentle and caring."

(Male, single, age 67) "Age 60, good-looking, beautiful physique, quiet type, agreeable, and who likes me."

(Female, widow, age 68) "About three to five years older, taller, not too heavy in weight, clean, gentle, blue eyes, dresses well, good, gentle attitudes toward life."

(Female, widow, age 63) "65, tall, dark, handsome."

(Female, widow, age 65) "60 to 73, tall and handsome, outgoing, a man who lives to travel, dance, go to a theater, so forth."

(Female, divorced, age 64) "Older than I, not too handsome, gentle and understanding."

(Male, divorced, age 69) "55 years. Pretty, clean, shapely, warm."

(Female, widow, age 63) "A man a little older than I. Youthful-looking with sex appeal and slim with intelligence if it's possible."

(Female, married, age 61) "Lover, age 70 and good-looking in the shower and in the bathtub."

(Male, widower, age 77) "A woman not too far from my age, not over twelve to fifteen years younger than I am."

(Female, widow, age 70) "65 to 75, not too tall, trim figure, neat and clean."

(Female, widow, age 72) "Ten years my junior, looks average type, six foot or over in height, brown eyes and compassionate toward me."

(Female, widow, age 88) "Close to my own age, good character and kind."

(Male, widower, age 74) "Late 60s, pleasant, intelligent, someone I can talk to, go to shows and a person who will not do embarrassing things such as talk loud."

(Female, widow, age 67) "He is a real person, unattainable, married, professional, educated, kind, ten years younger, not at all handsome."

(Female, widow, age 85) "If I had a lover I would prefer him to be near my own age; I would want him to look well-groomed, to be friendly, outgoing with high ideals and enjoy similar activities, to have a deep faith in God and be an honest upright gentleman, courteous and honorable."

(Female, widow, age 78) "70 years old, nice-looking, clean and good company."

(Female, divorced, age 66) "That's easy. My generation so we share memories. He is taller than I. He is an intellectual or very educated man—self-education is OK: he is a compassionate person, warm, tender, thoughtful of others. For icing on the cake he has gray or white hair and lots of it. He is not so sexually sophisticated that he wants sex to take hours."

(Female, widow, age 75) "About 60 to 65, slim and very good looking, neatly dressed and still young looking."

(Male, separated, age 74) "My age to ten years younger. Attractive, clean, personable."

(Male, married, age 80) "Tall, clean, not plump, age to 70, gray hair or white hair is fine. Neat clothing and cares about appearance."

(Female, married, age 70) "Sixtyish, lovable, warm, knows how to make a girl feel great."

(Female, widow, age 70) "Ten years my junior, average to tall, considerate, loving, giving and very, very passionate."

(Female, married, age 63) "From 50–65, tall, lean, muscular, resonant voice (the voice has always stimulated me), humorous, intelligent and he must be crazy about me."

(Female, divorced, age 77) "About my age. Average, gentle, kind."

(Female, widow, age 67) "About 65, dark, wavy hair. Latin-looking."

(Female, married, age 60) "My own age. Distinguished, well-bred, good manners."

(Female, widow, age 71) "Age 55–65. Rugged type with deep wrinkles on parts of face. Tall, black hair, sprinkled with gray. Good, full mouth, good teeth, neat and clean dresser. Good personality, loves music, dancing, sports, fishing, gardening, good cooking, etc."

(Female, widow, age 76) "Tall, good looking, my age (76)."

(Female, widow, age 65) "Tall, 65, blue-eyes, blonde, laughing, ready to go at all hours—dancing, walking, loving."

(Female, widow, age 76) "My lover is taller than I, older than I and just what I love all the way."

(Female, widow, age 66) "Since I am 66 years old, I would be interested in any male 60 years and over, short (like me). I am uncomfortable with tall or fat men. I like clean-shaven men, intelligent, good sense of humor, caring, likes nature, children and health foods."

(Female, divorced, age 71) "He would be understanding, attractive and medium build, enjoying trips and camping, about 60 years old or maybe 65, depending on his health."

(Female, married, age 70) "About 10 years younger, gentle, intellectually stimulating, trim, eye contact extremely important."

(Female, widow, age 64) "A healthy, tall, 60-year-old—preferably good-looking and with sexual desires to match mine."

(Female, married, age 62) "Slender, about my age, intelligent, monogamous, imaginative, sexy, desirous of companionship, kissable."

(Female, widow, age 75) "An intelligent man in his 70s with a zest for living."

(Female, married, age 65) "Someone my own age, gentle, gray-haired and blue-eyed."

(Female, widow, age 72) "Age 60-75, intelligence and character which are usually revealed on the face. Strong but not a male chauvinist."

(Female, widow, age 71) "Age 70, white hair, blue eyes, clean shaven, flirty, 6', no taller, good dresser, just enough money, no millionaire, no silly jokes."

(Male, widowed, age 76) "Since I am 5'5" and weigh 122 lbs., I like a lady about the same age, height and weight."

(Female, widow, age 65) "Someone near my own age who knows he is a man, who understands a woman and shows love, gentleness and respect."

(Female, married, age 60) "61, tall, craggy handsome look, intelligent, inventive, imaginative, a great lover."

(Female, widow, age 62) "Middle-aged, real good-looking, sexy type, 10"."

(Female, married, age 62) "60s, slim, blue eyes, intelligent, clean, dresses well; communicates, interested in my welfare and thinks I'm beautiful, intelligent and interesting."

As the responses to so many of our questions proved, it is merely the age of the respondents that is, finally, notable—and in this case, the ages of the ideal lovers they named. Otherwise, the descriptions are what we would expect from adults of any age without taking particular notice—"tall, dark, handsome, pretty, full of fun, virile." This familiar list of attributes is jarring only because it is coming from people who are thought to be "beyond sex." But if a 61-year-old woman can fantasize about a 70-year-old man who is "good looking in the shower and the bathtub," clearly age is no barrier to a sexual turn-on.

In some instances younger ideal lovers were described. While this tended to occur more often with male respondents, it was also true for some women.

(Male, married, age 75) "Good shape, slim type, long legs, red hair, twenty years my junior."

(Female, married, age 66) "I think a person between 35 and 45 who is thoughtful, gently exciting and with whom I can hope for a long-term relationship."

(Male, married, age 62) "40 years of age but doesn't look it, sexy-looking, knowledgeable, 120 pounds, 5'8", heavy breasts, long legs."

(Male, married, age 63) "16, nubile, attractive, excellent figure."

(Female, widow, age 81) "A nice-looking young man from 18 to 45."

(Male, married, age 63) "Young, beautiful, aggressive."

(Female, widow, age 69) "A handsome man about 48 years old, tall, smart and passionate. I like them younger than me."

(Female, widow, age 74) "Age 20s, tall, dark, handsome—Lawrence Olivier, Gary Cooper."

(Male, married, age 74) "Early 20s, tall, slim, well-built, pretty, wholesome face, fun-loving, affectionate, and passionate."

(Female, widow, age 71) "Middle-aged, handsome, gentle, kind, considerate with concern for his wife."

(Female, widow, age 66) "48, tall, slim, easy going, well-groomed, slightly gray and in love with me. He does not have to be rich, but money for dinners and shows, etc., is just fine enough."

(Female, widow, age 81) "About ten years younger than me. Prefer tall people with a sense of humor and well-educated. Cannot stand dumbbells—should know something by now."

(Male, married, age 60) "A woman 16 to 60—any race, color. Clean, thin to average measurements and capable of exciting me via voice, manner, etc."

(Male, married, age 75) "Young, good-looking Latin."

(Female, married, age 71) "30 years of age and willing."

(Male, married, age 66) "Age 35, teats should not be too large or sloppy. 5'5"–5'10"—from 120–150 lbs, should look intelligent, not necessarily pretty but that helps. Black or white."

(Female, married, age 73) "About 35, presentable, neat, good companion, kind, understanding, thoughtful, exciting, good conversationalist, traveler, loving and kind."

(Male, married, age 60) "Male or female, about 18. The looks of beautiful youth are a turn-on."

(Female, widow, age 73) "Dark complexion, 40ish, tall and handsome, romantic and sentimental."

(Male, married, age 69) "Young girl, sexy, hot-looking, nice shape, nice tits."

(Male, married, age 80) "Hair in a certain place, lots of it, nice breasts, age 30, looks slender."

(Female, married, age 65) "Age 25, tall, blonde, well-built and very attractive."

(Female, widow, age 67) "My ideal lover might be young (say 30) but mostly he would have a good healthy body, strong legs, beautiful hands, a sense of humor to match mine and an intelligent brain."

(Female, widow, age 74) "About 35 years of age, tall and pleasant-looking, masculine, gentle, and considerate in love-making."

For some, age was not as important as performance. As one 73-year-old married woman bluntly said, "Any age as long as he has an erection which lasts long enough to give me an orgasm." Others stressed the qualities of the person:

(Female, widow, age 75) "Should be educated, well-groomed, a professional type. Need not be young or good-looking. Considerate and kind."

(Female, widow, age 60) "The quality of the relationship. Age should not be the determining factor. He has to be someone I can be proud of."

(Male, married, age 61) "Age unimportant. Should be slim and attractive, educated, sensitive and really enjoy love-making and being in love."

(Female, widow, age 87) "A tender, masterful man."

(Male, married, age 74) "Sensuous type regardless of age."

(Male, married, age 70) "Age doesn't matter as much as the person's response."

(Male, married, age 61) "Mature, trim, stacked."

(Female, widow, age 65) "Personality—rapport."

(Female, widow, age 77) "Age does not make a difference. He should be intelligent and distinguished-looking and be the way he looks."

(Male, married, age 68) "Beautiful features, somewhat aggressive and non-complaining."

(Male, married, age 68) "The person must have same desires and liking one another for what they are. Knowing one another is far more important than age, looks, etc."

(Male, married, age 73) "Beautiful woman at any age."

(Female, married, age 66) "Seven or eight years younger than I am, pleasant-looking, dark or blond or even gray. But first the appeal to me is personality and a little cerebral. I can't go to bed with a dummy; would rather do it myself."

(Male, divorced, age 69) "Age is irrelevant. My ideal lover would have a certain glint in her eye, be quick to laugh and play, eager to experiment with any kind of sex and would find no part of my body unpleasant to touch or kiss."

Many older people spend a good deal of time watching television. In previous years they were heavy movie-goers. It is, therefore, understandable that the media would provide the food for some fantasies. Names like Marilyn Monroe, Humphrey Bogart, Clark Gable, Johnny Carson, and Hal Linden, among others, were frequently mentioned, more commonly by women than men.

That age is no barrier to sexiness is further reflected in the responses to Question 8, "What does it mean to be a sexy person?" Most respondents identify sexiness with qualities of the person, not age. "Passionate; someone who desires me; a loving, gentle person, attractive, rugged-looking; sensuous, lively and interesting; a good lover; a person with deep feelings." These descriptions and others like them are similar to the responses to the ideal lover question; they are qualities that transcend age.

Today, fantasy is viewed as an important vehicle for sexual arousal, essential for keeping long-term sexual relationships alive and renewed. Sex manuals recommend exercises for developing sexual fantasies and suggest that couples share the details of their erotic fantasies. Studies have shown that younger people actively fantasize during sexual intercourse. For example the *Redbook Report on Female Sexuality* cites a study of 141 housewives by E. Barbara Hariton indicating that erotic fantasies during lovemaking are commonplace and enhance sexual pleasure. Popular authors such as Nancy Friday have convinced us that erotic fantasies are an important part of the sexual "turn on." In *The Fantasy Game* Dr. Peter Dally warns of the danger of not using your fantasies: "All too often . . . marriages fail to develop, or decline and break up, because partners ignore or suppress their own and each other's fantasies, and boredom sets in." In *Nice Girls Do* Irene Kassorla suggests that couples share their fantasies about others to heighten the excitement.

Yet despite society's new openness and despite the fact that conceiving the ideal lover proved to be a rich source of fantasy among our respondents, more elaborate fantasies of sexual practices was still a taboo area, running a close second to the practice of masturbation. Like masturbation, indulgence in fantasy has the aura of self-indulgence and idleness, both counter to the turn-of-the-century ethics of hard work and denial of pleasure.

Some of our respondents have apparently broken the taboo about fantasy, but many have not. Thus in some cases, even on the question of the ideal lover, we find instances of total denial. Eight percent say they have no fantasy: "I have none. I am satisfied with my husband and don't fantasize," said one 73-year-old married woman emphatically, forgetting that she complained about her sex life elsewhere in the questionnaire. Another 64-year-old woman complained about her "dull" sex life because of her husband's lack of interest. Yet she too cited him as her "ideal lover." It was a typical pattern of denial to invoke devotion to the spouse in justifying not fantasizing. Our respondents seemed to be saying that fantasy is a betrayal of their sexual partner, unless it focuses solely on him or her.

In a few cases the respondents cynically skirted the issue of the ideal lover. As one 65-year-old divorced female put it, "An ideal lover is usually a bastard. Very few men are good lovers."

We pursued the question of fantasy further in Question 34, "What do you think about while you are making love?" Most of the answers concentrated on physical sensations (57 percent) without making any reference to fantasy:

(Female, married, age 61) "Ecstasy."

(Male, married, age 67) "Just take in the enjoyment and don't think."

(Female, married, age 61) "I think I'm in heaven."

(Male, married, age 72) "The grand feeling of intercourse."

(Female, widow, age 82) "Just what we are doing."

(Female, divorced, age 62) "A great sense of well-being."

(Male, single, age 66) "Of how wonderful I feel."

(Female, married, age 65) "My body."

(Female, widow, age 67) "My feelings and his reactions."

(Male, divorced, age 62) "How to have my partner and I enjoy every minute of it."

(Female, divorced, age 68) "Just making love."

(Female, widow, age 71) "Just relax and enjoy."

(Male, married, age 69) "I am not aware of thinking anything other than the sensations."

(Female, widow, age 67) "I don't think of anything except of the enjoyment I am experiencing."

(Female, single, age 65) "Sometimes a wide variety of things, but I have discovered I have to concentrate on what feels good in order for me to respond up to the point of orgasm."

(Male, widower, age 73) "Just how good it feels."

(Female, widow, age 70) "I become intensely aware of my own body and his and don't do a lot of thinking at all. It is purely physical and the need to be stroked and made love to generally is one of total involvement."

(Female, widow, age 64) "Nothing but releasing myself in total enjoyment."

(Male, married, age 62) "About what is happening—feels good."

(Female, widow, age 61) "How good it feels. Have never fantasized. Should I?"

(Female, widow, age 66) "How good it feels and hoping that I can climax before he pops off."

Twenty-two percent simply said they think about "the person I'm with." This frequently came across to us as a denial of fantasy, suggesting that thinking of anything or anyone else would be disloyal to the partner. Of course, in many of these instances the person referred to was the spouse, making it the expected response.

Another 7 percent totally denied fantasy by saying they thought of "nothing" during lovemaking.

A small percentage of respondents (5 percent) cited "abstract or diversionary" thoughts during lovemaking. These, too, seemed to avoid the question of fantasy.

(Female, married, age 79) "How much I love my husband."
(Female, married, age 60) "Anywhere from making a shopping list, wish he'd get it over with, to a mindless wish to have it go on forever."
(Male, married, age 67) "Beautiful things."
(Female, married, age 63) "I forget the whole world when I'm making love."
(Female, widow, age 80) "Thoughts disappear."
(Male, widower, age 74) "The joy of being alive."
(Male, widower, age 84) "Love."

Only in some instances (10 percent) do we get even a vague suggestion of a genuine erotic fantasy during lovemaking. "Spin fantasies from old descriptions in past reading," writes a 60-year-old married woman. A married male, age 63, rejoins, "A prior sexy situation or person," while a 72-year-old married female replies, "Often my first sweetheart." But in these hints of fantasy there is no elaboration or explicit detail provided. The evasiveness on the topic of fantasy is obvious when we consider the frankness of the responses to other seemingly more intimate questions.

Kinsey also noted little fantasy, particularly among his female subjects. These people, who are of the same generation as our respondents, are still not fantasizing many years later. Their low level of fantasy can probably be traced to their upbringing. However, Kinsey concluded that females required direct physical stimulation for sexual arousal while males could respond to a psychological stimulation (fantasy, erotic material, etc.). His conclusion ignored the fact that women born at the turn-of-the-century when the double standard was in its heyday had far more restrictions on their sexuality than men. Dwelling on sexual thoughts was simply not permissible for women. However, the proliferation of sex literature that now encourages both men and women to develop their potential for fantasy as a means of enhancing sexual response, seems to have fostered a high level of fantasy activity among young males and females. Dr. Aaron Hass found in his survey of adolescents that all teenagers today, both female and male, fantasize while masturbating. Surely succeeding generations of elderly will carry forward their heritage of more active sexual fantasy.

Sex and Marriage

What do our respondents think about sex outside of marriage for older people? Back in the late 1940s and 50s when our respondents were busy raising their 2.5 children and saving strong, inflation-free dollars for a split-level ranch house in the suburbs, sexual ethics were clear and simple. Sex and marriage were indivisible. Our respondents told their daughters, as they had been told before them, that sex should not be given away for free lest the prize of marriage be lost. The double standard gave boys a bit more freedom, but then the "good girls" were not available for sexual relations. The sex game became "What did you give?" for girls and "What did you get?" for boys, the giving and getting usually meaning something short of sexual intercourse. Young men could, of course, choose between "Crazy Shirley" (a real or mythical person in every neighborhood) or prostitutes. Masturbation, as Kinsey reported, was flourishing, especially for boys (girls were soon to catch up). Guilt about sex was rampant but relatively unquestioned, since it was assumed to be inherent in the sexual experience. Living together outside of marriage was almost unheard of, or at best very secretive. For most, it was neither an issue nor an option.

At that time most of our respondents would have been upset, even scandalized, if their children pursued the laissez-faire sexuality they see casually flaunted by their grandchildren and the young adult generation. Marriage was understood to be the only acceptable route to regular sexual relations.

All that changed in the 1960s when sexual morality burst out of the traditional mold. Betty Friedan's *Feminine Mystique* pierced the hearts and minds of the depressed daughters of our respondents, who were now approaching their middle years in the fulfilled if empty dream of affluence lived out in the "split-level traps" of a spreading suburbia. The feminist movement had been launched.

As we have noted, many of our respondents find themselves in a new world now, one where sex is available, where the sacredness of marriage is questionable, and the divorce rate is soaring. For many "till death do us part" has been played out. It is a reality. The ranks of the elderly are filled with a large number of widows and fewer widowers. Others can realistically anticipate the day when they will join the growing numbers of older adults without partners. The dilemma of these people leaves many of them pulled toward choices that challenge the traditional morality of their upbringing—affairs, homosexuality, sex without marriage, and living together without marriage. These "illicit" alternatives are often the only practical way for older adults to satisfy their needs. Can they do it? Do they do it? What do they think about the issue?

Question 29 asks, "How do you feel about older people who are not married having sexual relations and living together?" In the light of what we know about the moral training of our respondents and their previous undoubtedly traditional stance on sex and marriage, we could not have anticipated what we found in the responses to this question. An impressive majority endorsed these practices. A whopping 91 percent approved. Men (95 percent) and women (89 percent) gave similar responses, as did those who were sexually active (94 percent) and those who were inactive (93 percent). Many responses expressed unequivocal enthusiasm:

> (Female, widow, age 67) "I think it's great."
> (Female, married, age 73) "Fine. More power to them."
> (Male, widower, age 79) "I myself think it is ideal. I have lived for periods of time with widows."

(Female, widow, age 70) "No objection whatsoever. Highly desirable."

(Female, single, age 65) "I'm doing it and I think it's great."

(Male, married, age 71) "Great, leave them alone."

(Male, widower, age 74) "Good as long as they get satisfaction."

(Male, married, age 70) "Sex is a necessity and it is wonderful if a couple can satisfy each other's needs."

(Female, widow, age 76) "Very good. I am one of them. It took a lifetime to attain independence. I wish to keep it that way."

(Male, married, age 69) "It's a good way to go."

(Female, married, age 65) "As long as no one suffers from their actions, why not! If it's a mutual desire, go to it."

(Female, married, age 61) "I believe in it."

(Female, married, age 66) "Dandy."

(Female, widow, age 69) "Very good. Healthful."

(Female, married, age 64) "It's fine with me. May not make mistakes like our generation did."

(Female, widow, age 75) "It is OK. Nobody's business but theirs. Might be a better arrangement than formal marriage would."

(Female, married, age 62) "Super—beautiful—do it!"

(Female, widow, age 76) "Sometimes it is better not to get married because some men are nice before and change after—that goes for a woman too."

(Female, widow, age 67) "My feelings are—hooray!"

(Male, married, age 73) "I give them credit for their courage "

(Male, widowed, age 84) "I think it's wonderful for both."

(Male, married, age 60) "Beautiful."

(Female, widow, age 67) "I'm all for it. What bothers me is that it is assumed that age changes a person's nature. Men and women are sexual beings. Why should desire die before a person dies?"

(Female, widow, age 63) "I think it's OK. Living together is much better than a rotten marriage or being alone."

(Female, widow, age 68) "I'm in this category myself."

(Female, married, age 66) "One of the good things to come from the new morality."

(Male, widowed, age 78) "Good. What could be better? You only go around once."

(Male, married, age 67) "Fine, as sex is needed in life."
(Female, widow, age 60) "Fine. Who wants to be married again?"

Living together can be "great, desirable, healthful" or in general "a good way to go." Like the younger generation they can see the practical benefit of living together so as "not to make mistakes . . ."

Economic factors are the overriding consideration for many respondents:

> (Female, widow, age 75) "They need to be wanted and loved and can't afford to lose their social security benefits. It also takes two incomes to survive."
>
> (Female, married, age 61) "May be economically practical. Those I know do so to enjoy freedom—don't want to be tied down."
>
> (Female, widow, age 78) "If for economic reasons it is their thing it's all right with me. They should be allowed to enjoy their later years as long as they do not offend anyone."
>
> (Male, married, age 67) "Just fine—a mutual aid society without the legal entanglements."
>
> (Female, married, age 72) "In some cases it is a financial necessity so I don't criticize them."
>
> (Female, widow, age 77) "It is perfectly alright. Social Security laws are such that they are better off financially by not getting married."
>
> (Female, divorced, age 61) "A practical, economic arrangement. Social Security penalizes them if they marry. Separation doesn't have legal strings if it comes to that."
>
> (Male, married, age 76) "That is a matter of choice and I can't quarrel with it as I know widows who would lose pensions if they married. More power to them."

Perhaps the best insight into the open attitude of our respondents is the simple and factual acknowledgment that times have changed:

> (Male, widower, age 67) "It has become the thing of the time."
>
> (Female, married, age 72) "OK. Seems to be the trend."
>
> (Female, widow, age 68) "I don't see any wrong in it. You used to think, 'Oh, what will the grandchildren think,' but those days are gone. We'll hope it's for the better."

(Female, widow, age 65) "Nothing is wrong with it. Times have changed. It has been done since time began and will continue."
(Male, married, age 80) "It is a new way of life. You have to accept it."
(Female, married, age 62) "I feel it is OK. Everyone is doing their thing these days. To each his own."
(Male, single, age 63) "Fine. Why not in our permissive society?"

Taking their cue from the new spirit of liberation, some say that what is OK for the young should also be OK for older people. As a married woman of 62 put it, "I think it's just fine. If their grandchildren do likewise they should not be bothered."

We are used to young people sometimes belittling marriage and the marriage contract as the sanction for sexual relations. It is somewhat unexpected to find older people joining the same chorus. "Great. They are mature enough not to need that piece of paper," writes a widow, aged 69. "I cannot marry because I would lose my pension. He and I are mature enough that we do not need that piece of paper," agrees a 70-year-old widow. And a 66-year-old married man writes: "Great. What does a marriage certificate got to do with it?"

Others insist that the feelings and needs of two people supercede the standards set by society:

(Male, married, age 68) "They should follow their personal feelings. If it does not create a feeling of guilt or other rejection they have the right to have a response to their feelings."
(Female, widow, age 70) "I am not in favor of bedhopping, but where there is a real caring and for some a better arrangement, I think it is all right."
(Female, widow, age 78) "Let them have it if they want it. They are old enough to know what they are doing."
(Male, married, age 83) "No objection if the relationship is based on mutual understanding."
(Female, married, age 74) "If they love each other or just like each other and have much in common it's great."
(Female, widow, age 82) "OK, if they really enjoy each other."

Some who approve of sex outside of marriage have a more tentative view of living together:

(Male, widower, age 80) "Have sex relations but do not live together for you have children and grandchildren."
(Female, married, age 74) "Sexual relations if desired, OK. Living together, unless for financial needs, no."
(Female, widow, age 63) "Sexual relations, OK; but not living together."

The ambivalence of some was best expressed by the 74-year-old widow who writes, "I think that if that is what they want why shouldn't they, although it is a sin." Her conflict is what we might have expected from the group as a whole. But our data show much the contrary. Again we find that older adults not only respond to the revolutions of their times but also change with them.

8

Intimate Communications

John and Sue have just made love. "How was it?" he asks tenderly. "I'm still excited," she whispers. John promptly embraces her and continues the lovemaking until he helps her reach orgasm through manual stimulation.

This is surely a familiar scene to young couples. With the current emphasis on sexual satisfaction for both partners, there is greater freedom to express feelings and make demands. In previous decades, it might have been more typical for Sue to simply say "Wonderful" to John's query of "How was it?" Later she might have quietly masturbated to achieve the release she did not have during lovemaking or possibly have gone unhappily to sleep.

Sex between two people is an interactional process. To achieve maximum satisfaction (or in some instances minimal satisfaction) you have to communicate your needs and preferences to your partner. Everyone's sexual response system is different. Some people get aroused slowly, others quickly. Some people reach a high pitch of excitement from having specific parts of their body stroked—breasts, nipples, testicles, back, palms, etc. Almost any part of the body can be an erogenous zone for a given individual.

How do our respondents rate their sexual satisfaction? More importantly, what do they do when not satisfied? Popular belief has persuaded us that older people have routine sex, at best. Kinsey reinforced this notion with his finding that three-quarters of his male sample (the same generation that is now our sample of older adults) ejaculated within two minutes of entering the woman. This led to many jokes throughout the world about the "quickie" style of American sex: "If you only have a few minutes, we can do it American style." It also explained why many women were "frigid" or unable to have orgasms—their arousal systems simply required more time.

133

We, therefore, anticipated considerable dissatisfaction, particularly from our female respondents, when we posed Question 20, "Do sexual experiences leave you satisfied? What do you do when not satisfied?" Much to our surprise, most said they were satisfied (Table 20): 72 percent said "yes" unequivocally while 23 percent said they are satisfied "sometimes." Only 5 percent indicated dissatisfaction. In examining male-female differences, we find that male respondents say "yes" more than females—82 percent compared with 66 percent. But more females (27 percent) than males (15 percent) say they are "sometimes" satisfied. Of those respondents who are clearly dissatisfied, the figures for males (3 percent) and females (7 percent) are fairly similar.

Since most were satisfied, the majority of respondents addressed themselves only to the first part of the question. Many statements were emphatic:

(Female, married, age 62) "Yes, since my husband sees to it that I am satisfied whenever I feel the need."
(Male, married, age 70) "Always satisfied."
(Male, married, age 68) "Usually am satisfied."
(Female, married, age 72) "I'm satisfied."
(Female, widow, age 74) "They leave me satisfied most of the time."
(Male, married, age 82) "Always pleasurably satisfied even if full clima: hasn't been reached."
(Male, widower, age 67) "Almost all ways they do. Especially when both partners have their climaxes together like mine did."
(Female, widow, age 78) "Yes. It does leave a satisfied feeling."
(Male, married, age 76) "Always been satisfied."
(Male, married, age 86) "Yes. An orgasm reached equals satisfaction."
(Female, married, age 69) "Yes. I am always satisfied. For this has always been our agreement since we are older."
(Male, married, age 73) "With a good partner—yes."
(Male, widower, age 75) "Yes. Has not occurred."
(Female, widow, age 75) "Most of the time. Try to fake it if he is too tired to keep going."
(Female, married, age 62) "Yes. I'm always satisfied—completely happy—ready for next time."

(Male, married, age 76) "Yes. Leaves me satisfied. We are married 37 years and always have climaxed simultaneously."

Lack of satisfaction can mean a number of things. Clearly many women interpreted it simply as not having an orgasm. Some of the men based their answers on their difficulty in reaching orgasm or ejaculating, even though they were able to maintain an erection for a relatively long period of time. This 71-year-old widower expressed his view in no uncertain terms: "I have a lot of sex but don't come all the time. It really pisses me off. I used to be a tiger."

In some instances, the men felt dissatisfied when their partners didn't reach orgasm. For example, a 64-year-old man said: "I wish my wife would climax more often. I try hard to please her. I have no problem."

Among those who did tackle the second part of the question, 40 percent did not actively pursue sexual release. They mostly "went to sleep." (Table 20.5)

(Female, widow, age 80) "Go to sleep."
(Male, married, age 70) "Yes. Make the best of it. Try to sleep."
(Male, widower, age 81) "With or without—go to sleep."
(Male, married, age 64) "Yes. Seldom occurs but I fall asleep easily."
(Female, married, age 65) "(1) Of course. (2) Get up, wash my private parts with cool water, put out the lights and go to sleep."
(Male, married, age 67) "Most times, yes. Other times I am frustrated and in that case go to sleep."
(Female, widow, age 75) "Nothing. Turn around and go to sleep."
(Male, married, age 71) "I just kiss her and go to sleep."
(Male, married, age 72) "You forget it."
(Male, married, age 72) "Ordinarily, yes. Other times I just go to sleep, vowing to do better next time."
(Male, married, age 69) "Yes. When climax is not mutually attained, go to sleep."
(Female, married, age 66) "Oftener than not. Cool off and go to sleep."
(Male, widower, age 68) "1. Yes. 2. Go home."
(Female, married, age 66) "Kiss and go to sleep."
(Male, widower, age 64) "Relax and have a drink."
(Female, widow, age 71) "Usually. Go to sleep."

(Female, married, age 66) "Not very often. Turn around and go to sleep."

Others who did nothing for the moment looked to the next sexual encounter:

(Female, married, age 60) "Yes. I look forward to the next time."
(Male, divorced, age 67) "Generally they do because I usually wait for the right partner. If I'm not satisfied I cool it, thinking the next time will make up for it."
(Male, married, age 73) "Wait for the next time."
(Female, married, age 69) "Not being satisfied is rare. However, if it does happen, we forget it, and go about business as usual, knowing that next time will be better. It presents no problem so far."
(Male, married, age 67) "(1) Yes. (2) I say, 'You owe me one.'"
(Female, widow, age 64) "Yes. If not satisfied, hope next time better."
(Female, widow, age 64) "Yes. If not satisfied, I take it as a matter of fact saying there will be another time."
(Male, married, age 68) "Swear a little, then wait for next time."
(Female, married, age 74) "Yes. When not satisfied, we repeat it sooner, say in a day or two."

A sizable number of the dissatisfied group resorted to masturbation (20 percent). Some used masturbation along with other palliatives like "taking aspirin for pain or a warm bath," as was the suggestion of one married woman of 72. The responses were direct:

(Female, single, age 65) "If he ejaculates before I have orgasm, I am not satisfied and I masturbate. He is inclined to go to sleep at this point, which pisses me off."
(Male, married, age 60) "Usually they do. Masturbate."
(Female, married, age 66) "Not always, if my husband has only a partial erection. Sometimes I manage to get to sleep; other times I masturbate."
(Male, married, age 62) "Most of the time. If I feel frustrated, I fantasize and masturbate to the fantasy."
(Male, married, age 62) "Yes. Seldom have this experience. It might be a time to masturbate, maybe go to another woman."

(Female, divorced, age 64) "Yes. Resort to self-help."

(Male, married, age 70) "Yes. Masturbate."

(Female, married, age 61) "Usually. Masturbate or get up and read."

(Female, married, age 81) "Some, yes. If the pressure is great enough to be uncomfortable, I masturbate."

(Female, single, age 71) "Sometimes yes. Sometimes no. If I'm horny, I masturbate it through to climax."

(Female, widow, age 76) "Not always. Masturbate. I have a dry vagina and penetration hurts. I am trying to medicate the problem."

(Female, widow, age 63) "Either engage in mutual masturbation or roll over."

(Male, divorced, age 66) "Not always even in masturbation, but I attempt it less and find other things to do—I keep active in work or read good books."

(Male, married, age 75) "Sexual experiences with my wife, whom I love, do not generally satisfy. I generally masturbate next day."

(Female, widow, age 67) "Very seldom unsatisfied. When not, masturbate or have partner bring me to orgasm."

(Male, married, age 69) "No. I'm not satisfied with my performance and my wife will not permit any manual manipulation to bring her to an orgasm so she's unfulfilled. Sometimes I'll masturbate after an unfulfilling performance."

(Male, married, age 74) "Keep on trying by masturbating until I am satisfied."

Whereas some masturbated to relieve tension or even "pain" when left dissatisfied in their sexual experience, others (18 percent) could not shake their dissatisfaction and the tensions and pressures this produced. Both their physical and emotional pain were evident, showing that sexual satisfaction is not a casual matter.

(Female, widow, age 66) "If the man lasts, yes—but if he doesn't I stay uptight for days. I do nothing about it because it takes a partner for me to be pleased."

(Female, widow, age 65) "Cry—try to get busy with other things and distract myself with activities."

(Male, married, age 73) "Yes. If not satisfied, short temper and grouchy."

(Male, married, age 74) "Yes. Feel pressure of everyday life more."

(Female, widow, age 65) "Tense."

(Male, widower, age 63) "Yes. Feel frustrated."

(Female, widow, age 66) "I don't do anything but lay there and realize that I'm disappointed."

(Female, married, age 65) "Stay awake all night 'till about 5 A.M. when I'm so tired I finally fall asleep from praying."

(Female, married, age 68) "Usually, get mad."

(Female, divorced, age 68) "My last marriage did not leave me satisfied. I felt like crying."

(Female, divorced, age 77) "Sometimes I just feel yucky."

(Male, widower, age 72) "Yes. Irritated."

(Female, widow, age 68) "In marriage, I was often unsatisfied and was deeply resentful and sleepless."

(Female, widow, age 74) "Feel cheated."

(Female, widow, age 66) "No. I don't do anything but lay there and realize I'm disappointed."

(Female, widow, age 68) "Disgusted. Unhappy."

(Female, divorced, age 65) "Have difficulty sleeping."

(Female, widow, age 65) "Sometimes I feel cheated."

(Male, married, age 80) "Yes. Grouchy and cranky."

(Female, married, age 66) "Sulk, and go to sleep."

(Female, divorced, age 79) "I feel let down."

(Female, widow, age 70) "Sexual experiences leave me satisfied when I feel I have been desired by the other partner and given them a sense of satisfaction as well. I am not satisfied if I am rushed, not given much touching or kissing, and left without orgasm. When I am not satisfied, I do not communicate that fact but resent it inwardly."

(Female, married, age 67) "Not always. Suffer."

(Male, married, age 65) "Bitch about it."

(Female, married, age 65) "Take a cold shower."

(Female, widow, age 67) "Yes. I get very annoyed."

(Female, married, age 63) "No. Masturbate. Spend sleepless nights."

(Male, married, age 72) "Mostly satisfied. Severe frustration and anger when not."

(Female, married, age 72) "Yes. If I climax, I am satisfied. If not, there is disappointment and I feel cross."

(Female. married, age 69) "I am moody if not satisfied."

(Female, divorced, age 64) "Oh my—yes. I become either angry or worried that perhaps I am disappointing my mate."

(Male, married, age 65) "Yes. I get solemn and grouchy."

(Female, married, age 70) "If my husband and I have orgasm too quickly, later I seem to feel keyed up."

(Female, single, age 63) "Sometimes. Masturbate, grit my teeth."

(Female, widow, age 72) "Cry."

(Male, married, age 63) "I eat."

(Female, married, age 61) "If not, lay awake longer before getting to sleep."

(Female, widow, age 65) "Satisfied most of the time. If not, take a shower."

Another large group (18 percent) were more persistent believing in the motto, "If at first you don't succeed . . ." These respondents either seduced their partner or just continued trying until satisfaction was achieved. Considerably more men (32 percent) than women (10 percent) continued the effort to reach satisfaction. This is not surprising when we consider that men in our sample are more often the initiators of sex (Question 35—"Who usually begins the lovemaking, you or your partner?"). Only 8 percent of the women are consistently the initiators. Many of the responses in the "seduce/continue trying" category show a strong determination:

(Male, married, age 70) "Insist that we keep trying."

(Female, widow, age 68) "I ask my partner to help me and satisfy me before he leaves my bed."

(Male, married, age 64) "Just keep trying until I get there."

(Female, widow, age 65) "Yes. Why, I just tell my man and he takes it from there."

(Male, widowed, age 71) "Keep trying."

(Female, divorced, age 74) "Yes. Demand satisfaction."

(Female, widow, age 82) "Ask for more."

(Male, married, age 69) "Yes. Try it again."

(Female, divorced, age 65) "Yes. Could ask my partner to keep trying."

(Male, married, age 69) "Yes. Try it again."

(Male, married, age 82) "Try again."

(Male, widower, age 80) "Yes. Try again."

(Female, widow, age 74) "Start over."

(Female, widow, age 72) "Try another time."

(Male, widower, age 81) "Yes. Take a rest and try it again. Talk it over with your partner and see if you both can do better later."

(Female, widow, age 72) "Yes. Do without or try again."

(Male, married, age 68) "Very much so. Continue to try or wait until the next time."

(Male, divorced, age 61) "Very satisfied. Try again if I'm not satisfied."

(Female, widow, age 68) "Yes. Continue the sexual experience until I am satisfied."

A small group (5 percent) used an activity to take care of the tension:

(Female, divorced, age 66) "Usually. If not, I tend to get out of bed, smoke a cigarette, maybe have a drink (alcoholic) mild."

(Female, widow, age 61) "Usually. If not, smoke more. Possibly have a drink, or find something interesting to read."

(Male, married, age 75) "Work it off in the shop."

(Female, widow, age 66) "Walk or try to get over it."

(Female, divorced, age 64) "Physical activities. Brisk walks, thorough housecleaning, etc."

Communicating or talking about sex with a partner often proves to be a turn-on and a key to achieving satisfaction. It can also be a way of giving out medals or shouting one's grievances. In Question 38, we asked our respondents, "Do you talk about sex with your partner? What part of the sexual experience do you discuss?"

Almost a third do not discuss the sexual experience at all (30 percent males and 33 percent females). Their comments are, aptly, brief:

(Female, married, age 66) "We do not discuss it."

(Male, widower, age 72) "Seldom, after first five years."

(Male, single, age 72) "Very rarely."

(Female, married, age 61) "No talking."

(Female, married, age 60) "Not particularly."

(Female, widow, age 75) "Never did."

(Female, widow, age 69) "None of this."

(Female, widow, age 74) "We never talked about sex."

(Female, widow, age 73) "Not especially."

(Male, widower, age 81) "No. No need to talk."

(Female, widow, age 66) "I never talked sex, with or without a partner."

(Male, married, age 65) "Not anymore. We've had enough experience in fifty years."

Some respondents felt their partner was a barrier to open communication:

(Female, widow, age 78) "Men don't like to talk about sex."

(Female, divorced, age 64) "No. Present partner not educated enough."

(Male, married, age 73) "My wife never allowed talking about sex when she was willing, unless it was hurry up and get through."

(Female, married, age 67) "He refuses to talk about sex."

(Female, widow, age 63) "Often the conversation is one-sided. Older men don't seem to want to talk about possible lesser prowess."

(Female, married, age 71) "I'd have my head handed to me."

(Female, widow, age 68) "I was unable to communicate with my partner on the feeling level. He did not want to accept the fact that he could express his feelings."

(Male, married, age 64) "Very little discussion. She has sex hang-ups."

(Female, married, age 69) "It is very difficult to talk to him about sex. He doesn't perform and this hurts him I am sure so I don't discuss it much."

(Male, married, age 74) "Not enough talk. She is too bashful to talk about it and thinks it is dirty."

(Male, married, age 69) "No. It's not a discussable subject with my wife."

(Female, married, age 63) "With my lovers we talked entirely openly about sex. With my impotent husband, this topic is never discussed."

Of the 68 percent who do talk about sex, some use communication to reinforce the partner, to compliment and relate the enjoyment of the experience, or to heighten the eroticism:

(Female, divorced, age 63) "He tells me he wants to kiss my 'beauties' (breasts). I rave about his erection and the hardening of his balls and how I love to feel them filling up."

(Female, married, age 79) "Yes. How sexy each happens to be."

(Female, married, age 73) "Simply that we both enjoy it."

(Female, married, age 65) "Always, after sex, I ask if the act was good. My husband says it's beautiful and the best medicine in the world."

(Female, married, age 60) "Just how good it was."

(Male, married, age 72) "Yes. To see if it's OK."

(Female, married, age 69) "Yes. We talk, and we discuss all parts of it. What to do each time, how to do it, and how much we are enjoying it as it progresses. Finally, always afterwards, we discuss how great he was."

(Female, divorced, age 66) "Building each other up."

(Female, widow, age 67) "The effect on each of us."

(Female, divorced, age 62) "Yes. The ability to enjoy each other."

(Male, divorced, age 69) "Yes. How good it is, foreplay and four-letter words."

(Female, married, age 70) "Not much talk—except words of joy and encouragement."

(Female, widow, age 76) "Yes. How pleasing he is."

(Female, divorced, age 65) "Sometimes how we can better please each other—or just erotica or fantasy for fun."

(Male, widower, age 71) "How much we love each other."

A few people say they do not go into elaborate descriptions, but do tell their partners how good it is:

(Female, married, age 60) "Not much. Just how good it was."

(Female, widow, age 70) "Not much. I might comment it was a wonderful experience—he was terrific—but that's all."

A few believed in the adage "Actions speak louder than words." Their communications were nonverbal. They simply acted:

(Male, married, age 69) "We do not discuss it—usually act it out."

(Male, widower, age 79) "My steady lady, 40 years old, and I never

talk about it, after petting, etc. We both undress, and have our sex. Which is neatly done and without embarrassment."
(Male, married, age 83) "No need to discuss it. We kiss frequently, cuddle up and just sit quietly reading or watching TV."
(Female, widow, age 68) "We hardly 'discuss'—but check out how it was for each other."
(Female, married, age 63) "We don't discuss it. We do it."
(Male, married, age 75) "We do sex more than talk about it. There is body language, you know."
(Male, divorced, age 65) "Not very much. I believe in doing things rather than just talking about them."

Some people expressed the wish to communicate more and regretted that they did not:

(Female, widow, age 64) "Not enough discussion. Wish there had been more."
(Female, married, age 67) "Not much. Wish we could talk more."
(Male, married, age 75) "We do not talk about the sexual experience; this is part of our hang-ups."
(Female, divorced, age 65) "No, we don't. Never. Wish we could."
(Female, widow, age 61) "I wish I could."

Others indicate a change over time, saying that they had communicated but were no longer doing so:

(Male, married, age 68) "We talked about it when we were in our prime. It is seldom that we talk about it these later days."
(Female, married, age 73) "Not anymore."
(Male, divorced, age 68) "Not much anymore. No. Am not an expert in sexual matters at all."
(Female, widow, age 75) "Not anymore."

When our respondents did talk openly about sex with their partner, the communications tended to be clear:

(Female, married, age 62) "Yes, we do. How I would like him to touch me and what I would like him to do at the time."

(Female, widow, age 61) "Yes. All points, foreplay, position, mood, what have you."

(Male, married, age 74) "What we each enjoy most in our intimate relations."

(Male, divorced, age 69) "Yes, I do. We talk about what feels especially good or exciting. We sometimes discuss whether something is painful, such as pressing or squeezing breasts or testicles too hard, or anal sex."

(Female, widow, age 72) "Yes, to keep it up longer."

(Female, widow, age 73) "Our desires and preferences."

(Male, divorced, age 60) "Yes. Feelings during the sexual experience. What we like, don't like."

(Female, widow, age 60) "Yes. We would discuss sex, go to X-rated movies to see about different techniques and relationships. Never indulged in them but were stimulated, sometimes disgusted."

(Female, widow, age 64) "We always talked about lovemaking and what put me in a good mood."

(Male, married, age 66) "Yes, stroking, kissing and orgasm."

(Male, married, age 67) "Yes. The mutuality."

(Female, widow, age 66) "Yes, how much I enjoy him and what a great lover he is."

(Female, single, age 79) "Yes. What is most effective."

(Female, widow, age 80) "We talked, not 'discussed.'"

(Male, married, age 69) "We discuss what is pleasing to us and what to do for each other."

(Female, widow, age 72) "Yes. All of the ways."

(Female, widow, age 75) "Sometimes. Usually lack of orgasm."

(Male, married, age 75) "Yes. Touching and intercourse."

(Female, married, age 60) "His ejaculation before I am satisfied."

(Male, married, age 68) "Yes. Imaginary positions, more than one partner at the same time, etc."

(Female, widow, age 74) "Yes. I talk about what he did to make me more responsive."

(Female, married, age 62) "Yes. All parts. It's nicer discussed during the process of lovemaking. It enhances the thrill."

(Male, married, age 72) "We always discuss the important approaches and direct each other."

(Female, widow, age 67) "Yes. All of it. What is pleasing and why—what we'll do next time and how. What was particularly good this time compared to other times."

(Male, married, age 68) "Yes. How much it means to us and how much I enjoy her attention."

(Female, married, age 64) "We talk about fantasies, discuss what's suggested or brought to mind in sex magazines, movies or scientific studies."

(Female, married, age 67) "Yes. Love play, erotic zones."

(Male, married, age 76) "Certainly and without limitations."

In answer to Question 25, "How does your partner know what you like in sex?" 32 percent answered that just living together with somebody for a long time can generate awareness and sensitivity to a partner's needs (our "assumes" category):

(Male, married, age 69) "We have been married a long time and after 40 years, we should know each other's needs."

(Female, widow, age 69) "I guess after 40 years he knew. Otherwise tell him. Explore yourself so that you are able to explain."

(Female, widow, age 70) "My husband and I probably had as satisfactory a sex life as any I know of, and I think he did what he knew would be pleasing to me."

(Female, married, age 67) "He knows me too well."

(Female, divorced, age 82) "Mutual understanding."

(Male, married, age 78) "We have the same feelings."

(Male, single, age 72) "By repeating former experiences or by outright questions."

(Female, widow, age 78) "We understand our wants."

(Male, widower, age 73) "It takes time to get to know someone and to talk about sex and what you like."

(Male, widower, age 88) "Experience."

(Female, married, age 79) "He knows."

(Female, married, age 64) "After 43 years, he should know."

(Female, widow, age 78) "We understand our wants."

(Male, divorced, age 62) "She knows what satisfies me."

(Female, married, age 69) "He's lived with me for 39 years. He should have learned by now."

(Male, married, age 69) "After 40 years, why question?"
(Female, married, age 64) "Without any brains at all and with any amount of consideration for others, a partner learns this. We don't need most of these things spelled out or shown on film."

Simple direct communication seems to come naturally to half of the respondents (males 52 percent and females 49 percent).

(Female, married, age 71) "I tell him."
'(Female, widow, age 75) "You let him know."
(Female, widow, age 61) "I let him know when I find something different particularly pleasing. Or I make suggestions."
(Male, married, age 75) "I tell her. She tells me."
(Male, married, age 74) "We discuss our likes and dislikes about sex."
(Female, widow, age 80) "Mostly instinctively, sometimes by telling."
(Male, married, age 63) "We talk and we both know each other well."
(Female, divorced, age 63) "He is sensitive to my feelings and listens to me."
(Female, widow, age 67) "We communicate and feel free to tell each other."

Some use nonverbal gestures or body language only, but most used words and gestures to indicate their needs:

(Female, widow, age 60) "I tell him by body language and response as well as verbally—no need to verbalize that much."
(Female, divorced, age 64) "I guide, suggest, imply—or show."
(Female, widow, age 66) "By my response and satisfaction."
(Female, married, age 65) "Lead him on and guide him."
(Female, married, age 60) "Nonverbal body language."
(Male, divorced, age 69) "I guide her hand or body gently."
(Female, widow, age 70) "By my response."
(Female, single, age 65) "I tell him and show him."
(Female, divorced, age 63) "I let him know by my reactions."
(Female, widow, age 73) "Show and tell."
(Female, married, age 60) "I have shown him some of the things that were essential in order for me to reach orgasm."

(Male, widower, age 72) "Feeling rather than words."
(Male, divorced, age 60) "I act pleased—make pleasurable noises."
(Female, married, age 63) "I try to direct him with my hand and with my body."
(Female, widow, age 75) "By my behavior."
(Male, married, age 72) "I direct her."
(Female, widow, age 74) "It would be indicated by response. I am not inhibited."

For 9 percent of our respondents, communication is clearly difficult and the partner doesn't know sexual preferences. In these responses, the anger is sometimes most evident:

(Female, widow, age 74) "He doesn't know. You tell him."
(Female, married, age 63) "I've told him over and over for years. He doesn't want to hear me."
(Male, married, age 69) "Doesn't know. I give her hints occasionally."
(Female, widow, age 64) "I try to tell him, though communication is frequently difficult."

Though a person who lives with another for any extended period of time is often perceptive of and sensitive to the other person's needs, each of us is an individual, following his or her own special track. On that track, we are sometimes at one point while our lover is on another. When this happens, it is necessary to be able to work out some system acceptable to both. It could be that one person's needs are considered supreme; that negotiations for mutuality are in order or that some other form of understanding is evolved. We wondered how the "give and take" worked with people in our survey, so we posed Question 36, "What happens when you are in the mood and your partner is not?"

Similar to the responses on the question of sexual satisfaction, the largest group (46 percent) do "nothing" but, rather, accept the situation. This "forget about it now" group says:

(Male, divorced, age 69) "We usually just kiss and hug and go to sleep. Sometimes we say maybe we'll wake up later or make love in the morning. Sometimes I feel wakeful and go and read or watch TV."

(Female, married, age 73) "I read or go to sleep because I have found him unreceptive."

(Female, married, age 60) "I read or masturbate."

(Female, widow, age 61) "Find something else interesting to do—music or books."

(Female, married, age 60) "I let it pass and try again some other time."

(Female, widow, age 60) "Being considerate the reason is found—and do not make an issue of it. There's always next time."

(Female, single, age 79) "We wait."

(Male, married, age 66) "Postpone."

(Female, married, age 66) "Go to sleep."

(Male, married, age 74) "I do without sex."

(Female, widow, age 75) "Forget about it."

Others (26 percent) are persistent in seduction of their partner to achieve their goal. Surprisingly, this is more true for females (30 percent) than males (19 percent). The persistent ones are not easily thwarted:

(Female, widow, age 73) "I try to seduce him as subtly as possible."

(Female, widow, age 66) "I pet him and play with him in various ways to turn him on."

(Female, divorced, age 64) "Slowly, insidiously turn him on."

(Male, married, age 75) "Most of the time I finally get her so after kissing and massaging entire body."

(Female, married, age 65) "It doesn't matter. After a few minutes of caressing he always responds."

(Male, married, age 70) "Try to arouse her with caresses and kisses, especially in the genital area—this really works."

(Female, married, age 66) "I always try to be in the mood or get into the mood."

(Male, married, age 63) "She is often anxious to cooperate anyway."

(Female, widow, age 72) "Get into the mood."

(Female, widow, age 74) "Get him in the mood. Give him a rubdown."

(Female, married, age 71) "He gets in the mood quickly if that ever happens."

(Female, married, age 73) "I try to caress him and get him interested."

(Male, married, age 66) "Try to put her in the mood or try to persuade her to have sex as an accommodation to me."

(Female, widow, age 68) "Try to put him in the mood."

(Female, widow, age 74) "I gently try to stimulate interest."

(Male, married, age 68) "Try to make her in the mood. If not, she masturbates me."

(Female, widow, age 73) "A woman could always put her partner in the mood."

(Male, married, age 69) "It doesn't take long to change her mind."

(Female, divorced, age 67) "I try to arouse him—often successfully."

(Male, married, age 73) "I have to do a lot of love play—including kissing different parts of the body."

(Female, widow, age 67) "Since it happens so seldom, it is not too difficult to get him into the mood by special seductive caresses."

And here's what the ones who are never out of sync (18 percent) say:

(Female, widow, age 64) "This hardly ever happens. He reacts very quickly to any enticement."

(Female, married, age 61) "I'm always available."

(Male, widowed, age 71) "She's always willing."

(Female, single, age 65) "This hasn't happened yet."

(Female, married, age 69) "This doesn't happen. He is always ready."

(Female, married, age 86) "It never happens."

(Male, divorced, age 60) "Seldom happens."

(Male, widowed, age 67) "She never turns me down."

(Female, married, age 62) "I never had to contend with this. I don't know."

(Male, married, age 72) "Hasn't happened yet."

(Female, widow, age 73) "We are as one—always ready for each other."

Moods can be manipulated or managed. A lover can be seduced, encouraged, assuaged, or managed. But moods pass, and what happens when there is a problem with the male erection? Impotence is the most talked about subject concerning male sexuality. We explored the scope of this difficulty with Question 40: "It is said that older men have difficulty getting an erection. Is this true in your experience? Explain." Sixty percent of the men indicate an erection problem at one time or another. This figure is confirmed by 58 percent of the females, who also say "Yes" to the question.

Impotence, whether transient and an isolated incident or more serious, can be a source of intense anxiety and frustration to some because so much of the male self-image is built on sexual potency. For others, occasional failures or incomplete erection are taken in stride without interruption or curtailment of sexual experiences. No doubt this explains why so many of our male respondents were satisfied with their sexual experiences and considered sex now as good or better than when younger. However, in almost all instances where male dissatisfaction was expressed, it was the reduced erectile response that was implicated. We should also bear in mind that the incidence of impotence and male withdrawal from sexuality is probably greater in the general population than reported in our survey. Men who have withdrawn from sex are not likely to fill out a detailed sex questionnaire.

Curiously, although impotence is the chief cause of older men withdrawing from the sexual arena, over 90 percent of impotence is psychological in origin. Even most prostate operations should not cause impotence. Dr. Richard Milsten in *Male Sexual Function* states emphatically that only in the very rare cases of "radical prostatectomy, in which the entire prostate gland and the seminal vesicles are removed" does impotence result. According to Dr. Milsten, some men do use prostate surgery as an excuse to withdraw from sex; however, if they were functioning normally before the operation, they should continue to do so.

Male impotence has a dramatic impact on female sexuality. Pfeiffer, Verwoerdt, and Wang note that older women cease sexual activity a decade earlier than men. It is not that these women have lost interest or desire (certainly our data confirm this) but that their sexual lives are tied to men, often older than themselves, who become "impotent." Looked at in this way, impotence is not only a male problem. Older women have a big stake in overcoming male impotence and, perhaps even more importantly, the male's fear of impotence and failure.

The male erection is indeed a mystery. In adolescence it appears with uncontrolled frequency; it seemingly just happens. It has been humorously said that at any given moment among a group of adolescent boys three-quarters of them will have an erection. The experience of the confident, reliable erection is what lulls young men into the belief that it is their birthright and will always be that way. As the years go by, experience proves otherwise and men begin to worry. The failure to have an erection may occur for the first time at 25 or 30 after a late night out or too much to drink. The experience may be the first hint that the erection is not guaranteed. At 40 fears about impotence become epidemic. If a man is the worrisome type he might create a problem by concentrating on his anxiety rather than the sexual experience. This, in turn, can start a snowballing process in which fear escalates and frequency of failure increases until finally there is withdrawal from sex.

Many men feel ashamed of failing to have an erection when making love. Some have unrealistic expectations. The thought of "What will the woman think? Will she consider me a real man?" may prove so painful that he avoids the whole situation. Rather than risk failure, he now says that he is too tired, worked late at the office, has to get up early for a meeting, or is just not interested. The woman, sensing that something is wrong but unable or unwilling to talk about it, may cement the unspoken pact of mutual withdrawal. Sex becomes a memory of the past.

Total avoidance of sex is suspect. To preserve their sexuality women must become more assertive on this point. We have a number of responses from vibrant women who have had their sex lives short-circuited years earlier by such experiences. "My husband has been impotent for fifteen years so we do nothing," says a 67-year-old woman. Impotence does not explain doing nothing. Only fear and anxiety explain that, for there is much a couple can do sexually, even if the man is truly impotent. We learned this from the men who wrote that in spite of impotence they feel sexual and are very active, engaging in mutual masturbation, oral sex, or just kissing, stroking, and cuddling.

Men who withdraw from sex because of fear of impotence, occasional experiences of impotence, or actual impotence are ignorant of a dominant attitude among women, the scope of which even came as a revelation to us: Women are much more tolerant, concerned, and sympathetic about sexual performance than they have ever been given credit for. Having shed their sexual inhibitions over the years and still at a high level of responsiveness and desire, many older women feel committed to their partners and want physical contact and pleasure in spite of erection problems. The emphasis is not on the male erection but on the male. These women are perfectly willing to accept alternatives to genital intercourse. As one 66-year-old married woman writes: "He still makes me climax one way or another so it's not a problem for me. But I know it bothers him."

To get over the hurdle of real or imagined impotence, men must expand their concept of sexuality and couples must communicate their feelings openly. As we have constantly emphasized, sexual energy exists regardless of erection or ejaculation; it resides in the vitality of the individual. Therefore, it is possible to have powerful, fulfilling sexual experiences with or without an erection. It is what you feel and experience with your partner that counts, not so much what you do. If "impotent" men could accept these principles, they would have few sexual problems. They could reclaim, rather than disclaim, their sexuality. And, as an added benefit that is likely to occur when they least expect it, the erection may return.

We asked Question 43, "What can a couple do when the man is unable to have an erection?" to look at the solutions couples actually use. The majority of respondents (48 percent) suggest alternate methods of sexual satisfaction. Another 11 percent (16 percent of the men and 8 percent of the women) prefer oral sex:

> (Female, married, age 72) "They can still enjoy each other by touching tenderly in the sensitive places, etc. Just knowing the other partner is near and still cares, and remembering the many nice and wonderful times we have had together."
>
> (Female, divorced, age 63) "1. Be understanding; 2. Help in the ways he suggests; 3. Reassure him it's OK; 4. Be very loving in a truthful caring way, not patronizing."
>
> (Female, single, age 65) "They can do a lot of cuddling, manipulating with fingers. Find out if the inability to have an erection is of physical or psychological origin."

(Male, married, age 77) "A wife can induce an erection by being playful."

(Female, married, age 67) "Many times fondling and masturbation gives much satisfaction."

(Male, married, age 83) "Pet, kiss and relax."

(Female, married, age 62) "A woman should be able to rouse her partner with fondling, etc."

(Female, widow, age 71) "Woman can try to help him by caressing penis—or reassure him by saying it will probably be better next time."

(Male, married, age 75) "Massage each other—play with hands or [use] nylon penis for intercourse."

(Female, married, age 60) "Take pleasure in fondling and being affectionate."

(Female, widow, age 73) "Pet to climax or just cuddle and be loving."

(Female, married, age 60) "Have close physical communication and possibly oral sex."

(Male, married, age 69) "Caress, suck, talk, try everything—you never know when it happens. Keep trying."

(Male, divorced, age 69) "Manual and oral stimulation are good substitutes for penile-vaginal sex."

(Female, married, age 65) "Have oral sex or one can use the finger."

(Male, divorced, age 60) "Touch, rub, kiss, oral sex."

(Male, married, age 66) "Use oral gratification."

(Male, divorced, age 74) "Touch, suck."

(Male, married, age 69) "Fondling, kissing, mutual masturbation, oral sex."

(Female, widow, age 75) "Oral sex."

(Female, married, age 63) "Fellatio and cunnilingus."

(Male, divorced, age 66) "The woman must find a response which causes the erection. Helping penetration by hand, nude body, rhythmic contact."

(Male, married, age 63) "The only problem that can happen is if he lost all his fingers and tongue."

(Female, married, age 67) "Give him love, oral sex. Try as long as he wants to try."

(Male, married, age 73) "The female can play with his organ until completion of orgasm."
(Female, divorced, age 71) "He can help her to have an orgasm manually."
(Female, widow, age 74) "He can satisfy her to climax by clitoral means. She can use oral sex to stimulate him."

Twenty-four percent of the respondents accept the situation without seeking alternative methods of sexual gratification. Many of these emphasize love and understanding but do not suggest an active solution. Others (18 percent) see the need for professional help in dealing with this problem. More women (20 percent) than men (13 percent) are open to this approach.

(Female, widow, age 80) "Ask a doctor. If it cannot be corrected, the wife should be understanding and try, even to herself, not to own up to the fact that she is missing it. Her husband will make it up in tenderness."
(Female, widow, age 61) "Enjoy all the cuddling, touching and gentle words of lovemaking—and hope for better next time. Don't give up loving. Get a checkup."
(Male, widower, age 68) "Go to a doctor, someone well-versed in this. A physician and even a priest, minister or rabbi can help. He must have faith."
(Female, married, age 63) "They should find a means of gratification between themselves but the best thing to do is going to a doctor and he can help them."

Some, like one 73-year-old man, placed faith in vitamins—"I don't know, but I take Vitamin E." Others, like this 60-year-old widow, expressed a philosophical view: "Never thought about it. There's more to life than an erection." Others proved that patience was indeed a virtue, like the 73-year-old married man who said: "Happened only once in life. First night with my second wife. She knew I was nervous and excited and understood. Patience her motto next night *perfect!*"

It is startling how positive the answers were to these questions—especially if one considers the background of most of our respondents. The vast majority were taught little or nothing about sex (88 percent); when information was given, it more than likely carried with it the message that sex was "bad" or "sinful." Our attitudes toward sex are primarily conditioned by the home. Even if sex is a taboo topic and never mentioned, that noncommunication is a form of communication. Like white space in a drawing, it is a powerful message, an important shaping influence. Yet despite this training, many of our respondents (54 percent) were able to give positive information to their own children. They either communicated directly, answering questions openly, or they provided their children with books on the subject. Their answers to Question 41, "How and what were you taught about sex as a child? How and what did you teach your children?" were often detailed and expressive:

(Male, divorced, age 69) "I was taught little about sex as a child, except that it's irresponsible for a male to get a female pregnant without commitment. I think my father's 'fish skin' was left around purposely. I taught my child (a son) about condoms and supplied him with them."

(Female, married, age 86) "It was never mentioned. I always told my daughter, 'Don't believe a word about it. Do it now, marry later.'"

(Female, widow, age 80) "As a child, nothing, but I had hazy ideas about it, enough to know father and mother together bring forth a child, developing in the mother. I told my daughters more, about menstruation, so they did not get frightened like I did, and the reason for it. I explained how a woman is built inside. Also the beauty of love and creating a family with the right man."

(Male, married, age 74) "I was taught nothing about sex by my parents or in school—all learned from my peers—plus much misinformation. We taught our children every aspect of sex life from their youngest years and answered all their questions."

(Female, widow, age 70) "Sex was *bad* as a child. Taught my child that sex was natural—even birds and bees . . ."

(Female, married, age 69) "I had no sex education from my parents. I tried to enlighten my children as best I could."

(Female, married, age 66) "Nothing, Victorian mother! Anything the children questioned."

(Female, widow, age 74) "I had to find out for myself. I told them as much as I could and so did my husband."

(Female, married, age 60) "Badly. Strictly street talk. However, became self-informed through reading. An attempt was made to give our children information in this area."

(Male, widower, age 73) "I was taught it was dirty. No children."

(Female, married, age 76) "I was taught very little except about menstruation. I tried to talk to my daughter at 14. I talked to my son at 13. Both told me they knew all about the birds and bees."

(Male, divorced, age 74) "Taught nothing. Complete discussion with my child from age 12, continued until married."

(Female, married, age 62) "My mother didn't teach me anything. Having been a nurse, I tried to keep our children informed as to various facts. They all turned out well, so far."

(Female, widow, age 60) "Taught nothing, except to be alert to anything unnatural or questionable. Didn't have children due to early hysterectomy."

(Male, widower, age 73) "I learned about sex on my own. My wife talked to the girls and I talked to my son about keeping his penis clean."

(Male, divorced, age 60) "Was taught sex was sinful. Taught my children sex is beautiful."

(Male, widower, age 72) "Very little. Our principal advice was against venereal disease; and for responsibility for unwanted pregnancy. Referred to reputable books on physical sex acts."

(Male, single, age 66) "Keep myself covered. No children."

(Male, married, age 83) "Never taught anything by my parents. Our children always were free to ask questions about anything and always received honest answers, so gradually learned enough about sex."

(Female, married, age 65) "My mother said sex was degradation at its worst. My children were taught that sex with a loved one is a marvelous experience."

(Female, single, age 65) "I was taught that sex was never to be mentioned, talked about or thought about. Even the word 'pregnant' was taboo (too suggestive of sex). Sex was considered naughty, bad. Masturbation was taboo. I was told I must never touch the skin of that part as it was too delicate and could be injured. I've had one abortion at age 27—no child."

(Female, married, age 72) "It was a 'no no' and not discussed. When they were old enough to understand, I showed them illustrated pictures of the birth of a baby, which I believe were in magazine. Explained to my daughter about sex. My husband explained it to our son."

(Female, married, age 60) "Was taught nothing, told my children everything, especially techniques of multiorgasm."

(Male, married, age 63) "I was taught nothing. My children everything."

(Male, married, age 60) "I was introduced to sex by an older boy through masturbation. We bought our children good books on the reproductive system that also touched on love, sex and marriage."

(Female, married, age 62) "Taught that stork brought babies. Basically, sex was not in the English language. During teens mother said men wouldn't respect one who kissed. She was wrong on so many things that I never took her word as gospel. I taught my children the truth."

(Female, married, age 77) "As a child, taught on the street. Children were given the proper books to read."

(Female, married, age 64) "I was told 'don't.' As our children grew, their questions were answered. We had pets which demonstrated sex. They grew up knowing sex is beautiful and could result in babies. As adults, they say they don't remember a time when they didn't know of the joys of—and responsibilities related to—sex."

Some respondents told us their sex education came from experience. One 64-year-old divorcee said she "found out with a handsome guy." Another 74-year-old widow said she got her education from "on-the-job training."

A small number repeated the pattern of silence and did not educate their children. Taught little or nothing, they followed the same pattern:

(Male, married, age 69) "I was not taught. I did not teach."

(Male, married, age 72) "Nothing. Nothing."

(Female, widow, age 71) "Nothing and almost nothing."

(Female, widow, age 69) "My mother in my days she didn't teach

me nothing about sex. I didn't teach my children. They learned all this stuff in school and on the television."
(Female, widow, age 74) "I was taught nothing about sex. Neither were my children."

Some responses, almost exclusively from women, were striking for the ignorance about sex which they carried with them into early adulthood. Typical was the answer of the 78-year-old widow who said, "Nothing. When I was having my first child at 23. didn't know where the baby was coming from." Others said:

(Female, divorced, age 68) "My sexual problems with my marriage I feel now were greatly caused by what I was taught as a child. I was taught a man took advantage of a woman—was always wanting sex—all the man ever married for, etc."
(Female, single, age 69) "Told *only* to be careful with boys who are bad—that I could have a baby. Didn't have an inquisitive attitude about birth of babies—was over-careful about boys who wanted to kiss me or did kiss me. Always enjoyed platonic friendships with boys and men and never let these friendships get to the 'sexual' stage."
(Female, married, age 63) "My husband taught me. I had no mother and father. Sister was very strict. I got married at 28 years of age and didn't know anything. . . . I taught my daughter about menstruation and told her about boys, etc."
(Female, married, age 70) "When I was 16 I asked the girl across the street if I could get pregnant because I had kissed a man. I think there were some girls at my son's college that taught him the facts when he was a freshman. . . . He was quite shocked so maybe I didn't teach him very well."
(Female, married, age 70) "Knew nothing."
(Female, widow, age 74) "Picked up by 'osmosis'—'dirty' 'sublime' 'beastly' 'natural'. No children."
(Female, widow, age 78) "I was always told *never* let a man touch me. I had no children."
(Female, widow, age 68) "Sex was naughty. I wasn't to look at myself in a mirror. I carried some of my early beliefs into my acculturation of the children."

(Female, widow, age 75) "It is wrong and bad to experiment with sex before you get married or else you get pregnant each time."

Then there were those who regretted not having been more open with their own children:

(Female, widow, age 70) "I was taught very little as a child and fortunately was not under the pressures of our modern youth. I did not do a very good job of teaching sex to my children but we were able to discuss it more than I did with my parents."

(Female, widow, age 75) "Very little as a child. Probably too little with mine."

(Female, widow, age 65) "Nothing. Taught my children very little, *regretfully.*"

(Female, married, age 60) "Very little, but I had loving parents who kissed each other and me. I taught mechanical aspects of sex but I did a poor job on relationships and responsibilities to a partner."

(Female, widow, age 69) "I was taught it was bad. If I had sex, it was naughty. Lots of fear and guilt went with sex. I wasn't comfortable talking sex with my children. I hope I didn't pass on any verbal crap about sex."

(Female, married, age 63) "The subject was taboo. I got a lot of misinformation from teenage relatives. I felt embarrassed with my own kids and probably didn't give them much information."

As these responses show, the present generation of older adults has had a tough road to pave in developing communication skills, especially around sexuality, since it is so foreign to their training. Nevertheless, what we heard reinforced the lesson we learned repeatedly in our survey: That older adults listen, learn and grow. Their communication on this score is startlingly clear: "We're here, we're alive, we receive and send messages, we take ourselves and our needs seriously."

If there is a quality to most of their responses on the issue of communication, it can best be described as mellow—soft lights as opposed to harsh glare. Behind this tone is the fact that most of our people have had many years of living with their lover, usually a spouse. Satisfied in their sex lives with their partners, they are willing to be flexible when there is dissatisfaction. Masturbation is one answer. So is the "Tomorrow is another day" motto. The partner is not criticized, rejected, or ignored.

These older adults are the survivors who have learned to cope and adapt over many years. Willingness to accommodate is built in, perhaps even to the extent of deceiving themselves about their degree of satisfaction. Coping can mean watching television or reading when your partner is not in the mood for sex. It can also mean seducing him or her subtly or directly.

Most interesting is the fact that the women are not only sympathetic to the male with erection problems, but are also willing to take an active helping role. Oral sex is one prescription that comes up frequently for helping the male. This seems astonishing considering the era our respondents were raised in—that "plain sex" was suspect, and anything "fancier" was totally taboo. This is blatantly apparent in their responses concerning their own sex education. Yet many have been able to surmount this training, teach sex and love to their children and, most importantly, be active participants themselves. For many, the taboos of childhood, along with fears of monsters and witches, have been abandoned in favor of the pleasure of sex. Resentments are dissolved in activities, and blame is not a preoccupation. Patience and tolerance are easily blended. In a society which in the past has tended to push the older person into the role of passive observer, our respondents reflect a life pulsing within.

9

Older Women Alone

"The men walk into a singles' bar and have a field day. The women are stretched out like wall-to-wall carpeting. Men have their pick and they go for the young ones, just out of college sometimes. For the women, the scene is a disaster."

The woman expressing this is a 40-year-old widow. She has been alone for close to a year and is getting "adjusted" to the cosmopolitan single world. She elaborates: "I'm a sharer, but now there's no one to share with. I have to go it alone and that's hard." Her friend, divorced, also middle-aged, states: "I get scared at night when I'm not feeling well and worry about who will take care of me; how will I manage if I really need someone. It's especially scary late at night when you can't easily wake neighbors or call friends." She hesitates, fidgets with her ring now on her right hand, sighs, and adds: "There are some good things about being alone, too. I like not having to ask anyone's permission to do something. I'm totally free. I can go anywhere, do anything and not have to report back. But sometimes I feel like the slaves must have felt after the end of the Civil War. You're free and the chains are off, but where do you go?" Her friend shrugs her shoulders and looks blank. The answers seem out of reach.

If middle-aged, attractive, professional women fear a life alone—which for them means loneliness—what about older women without partners? According to the U.S. Senate report on aging, 53 percent of women 65 and over are widows, while 77 percent of men that age are married. At any point of time after age 65, there are five times as many widows as widowers of the same age. In 1976 there were 13.6 million women over 65, to 9.4 million men that age. Projections for 1990 are that, for people over 65, there will be 67.5 males to every 100 females; and that at age 75, the ratio will decrease to 57.8 men for every 100 women. The woman at 65 currently has an additional 17.5 years to ponder this dilemma. The man has 13.4 years.

For the widowed, single life often comes as a shock. Sure they knew it was possible, even probable. The evidence was all around them: Aunt Sadie widowed at 58, Cousin Cathy widowed at 64, and Mrs. Jensen down the block widowed at 61. But the "it will never happen to me" syndrome pushed the thought out of mind until the fateful day arrived.

Adele Nudel in her book *For the Woman over 50* notes that many older women feel "a big hoax" has been played on them. They were taught and grew up believing that if they were "good mothers and grandmothers" they would be "honored, respected and loved" in their middle and later years. For the older widow the hoax is a double whammy. Not only does the older widow feel unloved and unwanted, she is suddenly abandoned and on her own.

Most widows do not choose to live alone, yet that is the state of their world and they must deal with it. Many women in the present over-60 population have defined their existence within the marital relationship. Descartes said, "I think, therefore I am." But the older woman almost seems to say, "I am with you, therefore I am. You confirm my existence." With this assumption, the loss of a spouse is, in a sense, the loss of self.

Adjusting to a single life style can be a formidable task when you are over 60. Most older women never developed the social skills necessary for their new existence, so they must invent them. How do you enter the mating and dating game at 72, when you were married at 18 in a different era? Dating in the days of crinoline, punch, walks in the park, and chaperones was different from dating in an age of instant intimacy. And widows quickly learn that available men are few and the competition for them fierce.

Then there is the "third-party syndrome": Mary has been a widow for several months now. She and her late husband had been friends with Ethel and Henry for over thirty years. Sensing her friend's aloneness, Ethel has begun to invite Mary to dinner or the theater, etc. On a few occasions their plans also include Henry. On such occasions, Mary's dilemma is as follows: "We go into the restaurant and I don't know what to do about the check when I'm with my old friends. Before either my husband picked up the check or else Henry would. I would tune out what I knew to be the men dividing the bill, each trying to be fair, each trying to be generous. As I got up from the table and put on my coat, I would hear things like: It's OK, Henry, next time you'll make up the difference. After all, we had the two drinks, not you. Now I don't know if I'm supposed to assume that Henry will pay for me because I am the woman. Or am I supposed to pay for myself? Maybe he expects to split it with me? I just don't know and start feeling like the third party almost immediately after I accept Ethel's kind invitation. Yet I go, for to stay home means loneliness, and I also don't want to give up old friends. Sometimes I hate myself as I find myself thinking that it would all be so much easier if Ethel were also alone, like me."

Ethel is in an equally awkward position. "I go home with Henry and fight with him because he keeps saying he doesn't need two wives for the evening. I keep saying that she is my very dearest friend and ask how he could be so unkind?" The three of them are caught in a bind, for society has set no rules, no guidelines for the widow or woman alone in the company of a couple. With no ground rules, how do you play the game?

Other widows may not have friends as sympathetic as Ethel. The fact is that widows and divorcées of all ages are promptly discarded by their friends—even friends of long-standing. This sad state of affairs was confirmed repeatedly in the embittered comments we heard. A typical instance was the very sophisticated 62-year-old women whose husband, a physician, had died a few years earlier. The social circles that she traveled in with great ease and acceptance were immediately closed to her upon her husband's death. After a period of depression, she decided to move to a different city where she now has an active professional life of her own with a new circle of friends, predominantly women without partners.

But what about the woman who has never had to fend for herself—who has never had to put up a shelf, hang the drapes, or get the car fixed; who has never had to balance the checkbook, pay the mortgage, or deal with a life insurance salesman? These women grew up in a generation where male and female roles were clearly defined and separated.

The new widow, a housewife and mother for all of her mature years, must suddenly take on new roles for which she was never trained. But how does she acquire these skills? One woman told us she would "most likely call my son" to help her with any problems or decisions, blushing and lowering her eyes as she said this as though aware that she was sticking to her training and could not break out. How many can?

Some widows choose to concentrate their gratification on the "extended family" of children and grandchildren. But the extended family which used to be huddled in one house, neighborhood or city is now dispersed far and wide. You may live in New York and the children in California, Michigan, Georgia, or even London. If the children are within driving distance, the weekly or monthly visits are likely to take on a tinge of obligation—hardly the fabric on which to build a life.

The dilemma of the older woman alone is magnified in her sexual life. She has strong sexual needs, she's likely to be highly responsive— and her outlets are few. We repeatedly heard the cries all around us as we traveled to senior centers from the East to the West Coast: "We're ready, we're willing, but where are the men?" The shortage of older men is real. If it is apparent to the middle-aged woman, it is transparent to the older one. This is compounded by the fact that some older men seek out younger women. Younger lovers for the older man are condoned; for the older woman they are often just not available since her likely choice, for example, the middle-aged man, is probably also looking for a younger woman.

The lack of males in the later years was as evident to us in our talks to our audiences as was their curiosity about us as the "sex lecturers." Inside any auditorium, hall, or meeting room, one glance showed us that the majority of persons attending were women. The professionals who had invited us were also sensitive to this fact. They often acted as if they were offering us a "give-away" or bonus when they could make statements such as "We have a lot of men at this center," or "We have lots of couples, too."

After our talks the women who clustered around us were eager to share their feelings, experiences, and aloneness. They echoed feelings similar to our middle-aged female friends: "I like coming here, but wish there were more men around" or "I have sexual feelings. You know my husband died. We were married thirty-five years. But what can I do? There are so few men!" Some struggled with their words in admitting to us that they had stepped out of their morality. "I'm having an affair," said one woman. "He's married and I wasn't brought up that way. But she's sick, I'm well, and . . . you know what I mean." The exchange of looks gave closure to the statements. But the open pain, the discomfort was evident. Yet solutions were being found by many women, and we were curious to find out what they were.

Accustomed to a life with another person, having taken their sexuality for granted, what did these women do? We phrased some direct questions to get at the answers. Question 31 asked "In the later years there are more women than men. How can older women deal with this?" And Question 32 stated: "How can older people deal with their sexual feelings if they are not married or if they do not have partners?"

Many women in our sample suggest some form of sublimation or diversionary activity (43 percent on Question 31 and 44 percent on Question 32). Aware of their sexual needs, they reroute those needs when they can not act on them directly:

(Female, widow, age 73) "Only by keeping busy. Keep occupied with various activities and friends."
(Female, widow, age 71) "Have as many hobbies as you can. Keep busy."
(Female, widow, age 69) "Become active in certain community affairs, clubs."
(Female, widow, age 88) "Do physical exercise. Have many interests, hobbies."
(Female, married, age 79) "Become active in a lot of women's groups."
(Female, widow, age 73) "We just have to accept it and interest ourselves in other things."
(Female, widow, age 71) "Find interesting vocations, hobbies, etc."
(Female, married, age 66) "They have to cope with their life without men, getting involved in other interests."
(Female, married, age 67) "They should join organizations. Make one or two sincere friendships."
(Female, married, age 61) "Go to different socials and keep busy. Hobbies."

(Female, widow, age 82) "Keep busy doing something you like to do. Voluntary jobs, play cards, etc."

(Female, widow, age 67) "They should all have hobbies of one sort or another."

(Female, married, age 66) "Keep busy. Use time creatively."

(Female, widow, age 68) "Learn to live alone. Become involved in volunteer work or things of interest to you."

(Female, married, age 70) "Seek satisfying interests and friendships."

(Female, widow, age 67) "Exercise."

(Female, widow, age 64) "Try to divert themselves with anything: work, friends, etc."

(Female, widow, age 72) "Sublimate, activities."

(Male, widower, age 80) "By answering forms like this one!"

(Female, married, age 67) "Keep busy with different activities."

(Male, married, age 67) "Try sublimation via shows, books, group dancing, yoga, etc. Join worthwhile organizations and so in the course of things, probably establish promising relationships."

(Female, married, age 66) "Keep busy. Use time creatively."

(Female, widow, age 71) "Find interesting vocations, hobbies, etc."

(Female, widow, age 67) "By turning to music or other arts, painting, dancing is excellent . . . using nurturant qualities, loving pets, the elderly, the shut-ins. Reading, hiking . . . lots more."

(Female, single, age 79) "Find meaningful activity."

(Female, widow, age 73) "Keep busy. Occupied with various activities and friends."

Some elaborated, as did this 68-year-old widow who said: "I do not dwell on sexual feelings. By doing, keeping active physically, mentally and spiritually, join groups, work creatively with my hands, read, talk, discuss. I find sexual tensions abate naturally, particularly with exercise and a good diet." One single woman of 63 said philosophically: "Keep as busy as possible and do not dwell on what can't be changed." A 71-year-old widow rationalized this way: "Why allow the dog's tail to control the dog's life?"

Others mention the need for control:

(Female, single, age 72) "Control the mind. Become active."
(Female, married, age 66) "Either casual relationships or grin and bear it."
(Female, widow, age 65) "Suffer. Grin and bear it. Keep active."
(Female, married, age 86) "My mind controls my sex desires."
(Female, widow, age 69) "Well, they will have to go and take a cold wash."
(Female, widow, age 74) "Try and think of something else."
(Female, widow, age 69) "Control."
(Female, widow, age 66) "Forget it until someone feels as they do."
(Female, widow, age 64) "Learn to live without it."
(Female, divorced, age 74) "Don't think about it."

This group was summed up by a 74-year-old widow, who said, "That's their problem. As with all other problems, they have to learn to cope." Another married woman of 76 expressed a similar adaptive point of view: "They have to make the best of the situation." But one 61-year-old widow cautioned: "Try to ignore it. But you may become neurotic."

Understandably, the men in our sample having greater social and sexual options are less sensitive to the dilemma of older women alone. Consequently, the men lean more toward the direct action of "find a partner." Therefore, 21 percent of the men, compared to 43 percent of the women suggest sublimation in response to Questions 31 and 32. But when we look at the "find a partner" category, approximately 40 percent of the men urge that solution. But only about 19 percent of the women, having a more realistic awareness of the unavailability of men, adopt this alternative of a partner.

Traditional role concepts put the older woman without a partner at a disadvantage. Overtrained to be seductive and "get the prize with the honey but not the net," how is she to deal with her current life situation? She is expected to fit the Doris Day image of the seductive, "feminine," manipulative, but essentially passive woman who sets the trap and waits.

But those women who do place primary emphasis on getting a partner indicate that they have already broken the traditional role concepts in which the woman may be manipulative but is essentially passive in waiting for the man. This new role is sometimes encouraged by men.

(Female, married, age 66) "Enter the stiff competition."

(Female, married, age 76) "Become more aggressive."

(Female, married, age 63) "If she wants to compete she has to get out and work at seeking sex."

(Female, widow, age 69) "Let the best woman win!"

(Female, married, age 72) "Go where the man is. Be interested in him."

(Female, widow, age 73) "Actively look for a husband."

(Female, widow, age 73) "Be alert, interesting and attractive to the man. Go where he is."

(Male, married, age 70) "Outdo their competitors to get men."

(Male, widower, age 64) "They must get out and be more aggressive and let men know what they want and how they feel about sex."

(Male, single, age 67) "They can try harder to overcome competition from the other women."

(Female, married, age 61) "Find someone to love."

(Female, widow, age 62) "Find a nice man."

(Female, married, age 61) "When they go out socially, they will meet someone."

(Male, widower, age 67) "Get a mate or a sex partner."

(Female, widow, age 69) "I would get a friend for these feelings."

(Female, divorced, age 68) "By being more forward."

(Female, divorced, age 74) "Look for a compatible partner and hold on to him or her, but not to be possessive."

(Male, married, age 83) "You can find a partner."

(Male, married, age 74) "Find a compatible partner."

(Female, married, age 64) "Try to get a single man or woman."

(Male, married, age 69) "Have to try to find someone."

(Male, married, age 71) "There are many objects on the market."

(Male, married, age 74) "Make the best of it or proposition someone without soliciting."

(Female, widow, age 65) "Find a partner if sex is *essential*, irrespective of other feelings and considerations."

(Male, married, age 73) "I think older women would have no trouble finding sex if they tried, and I don't think they would have to try very hard."
(Female, married, age 60) "If sex drive strong enough, a partner will be found somehow."

The approach of these respondents is an active, seeking one. Unwilling to be relegated to a position in which they are disengaged from life, this group advocates mastery of the environment—that is, do something, look, try, and don't give up. Hope is the essential ingredient.

The answers are reminiscent of the late Sally Rand, the famous fan dancer who died in her 70s and was still fan dancing. Asked toward the end of her life why she continued to fan dance, her answer was: "Beats crocheting on the front porch."

One 71-year-old widow, obviously frustrated and angry, responded: "Let women, not men, go to war. It would help the 9:1 differential!" Another woman, single, age 65, expressed her shock at the uneven ratio: "This knowledge has freaked me out for years. Twenty years ago I was told that for every man over forty there were ten women looking for him. I can't imagine what the number must be now. My solution has been to belong to a peer counseling organization with the idea that the more together I am, the better I can find a partner." A 63-year-old widow summed up the determined, hopeful attitude, with the advice: "Get one. It's up to you."

For those who do not accept alternatives to direct expressions of sexuality, modifications may be necessary. Several alternatives are suggested, but masturbation is high on the list for some women—11 percent on Question 31 and 27 percent on Question 32. The percentages for men on this category are very similar—9 percent and 25 percent:

(Female, widow, age 69) "Masturbate with artistry."
(Female, married, age 70) "One gets used to living without intercourse but, I believe, masturbation is one answer."
(Male, married, age 70) "Try to find a friend who can satisfy her needs, or masturbate."

(Female, widow, age 70) "Be celibate. Masturbate or search for a partner."
(Female, married, age 60) "Sublimate through masturbating activity. Or hobbies, or advertise."
(Female, divorced, age 73) "Fantasize and masturbate."
(Female, widow, age 73) "Fantasy and vicariously through reading, make emotional ties to other women. Masturbate."
(Female, married, age 66) "Sublimate their libido into constructive channels. Masturbate."
(Female, married, age 65) "Get an artificial penis with a battery; when it vibrates, it does the trick."
(Female, married, age 72) "Learn to live with it or masturbate."
(Female, divorced, age 61) "Masturbate and fantasize. What else is there?"
(Female, widow, age 65) "Masturbate or forget it in wet dreams."
(Female, married, age 70) "Rush around like mad in volunteer work, or stay home and masturbate like mad."
(Male, married, age 66) "Should masturbate."
(Male, divorced, age 69) "I suppose primarily by masturbating. But finding other people who want sex (even one-night stands) or finding prostitutes would be other ways too."
(Female, married, age 61) "Let them pleasure themselves."
(Female, single, age 71) "Woman-woman relationships, masturbation, even more tenderness toward themselves, children and others who may be lonely."
(Male, married, age 87) "Masturbate, if they wish."
(Female, married, age 63) "Use a false prick."

The fact that this sample of older adults, who were brought up in an era when "pimples" were preferred to masturbation, offered this activity as a substitute for sex with another person is striking. Some even suggest sharing the male, the "valuable asset," along with other maverick solutions (10 percent):

(Female, widow, age 63) "We deal with this by being able to share, because some men require more sex than others."
(Female, married, age 60) "Maybe we ought to consider sharing the wealth or get ourselves surrogates—other women, if not men."

(Male, married, age 66) "Work the men overtime."

(Female, married, age 61) "Masturbation. Homosexuality. Find a younger man."

(Male, married, age 69) "Be less selective on one night stands. Take some risks with affairs or lesbian relationships. Masturbate."

(Female, widow, age 75) "I would like to say something funny. The man should have two women."

(Male, divorced, age 60) "By having sexual experiences with other women and by encouraging men to have more than one lover."

(Male, single, age 72) "Not to be averse to sharing a man."

(Female, widow, age 69) "Polygamy."

(Female, married, age 66) "Learn to take turns."

(Female, divorced, age 63) "Share. Why not?"

(Male, married, age 73) "Share the men. Polygamy. Plural mating."

(Male, married, age 68) "If sex is important—masturbate, shack up or hire a gigolo."

(Female, widow, age 66) "Maybe becoming a lesbian."

(Female, divorced, age 69) "Love women."

(Female, widow, age 62) "Homosexuality; masturbation; repression; activity in movements."

(Female, divorced, age 65) "Share-a-mate, abstain, cultivate loving relationships with people of all ages."

(Female, widow, age 75) "Several women sometimes share relationships with the same man."

(Male, married, age 65) "Seek out partners. If need be, go lesbian."

(Male, divorced, age 60) "By having sexual experiences with more than one woman and by encouraging men to have more than one lover."

(Male, widower, age 81) "Share the boy friends at hand and all have a good time. Why be selfish?"

(Male, single, age 68) "Well, as a single guy, I should try to keep in good physical condition to keep more women happy. In other words, more sharing is necessary."

One 65-year-old widow, obviously frustrated, sought a solution in companionship: "That's what I'd like to know. However, I have more women friends than I ever had before in my life." Another widow, age 66, expresses the need to get out of habitual grooves: "It is quite difficult. Women must have friends and go places together. Life is very upsetting but everything becomes a habit." A 69-year-old divorced man offers several suggestions, some novel: "By living in group intergenerational communities. Having relationships with younger men. Having sex with other women or masturbating."

Whereas most of our sample lived their lives in traditional, monogamous relationships, some (if only a small adventurous minority) are willing to entertain alternative styles including sharing, polygamy, communal living, and lesbianism. But let's not forget that the possibilities of today may be the realities of tomorrow.

For only a negligible few did a younger man seem to be a viable solution for older women (less than 4 percent of our total sample).

> (Female, married, age 83) "Find a younger man, I presume."
> (Female, widow, age 67) "Younger ones, I guess."
> (Male, married, age 69) "Pay younger men."
> (Female, married, age 75) "If they are interested, they can obtain sex from younger men, prostitutes and masturbate."
> (Male, married, age 64) "Find a younger man."
> (Female, widow, age 72) "Some aggressive women find outlets. Go with younger men."
> (Male, married, age 68) "Don't know. Probably marry younger men, say five years younger."
> (Female, married, age 66) "Getting younger men and if sex is that important, not be discriminating."
> (Female, married, age 70) "Go for younger men."

Mechanical, if not magical, solutions are sometimes longed for, as in the statement of this 64-year-old widow: "I wish I knew. There should be a clearing house for all single people so that they could look around for a matchmate." One 79-year-old widow confirmed the problem by her sympathetic observations: "I find this to be true as I coordinate Saturday night dances. I notice there are seven to eight women to one man at our dances. I can not solve the problem for the women. I do feel sorry for them."

Another 70-year-old widow echoed this, highlighting the feeling of humiliation: "This is a serious problem and has affected me directly.

However, there are ways to deal with it. Getting involved in activities of various kinds, socially, intellectually, physically, can bring you into more contact with the other sex. Going to dances is one way to meet men, but there the fact women outnumber men by such a marked degree has its difficulties. Also, it is humiliating to a woman to wait to be asked to dance. Folk dancing is a much better way in this respect."

Our society is in many respects both ageist and sexist. This is obvious in its attitude toward the "dirty old man," the older man interested in the younger woman. We outwardly say we disapprove, yet when one sees an older man with a younger female, there is often silent applause and admiration. The feeling is: "John can still get young women. Great for him."

But what about the older female? Can she get younger lovers? More importantly, does she want them? Question 44 asked: "How do you feel about older men having younger lovers? How do you feel about older women having younger lovers?"

The consensus of our survey not only sanctioned but was enthusiastically for the older women/younger men combinations (83 percent). Similarly, our respondents endorsed older men/younger women combinations (86 percent). Men and women had similar opinions on these two questions (Tables 44 and 44.5).

(Female, widow, age 74) "Great. In both cases."
(Male, widower, age 77) "I feel they should have whoever appeals to them."
(Female, married, age 66) "Why not?"
(Female, widow, age 70) "Wonderful for both."
(Female, married, age 66) "More power to them."
(Male, married, age 68) "Fine."
(Female, widow, age 63) "Age makes no difference in how a person feels."
(Male, widower, age 63) "It's OK."
(Male, divorced, age 62) "It's been going on for centuries."
(Female, widow, age 80) "It's up to them."
(Male, married, age 66) "I approve in both cases."
(Female, widow, age 74) "I think it is fine if they love each other."
(Female, married, age 73) "If it makes them happy, go ahead."

(Male, married, age 69) "To each their own. Why not?"

(Female, widow, age 67) "I see nothing wrong with it for either sex."

(Male, married, age 67) "More power to them."

(Female, married, age 60) "If they want to, fine. It's especially satisfying all the way around in an older woman, younger man relationship."

(Female, widow, age 64) "There's enough unhappiness in life, so I say it's fine with me. May they enjoy it."

(Female, divorced, age 68) " I think it's fine either way, so long as they are happy."

(Female, widow, age 74) "If a younger partner is helpful, why not?"

(Female, married, age 60) "With men, it has to be wonderful if he has enough *money* to attract young women. With a woman it's no good *unless* she is an unusually beautiful and shapely person."

(Female, widow, age 75) "If it helps, go to it."

(Male, married, age 69) "Older men tend to have younger lovers. Older women should also have younger lovers but society's attitudes are strongly against."

(Female, divorced, age 71) "Great for anyone who can get a younger partner."

(Female, married, age 62) "Great! Even better now that it's OK for women also."

(Male, married, age 66) "Both instances are great."

(Female, widow, age 71) "Very good. Makes me feel good that I can still keep up with a younger person."

(Female, widow, age 67) "It gives them a great sexual desire. It makes the woman feel younger."

(Female, divorced, age 68) "More older women should try younger lovers."

(Female, widow, age 76) "Let them enjoy themselves. I wish I had one for myself."

One 69-year-old widow ignored the first part of the question, but circled the older woman/younger man phrase and exclaimed: "It's great." Some, like a 66-year-old married woman, insist that standards should be equal: "I cannot fault a man who wants a more attractive younger woman, but the same tolerance should go for the woman."

One married woman of 61 circled the first part (older man, younger lover) and wrote: "Annoyed—so he's trying to be young." For the second part (older woman, younger lover) she wrote: "Good!"

Some, however, see problems in obtaining this type of match:

(Female, widow, age 63) "Great, if it's possible."
(Female, widow, age 65) "Not bad if you can get them."
(Male, divorced, age 67) "In my lifetime I have had generally younger lovers, approximately ten to twenty years younger. In the case of older women having younger lovers, the problem arises where the man reverts to type and seeks a younger lover."
(Male, married, age 83) "Great, if they can afford it."

Others dismissed the age factor as a jarring intrusion. After all, who would question the age of the artist of a masterpiece?:

(Male, divorced, age 69) "People are people and 'making love and revolution,' as Maggie Kuhn said, is good. Age is irrelevant."
(Female, widow, age 68) "Chronological age does not in my opinion have much to do with love. Real love—having a 'lover,' whatever the age of the persons involved—is the factor."

One married woman of 67 said: "Age is only one criterion—there are many others. Why not have younger lovers?" Another, a widow of 60, added a touch of irony: "Nothing wrong with this. What's good for the gander is good for the goose—provided in both instances they've at least reached the age of consent!"

Some are for it, but qualify the age of difference with a cut-off point:

(Female, divorced, age 66) "If about fourteen years difference, yes. But not more than that."
(Female, widow, age 62) "I myself can't see having sex with a very young man like 35 years old. But I also can't see having sex with a man of 78 or 80. It's up to the individual."
(Female, single, age 65) "All right if not old enough to be his mother. I've seen this latter and it ended in divorce."

A married woman of 66 said, "It's OK, but not half your age." A small number see the combination as potentially problematic:

(Female, widow, age 73) "If there are large gaps in age, I think in either case they are playing with fire."

(Female, married, age 66) "For the man, he'll die trying to keep up; if the older woman needs sex, I think it's OK."

(Female, married, age 73) "It's OK for women to have younger lovers, but not for men—bad for them—they should stick to women closer to their own age."

Some express a conflict:

(Female, widow, age 70) "Being an older woman, I think I am jealous of the young lovers. I would not feel comfortable with a younger lover, and by young lover I mean where the difference in ages was great. I do not believe the calendar age is as important though as the psychological age."

(Female, widow, age 69) "Sure. Gives the male good self-image. Lovers, yes, but marry those—seldom. The female may need to feel she can still attract the male—in charm, in companionship, in femininity. The male is so pleased that he can still perform. He knows he is still potent. The woman, on the other hand, is not the potent performer but the female who can still catch."

While the vast majority are approving, a smaller group is disapproving (Tables 44 and 44.5). Younger lovers are seen as "ego trips" for women, with disappointment at the end of the road and discomfort on the way. Others express ambivalence:

(Female, married, age 70) "Great, but would feel better with own age group."

(Female, married, age 76) "It is unusual but very possible— particularly older man having younger lovers."

(Female, widow, age 63) "Each to his own. As for me, I like a lover nearer my age."

(Male, married, age 75) "I think they both should have someone close to their own age."

(Female, widow, age 60) "I think it's an unsure ego trip that will eventually let you down too hard and be depressing in the end."

(Female, married, age 73) "I think people have a better rapport with people their own age. There are exceptions, of course."

(Female, single, age 65) "I tend to feel scornful when older men marry young women, i.e., Dr. Spock at 75 marrying a woman of 35. I am suspicious that men need a prop to help them feel young and that the younger woman does it for the fame and/or the money. If the man were psychologically healthy, he wouldn't need this kind of boost. But if it's just an affair, it seems OK for either sex."

(Female, married, age 69) "I think men like the flattering of their ego by having a younger woman; and in the case of women, it is usually a very sexually active woman who feels a younger lover can better satisfy her."

(Female, widow, age 66) "Some women need older men to really mature. Older women sometimes can't really take it if the young man likes it often."

Some, like this 66-year-old widow, accept the principle but reject the application for themselves: "OK by me, but not my cup of tea." The other end of that continuum is expressed by an 80-year-old widow, who said, in speaking of the woman with a younger lover: "She's crazy and dirty."

However, the majority's feelings can be summed up by a married man of 69 and a widow of 71. Said he: "I think it must be great to try, whatever the results. I have not, but would love to." Said she: "Men have always liked younger lovers. And I think the women are getting wiser in this direction!" While it is not likely that many of our respondents are having relationships with younger lovers, their clear endorsement of the concept may point to future trends.

While our survey clearly shows that older women are as interested in sex, if not more so, than older men, our respondents still cling to the stereotyped beliefs. In response to Question 28, "Who do you think is more interested in sex, the older man or the older woman? How are they different?" most respondents—both men and women—say the older man. Only 21 percent said the woman is more interested while 47 percent said the male; another 32 percent said there was no difference (Table 28). A contradiction was sometimes amusingly driven home to us when the belief that older men are more interested in sex was even stated by women who showed a powerful sexual interest on other questions while at the same time indicating that their partner was impotent or not interested in sex. Myths are capable of surviving the most blatant factual assault.

One 83-year-old man writes: "Man has a longer span of interest. Woman sees partner as less desirable as he ages," while a 74-year-old widow says: "The older man because it is up to the man to make the advance, although from what I hear and see, things are changing." Inculcated with the man-chasing-female image, she is, however, aware that our society is changing. But, the change for many is still to come. A 75-year-old married man says, typically: "The older man. A woman accepts her fate but a man keeps it in his mind." The woman is accepting, the man is driven we repeatedly heard. "It's part of the older man's self-esteem" writes another married woman of 65 as she designates him as more interested in sex while a widow of 74 says: "I think the older man would like sex more." Aware of our society, a 64-year-old married woman says: "1. Older man 2. The macho syndrome." Others feel the same way but give different reasons, as does a 68-year-old widow: "The older man is more interested. Men feel their time is running out." A 66-year-old divorced man writes simply: "The older man. Our society." He does not explain. He does not need to. "The older man. He looks for younger women" says a 66-year-old married man while two women, both married, one 69 and the other 72 merely circle the words "older man"; they too feel that no explanation is needed. A few see the woman as more interested and explain why. "Older man *seems* more verbal but I think the older woman is more interested in sex. She seeks closeness and views sex as a nurturing act," says a 60-year-old married woman. Another married woman of 63 says: "Older woman probably. It's always on a man's mind, but . . ." She does not conclude her thought. Possibly she is thinking that she needs to find a reason for suggesting that the woman is more interested.

In perpetuating the belief that men are more sexual, older women, particularly those without partners, place an additional restriction on their lives. Not only are there few men to compete for, but older women must withhold their assertiveness to fulfill society's image of the acceptable female role. Nevertheless, the feminist movement has made women more aware of their sexuality and the need for sexual assertiveness, and the restrictions are loosening.

In probing the question of what to do when you don't have a partner, we asked Question 23, "How do you feel about older men and women without partners going to prostitutes to relieve sexual needs?" Many were for it (68 percent); 64 percent of the women and 74 percent of the men approved (Table 23). Some were enthusiastic.

(Female, widow, age 87) "Where are these places? I would like to know."

(Female, widow, age 70) "I think it would be a good idea if such a place could be arranged under medical supervision and screening of all persons involved. I have always known of places for men to meet prostitutes, but I think we would have to be conditioned before we could accept that the 'Nice Lady' would go there too."

(Male, divorced, age 67) "I very much agree with this manner of relieving sexual needs and practice it."

(Male, widower, age 68) "More power to them."

(Female, widow, age 75) "I agree they should."

(Female, widow, age 70) "If there is no other person than a prostitute, go ahead."

(Female, married, age 74) "I see nothing wrong with it."

(Male, married, age 80) "It is necessary."

(Male, married, age 71) "That is a good way to relieve your tension."

(Male, married, age 69) "I think it is a good idea. Whenever it can be had should be the guiding rule."

(Male, widower, age 67) "More power to them if they need to relieve their sexual needs."

(Male, divorced, age 62) "I feel it is natural."

(Female, widow, age 68) "It's good but make sure the prostitutes are clean."

(Male, widower, age 66) "Think it's the thing to do but I can't get up the nerve to do it myself."

(Male, single, age 63) "I feel it is a good idea. Better than auto-sexual release."

(Female, widow, age 69) "See no harm but men have the advantage because there are places for them. Little has been done in this respect for women."

(Male, married, age 73) "It is very sad but one needs the closeness of someone they like and care for. Even a prostitute can help."

(Female, divorced, age 69) "Why not? I don't see age as making any difference. Desire is desire as is need and want."

(Female, divorced, age 62) "OK but no places for women to go."

(Male, married, age 64) "Perfectly understandable. No stigma."

(Female, married, age 63) "I say if you need it, get it where you can."

(Female, widow, age 73) "It's right for them if it's their need."

(Female, married, age 63) "Why not? Everyone should do their thing. Should have it for widows too."

Another group were for it, but had some reservations:

(Female, widow, age 68) "To each his or her own. I'm not a prude. If they have no other outlets, let their conscience guide them."

(Female, divorced, age 63) "It's unfortunate that people can't care enough to find someone else who cares—not to have paid love. But 'any port in a storm.' If it helps them, fine."

(Male, married, age 75) "I feel sorry for them and I sympathize with them. It's probably better than nothing."

(Male, widower, age 74) "If they cannot find a decent person of opposite sex, OK."

The popular opinion, in this case, could be summed up by the 67-year-old widower who wrote: "OKAY." One 73-year-old widow looked at the issue in the context of options for younger people: "They have the same rights as the younger generation."

A minority view gave the right to the man but not the woman. The comments of these two women, both married, one 86 and one 79 expressed this opinion. The first said: "Men yes. Not me." The latter: "I think it is natural for a healthy man to get sexual relief at a clean prostitute house where females are medically taken care of and are clean. Women, no." Some people took a contrasting view—that due to the plentiful supply of women, men need not go to professionals. "I do not feel that is necessary with so many women around for them to choose from," said a 72-year-old widow. A widow of 67 echoed her sentiment: "Why? There are plenty of women."

Another widow of 78, aware of our society's sexist position, "flipped the coin" and saw the other side. She said: "I think it would be a good idea if such a place could be arranged under medical supervision so that everyone would be clean. I think women should be able to frequent such places too. It is they, after all, not the men, who have the problem of no partners. Yet we have concentrated only on the men. Why?"

A smaller group of 32 percent clearly disapproved:

> (Male, divorced, age 66) "I've never been in a house of prostitutes. I'd rather jerk off."
> (Female, married, age 67) "Disgusting."
> (Female, widow, age 84) "Foolish."
> (Female, widow, age 71) "They have lost their perspective."
> (Male, widower, age 80) "I don't agree."
> (Male, married, age 68) "Don't approve."
> (Female, widow, age 73) "I can't agree with this practice."
> (Female, single, age 66) "Good counseling of both partners could avoid this."

Some in this group offered alternatives, while others talked of the dehumanization in the act:

> (Female, divorced, age 68) "I would like to have someone I know and respect."
> (Male, married, age 67) "I think they are pathetic and foolish. Masturbation would be much safer and just as relieving."
> (Female, married, age 65) "Men don't need prostitutes. There are many widows around hungering for a chance to get some love. Or is it just sex?"
> (Female, widow, age 74) "I never found it necessary. I don't believe in prostitutes because of the danger of contracting VD. There should be regular contact with the same person to get the most out of sex."
> (Female, widow, age 68) "Since this practice negates the humanness of another human being, I do not approve."

The reaction of one 61-year-old married woman was even more emphatic: "People aren't *things* to be *used,* regardless of age."

In accord with statistical expectations, the *majority* of the women in our sample (61 percent) are widows or single and divorced women who face a life of aloneness. But true to their style, many have the resiliency to cope once again. For these older women, aloneness is not necessarily equated with loneliness. Some have the self-confidence and social skills to compete for the small number of desirable unattached men. Others find that keeping busy or sublimating works for them. Another style is to develop new patterns of nonsexual intimacy with women friends. Masturbation in combination with other solutions is also a way. Still others are able to consider, if not participate in, maverick alternatives such as younger lovers, communal living, and lesbianism.

To survive in their new world, many have begun to move away from the traditional conception of the sexless, neuter grandmother. They still love their children and grandchildren, but at the same time are carving out a gratifying life for themselves. It is not all baking apple pies, rocking on the front porch and babysitting while their grown children live the "real" life.

Change and transition are not easy at any age. There is often pain and suffering. We see the pain when we speak to old people. We also note it in their responses to our questionnaire. It is a pain which awaits us all, at least in a society like ours which does not prepare us for the later years. How can we prepare our daughters and ourselves for such aloneness? How can we prepare a woman who has lived for many years with a man she loved to compete again; be super-attractive again; to repackage herself for presentation in a fiercely competitive, demanding market?

The answers, like the many hands of the god Krishna, seem not to point in only one direction. It would seem that we should first be aware of the human suffering that surrounds us; we have been blind to it. We need to reshape our thinking, to fashion creative social support systems for those who need them—networks which, like the loving mother, can offer succor, nurturance, love, and warmth. These external agents can be turned to along with the wisdom of life experiences, the memories, the images, the "pictures" inside ourselves that give us pleasure whenever we turn to them. There would thus be an outside nest as well as an inside one. The wasteland of this suffering of so many older women could give way to fertile land.

Above all, we could provide the nourishment to allow our people—older people—to take risks, to trust themselves, to embark on anything and everything that is not hurtful to others and that can give pleasure to themselves. We can provide a secure backdrop for this type of exploration. As one woman said about new sexual experiences: "I haven't tried them, but would love to."

An open society is one that promotes true independence, like the mother who wishes to foster autonomy in her children and allows them real freedom to be their own selves. It involves risk taking. But, as Ortega y Gasset said: "While the tiger cannot cease being a tiger, cannot be detigered, man lives in the perpetual risk of being dehumanized." For us to be aware of the pain of older women and do nothing is to promote such dehumanization. Women of all ages must understand that we are talking about their destiny. Sooner or later the problem affects everyone.

10

Looking Backward,
Looking Forward

Why don't we want to perceive the sexuality of older people? On some level of awareness, many of us do not want to look at what we believe is our destiny. But on a more subtle level, there is the issue of power. Sex in our society is clearly identified with power, a power that younger people would like reserved for themselves. What they don't consider is that they are eventually dooming themselves—for all of us, when we grow old, become the victims rather than the perpetrators of the stereotypes that we supported earlier.

It is interesting that we do not question the sexuality of older people who are otherwise powerful. When a rich and famous politician dies under questionable circumstances in the company of a young woman, the press may be interested in the details for their scandal value. But people do not question the plausibility of a relationship between the powerful politician and the young woman. Similarly, we may smile at the sight of aging actors and actresses, authors or artists with young companions of the opposite sex. We accept sexuality in these instances because these older people are powerful; and if powerful, they are allowed or assumed to have sexual power as well. But this is not supposed to be true for ordinary people.

We have seen older people themselves express their sexual needs strongly and forthrightly. One of the most fascinating aspects of our survey is that here we have a group who can look backward over a lifetime of sexual experience. So many young people fear growing old that they invoke magical devices of denial. They close the door on aging and pretend it doesn't exist. The advertising media support the denial by bombarding us with youthful images, as if the world were peopled only by the young. It's almost a fairyland of toffee candy and hot fudge sundaes. Then conversely, it's no wonder the young and middle-aged are terrified of aging. But what the older people are telling us is that if they have regrets about their sexual experience, it is over something they did or did not do *when they were young*.

We posed Question 49, "Looking over your sex life, past and present, what would you want to change?" to find out how older men and women would evaluate their past, and also to find guidelines that might help young adults reexamine their current sex lives and relationships. Half of the respondents (51 percent males, 49 percent females) said they are satisfied and would change nothing.

> (Female, married, age 69) "I feel that I have had a fulfilled sex life and don't know what I would have changed."
> (Female, divorced, age 61) "No regrets. I'm liberated and feel sorry for women who aren't."
> (Female, widow, age 82) "No regrets in the past. Might welcome a little now with a close friend with no complications."
> (Female, widow, age 85) "I had a very good sex life. If I had to do it all over again, I would want nothing to change."
> (Female, widow, age 69) "Since I have looked over my sex life, I don't see anything I would change since I had my fun when I was young."

Of those who do have regrets, 32 percent talk about the inhibitions, restrictions, neglected opportunities, and lack of variety in their sexual experience:

> (Female, married, age 66) "Everything. Would certainly try sex before marriage and not save myself as I had a lot of temptation."
> (Male, widower, age 72) "Had I experienced sex with a greater variety of partners, I might have better understanding of sex problems."
> (Female, widow, age 70) "Get instruction when eighteen. Get instruction with my husband in engagement, three months later— and more if needed. Hooray for our times which gives us such lovely books on sensuality. I never knew anything."
> (Male, married, age 74) "Be more open in expressing my own feelings about sex."

(Female, widow, age 65) "Would have liked to have experience with more than one partner, if only for comparison."

(Male, married, age 70) "Should have tried more of it with different partners."

(Female, married, age 75) "Wish I had been more sexual."

(Female, married, age 66) "At first I thought to have one man who was the best. But then I'd have missed a chance to compare."

(Male, married, age 63) "I was a virgin until marriage. Kind of regret I wasn't more active."

(Female, widow, age 63) "I wish I was as open as a younger woman as I am now."

(Female, married, age 60) "I would have wanted it more often in my youth. I am very satisfied now."

(Female, widow, age 70) "I have a difficult time to keep from being resentful because my husband died at a rather early age. I would make more of an effort to find another mate."

(Male, married, age 77) "I look back and I think I would have liked to have had sexual experience with another woman."

(Female, widow, age 70) "Accepting it without guilt when I was younger, and enjoying it to the fullest. Now I feel freer but have less opportunities since I can't seem to meet men I am attracted to or who are attracted to me."

(Female, divorced, age 63) "I wish I had started earlier. I wish I had continuous years and not had so many years of denial in between two marriages."

(Male, married, age 69) "I would like to have started earlier in life, experienced sex with more partners."

(Female, married, age 63) "I wish I'd laid half the town (the male half)."

(Male, married, age 64) "Only the beginning of my sex awareness. I would change the ignorance, ineptness, clumsiness, fear. I would want to be totally sex educated."

(Female, married, age 62) "Make it more spontaneous and at odd times."

(Female, married, age 63) "I think I would like to have had some lovers."

(Female, widow, age 82) "I think it might have been pleasurable for my husband if I had sometimes initiated the sexual experiences instead of leaving it always for him to make the sexual advances."

(Female, married, age 55) "It would have been nice to have been more communicative about it earlier."

(Male, married, age 72) "Doing it more often when we could have."

(Female, widow, age 74) "I would like to have been made more aware when I was young that morals that were instilled by parents were not correct in married sex life and so would have made my sex life less inhibited."

(Female, married, age 60) "I would have wanted it more often in my youth."

(Male, married, age 62) "Different and more varied partners."

(Female, widow, age 63) "To be more responsive to initiate the lovemaking sometimes."

(Female, married, age 75) "In younger years, I was often uncooperative. In later years, I wish I had taken full opportunity to promote enjoyment."

(Male, widowed, age 74) "Wish I had been more adventurous and had more experiences before I was married."

If some of these respondents focus on the lack of quantity and variety of their sexual partners, others regret that they did not go in for experimentation:

(Female, married, age 60) "Wish I had discovered the vibrator earlier."

(Female, divorced, age 66) "I'd have less quantity and more quality. It really took me until I was 34 to know what satisfactory sex was."

(Male, married, age 69) "That's easy. Try everything and everyone possible. Take more risks."

(Female, divorced, age 64) "I would like to have been less inhibited in trying unorthodox sex and more foreplay."

(Female, divorced, age 65) "I probably would try a homosexual experience. Perhaps I'd have liked a bisexual life style."

(Male, widower, age 74) "Wish I had been more adventurous and had more experiences before I was married."

(Female, widow, age 60) "Wish I could have lived in age when sex without marriage was not frowned upon."

(Male, widower, age 73) "I would have liked to join a nudist camp before I was married."

(Female, married, age 60) "I would want more frequency, experimentation and stimulation."

(Female, widow, age 67) "Yes—less inhibition, not so serious, more playful."

(Female, married, age 69) "I would have liked to have been more adventuresome in the acts. I would also have liked my husband to come more than once a night. I could have."

(Female, married, age 64) "It is interesting to think of the possibilities of assorted sex partners. Sometimes I daydream about more experiences with other men."

(Female, married, age 62) "I'd indulge in more wild sex if I were young. All kinds of sex experiences."

Some respondents (9 percent) attach their regret to the choice of mate. Of these, a number are blunt in saying they would have preferred a different partner.

(Female, widow, age 74) "I would skip my husband."

(Female, married, age 66) "On my husband's side more demands. Would have been nicer to take the initiative willingly."

(Male, divorced, age 61) "Believe I should have gotten a divorce several years sooner. Lost out on several years of potential lovers."

(Female, divorced, age 72) "I'd like a more loving, listening man. I felt a barrel in a bunghole and any hole would have been as good to my ex."

(Male, married, age 63) "Should have changed partners sooner."

(Female, married, age 71) "Make my husband drink less and make love more."

(Female, widow, age 75) "Would be more selective in choosing a life partner and cultivating better sexual responses."

(Female, married, age 70) "I would have liked a hotter husband."

(Male, married, age 69) "Wish my second wife had been my first. First wife never liked sex."

Widows sometimes talk about their loneliness and the desire for a partner in the present. In some instances the regret is for not having responded enough sexually when the spouse was alive. As a 64-year-old widow poignantly writes: "My only regret is that I did not seduce, entice, and tell my husband more often that I loved him dearly." But in general the respondents call for expanded sexuality in different forms. The words of a 72-year-old widow sum it up simply and directly: "Just more sex."

Sex and Retirement

Does retirement have to be the dreary end of the road portrayed in the mid-life fantasies of gloom and doom? Surely there is more leisure or discretionary time after retirement. But is it time to wait out a meaningless existence filled with mindless busywork? Is the idea of productive, creative retirement just a seductive ploy to sugar-coat the harsh reality?

Reality is filtered differently through the eyes of each of us. We heard various interpretations of the reality of retirement in our discussions with audiences around the country. One man of 69 said he was preparing to retire in the coming year since his company made retirement mandatory at age 70 and that "I am frankly delighted since I can then play golf all I want and am even thinking of changing my whole lifestyle by moving to a warmer climate. My wife has also been working and is looking to quit. It will be good to do a lot of things together again, like when the kids were young and all of us went places together. Somehow, when the kids were grown and we each were working all day long, work became the center of our lives. Time for a change." He then went on to say that he was attending our lecture on his day off but that, in the future, he could attend any and all lectures when, where, and how often he wished. We sensed in this man a looking ahead to a new kind of freedom in himself. He could not wait to explore worlds lying right ahead, and his enthusiasm was genuine.

Yet there were others, and we saw their side, too. For example, a trim, attractive 62-year-old woman confided that she had looked forward to her husband's retirement. "He was a real workaholic but I thought that when he retired at least he wouldn't be tired all the time and that things would get better. I was wrong. He still isn't interested." From her other comments, we got the impression of a depressed man whose identity was still tied to his job. Stripped of his sense of personal worth, he could not mobilize energies in other directions.

Another man told us he had recently retired. He was just past 70 and had dedicated his life to work, raising a family, and "accomplishing." "I did my job and a darn good one at that," he said with obvious pride. Then came retirement. He had looked forward to it. But something he had not anticipated happened. His initial happiness was pierced by his wife's displeasure. It was not that she did not care about him, he was quick to add. It was just that he, the new "daytime person," was "in the way." She explained to him that, with him working all those years and her being the homemaker, she had developed a life of her own. During the day they were, she said, on "parallel tracks" but at a distance one from the other. "I have established my own routine and don't want to give that up. You know each day I have plans—I have my bridge game each Monday, I go shopping with the other women on Tuesday afternoons," etc. The unexpected, he said, came when she added: "And don't think I welcome the idea of your hanging around at lunchtime each day. I'll be there for dinner but the daytime is mine, as it has been since the kids were gone—almost 20 years now." The perplexed look on his face showed how totally unprepared he had been for what was happening to him. He had, he added, relied heavily on his wife's being there to help him explore new worlds, and was now at a loss as to how to cope with the situation that existed. As much as the first retiree had looked gleeful, this newly retired man looked defeated. For one, retirement was a plus; for the other, at best a minus, at worst a cruel hoax.

Traditionally, the older woman has been a homemaker, and her role has remained constant throughout her life. The man in his new identity as "retiree" is role-less. He has no status, no title, no fixed hours, no routine and—no precedent in his experience. Like the bug in Kafka's "Metamorphosis," one day he is a man, and the next—a different species! Having lived a life with fixed schedules, he is now caught in unlimited time/space dimensions.

To compound matters further, there is the he/she part of this dilemma that now must be faced. Whereas "he" went to work each day, "she" either stayed home if she was a traditional woman or had a full- or part-time job once the kids were grown and away. Either way, their time together was fragmentary and geared toward short evenings and week-ends. During those times, chores had to be done and preparations made for the work week soon to begin. It was a busy schedule. Much as the busy work of the younger years in a new marriage centers around household routine and performing for children, so too does this extend into the later years when people are working. There is little time for the "togetherness" lauded as the model for American families. But then—almost suddenly—togetherness is upon the couple, not only on Sundays, or after dinner dishes are cleared away on weekdays, or on mad dashes out the door to work, but each day. For some, this can be a boon—unanticipated delight and pleasure in togetherness; for others, it can be the flip side or worse. The seeds for either, of course, have been there all along, but concealed from view until now, in retirement, when the moment of truth comes. For some, like our recently-retired male, the disappointment in his wife's response is keenly felt. For others, like in the not-yet retired man, the anticipation of the togetherness is joyfully planned. How often we heard the discordant responses: "I very much want to move to a different part of the country but he is attached to this neighborhood," said one woman to us after her husband told us that he was about to retire and pleased about it. That a compromise was intended was evident in his look, as he turned to her and us and said, "We'll work it out—we can always move and I can come back to the old block when I miss it too much." She seemed appeased.

Our working world has molded us into a very special mold. We assume an identity related to that work role. We say, when asked what and how we are doing, "Oh, I am a salesman doing fine" or "I am working in a factory and pretty bored with that," etc. But actually, the work role is only one, and besides being a worker we have other roles, e.g., the churchgoer, the homemaker, the father/mother, the wife/husband/lover, the card-player, the music-lover, the theater-goer, and so on. Our identities are many, even while we stay within that major identity—ourselves.

Each of our roles adds a dimension to our experience, the totality creating the complex person we are. Yet upon retirement, when asked

"What are you doing?" we can only respond with the simple answer, "I am retired." It is almost like saying we fell off the face of the earth, for we are now out of the work force, out of a job, out of . . . Little is said or spoken about what we are, conversely, *in-to*! New experiences can, potentially, lie ahead for all of us, for we can upon retirement become the *new* painter/thinker/poet/writer/user of leisure/card-player/golfer, etc. The list is infinite. Yet the words used about retirement do not suggest what can lie ahead, only what was before and lost, sadly and irretrievably. No wonder so many of us, in the middle years, fear retirement. And many fears and predictions become realized or "self-fulfilled."

Though we do not yet have models for retirement, it seems to be self-evident that our work week will be getting shorter, and that our work lives will offer more choice in retirement. Yet we need to be prepared, for as with much of life lack of preparation makes for ambiguity, and uncertainty causes confusion and anxiety. Stripped of a role, we know not how to perform, yet some of the best "performances" are preparing for just that uncertainty of experience—the yet-to-be. But this is true only if there is preparation from within, if we are unafraid, and look toward limitless time "to do" or "to be" with pleasure. Then, even if stripped of a familiar role, we have our core identity to fall back on. This is also, ultimately, the most reliable person to take into our new leisure-oriented role.

As we move toward a leisure-oriented society, will we be able to fall back on inner resources and use discretionary time intelligently, creatively, and with personal satisfaction? Imagine yourself having nothing to do for the next five hours. Would that be pleasing? Suppose you had a week with no commitments or constraints on your time. Would it be desirable for a month? For a year? How about a lifetime? Freud coined the term "Sunday neurosis" to describe the depression and anxiety that occurs on that sought-after day of rest and leisure when it finally arrives. Would your Sunday neurosis extend to the whole week if you were retired?

As Gordon Dahl writes, "The leisure that people need today is not free time but a free spirit; not more hobbies or amusements but a sense of grace and peace which will lift us beyond our busy schedules." In the Greek tradition, leisure should ideally be an end in itself, desirable for its own sake. Looked at in this way, leisure can be a precious gift of the retired.

What if you had more time on your hands? Would you fit the image of the old song with its refrain: "Time on my hands, you in my arms?" Would you play or use play as work? Would you try to stay perpetually busy? Would you still be bound to the external clock or your own internal one? What, in fact, would you do with your time after retirement?

Sex and lovemaking would seem to be natural and appropriate components of retirement, although they are rarely if ever mentioned. We decided to explore the impact of retirement and leisure on sexual behavior with Question 30, "It is said that older people have more time on their hands. How does this affect sex?" Only 9 percent said more time has a "negative" effect; 91 percent believe that time has a "positive" or "no effect" on sex. Half of these 91 percent said that leisure can enhance sexual activity.

(Male, divorced, age 61) "Should make their sex life that much more enjoyable. Eliminates need of adjusting sex time to work hours."
(Female, married, age 81) "It gives them more time for sex."
(Male, married, age 70) "More leisurely sex play."
(Male, married, age 63) "Provides more opportunity. But not a substitute for other activities."
(Female, married, age 66) "Beautifully, if they are so inclined. They have more time for it."
(Male, married, age 68) "I suppose it could give them a relaxed feeling of no rush of time."
(Female, widow, age 70) "I think they have more time to devote to one another and could possibly enjoy each other more—with or without sex. But sex is fine if possible."
(Female, divorced, age 65) "More opportunity for good sexual relationships."
(Male, widower, age 74) "Great. Now you can do things that you could not do before."
(Female, widow, age 68) "It helps it. The husband isn't tired from his job and the children are gone."

(Female, married, age 60) "It should make sex more available since they have mornings and afternoons free."

(Female, widow, age 69) "More time on your hands. That's good for sex."

(Female, widow, age 67) "You can relax and enjoy it much better."

(Female, widow, age 71) "Makes them more sexy. They are relaxed and rested."

(Male, divorced, age 69) "People who have avoided sex in their younger years will find busy work to fill in their time. But people who haven't can take the time to prolong and enhance sex."

(Male, married, age 73) "Older people have more time and think more of sex."

(Male, married, age 80) "Better."

(Female, married, age 69) "With children out of the home, it is nice to be able to indulge whenever the notion strikes; otherwise, there is no change and our sex life has not been affected yet."

(Female, married, age 69) "It is better for us. I think it depends upon how good their sex life was before they became older. Some women didn't enjoy sex in their earlier years and I don't think they will start enjoying it in later years."

(Male, widower, age 74) "Gives them a good chance to evaluate sex in a different perspective."

(Male, married, age 70) "They can do it at their leisure and feel great."

(Female, widow, age 68) "I find I think about sex more since I retired."

(Male, divorced, age 67) "In my case it would give me more time to enjoy sex to its fullest, to make a 'production number' of it rather than a quick thrill."

(Male, divorced, age 69) "Time to have fantasies."

Unobligated time for these respondents is the critical ingredient. Sex can be "more leisurely" or "relaxed" and a couple can have "more opportunity" and "enjoy each other more." Our respondents viewed sex as an activity to "fill in the spaces," a very special way of using energy, imagination, and ingenuity.

For one 60-year-old married woman it is essential in an active
life: "If they sit and rock, they become too lethargic. If they are active,
then sex is a joy." For still others the extra time factor increases desire:

(Male, widower, age 63) "They desire sex more often."

(Male, single, age 62) "Think of it more often."

(Female, widow, age 76) "They would want sex because they are
relaxed and happy. But sometimes women and men become impotent after many years of abstinence."

(Male, married, age 63) "More time, more opportunity."

(Female, widow, age 66) "More time to think about it."

(Male, married, age 74) "It might stimulate sexual desire, if in contact
with a male or female that one is fond of."

(Female, divorced, age 74) "More longing for attention, which is
part of sex."

(Female, widow, age 77) "You want more."

(Male, married, age 73) "It sure helps when you have more time.
You think more about it."

(Male, married, age 64) "It enhances it."

(Female, divorced, age 77) "You want more of it."

(Female, widow, age 75) "Time makes better."

(Female, married, age 64) "With a willing partner available, I'd
expect they'd have more sex."

(Male, married, age 72) "I believe it induces more sexual contact."

(Female, married, age 65) "It's nice not to have to calculate how
getting amorous might upset the morning routine."

(Female, widow, age 67) "It makes it easier for them. When you are
younger, you worry about being interrupted."

(Female, widow, age 66) "More time in bed."

For many of the 46 percent of respondents who said that more time
has "no effect" on sex, busy life activities continue at a rapid pace. The
72-year-old married woman who says she is "too busy doing other
things to the limit of my strength" is typical of a number in this group:

(Male, widower, age 68) "I find twenty-four hours a day not enough for me to do what I'd like. I guess for those who have time on their hands sex comes easy."

(Female, divorced, age 72) "I don't have extra time. Too busy."

(Female, widow, age 73) "Most older people I know are quite busy, as am I. But certainly leisure is good for sex."

(Female, widow, age 82) "Don't know. Always busy."

(Male, married, age 68) "Not so. Time passes much faster. I have the Elks, the community center and other outlets. Gives me something to do all the time."

(Female, divorced, age 63) "I don't know. I'm eternally busy in all the things I do and can't relate to this."

(Female, widow, age 74) "I don't know. I'm always on the go."

(Male, married, age 63) "I can't say because I have less time now than I had when I worked."

(Male, divorced, age 66) "I find there is not enough time in a day for me and can't see what this question has to do with sex in us older people. I was a young man in the Depression and found myself and my wife always screwing."

(Male, married, age 74) "We are busier in many respects now than prior to retirement. It has made no difference to us."

In recent decades there has been a marked decline in the Puritan concept of all work and no play. Less distrustful of pleasure, our society is learning to take joy in many areas, including sexuality. This is most evident in the new music, art, and lifestyles. These trends can be related to a loosening of restrictions as we encourage people to "do their own thing." But for 9 percent of our respondents, time to experience pleasure may mean troubled time:

(Female, widow, age 75) "They are more on edge and restless. When frustrated with too much time on your hands, they can't relax and enjoy sex as often as the younger generation."

(Female, widow, age 86) "More time, more problems."

(Female, divorced, age 82) "Idle time is trouble time. Keep busy. It's more helpful or beneficial."

(Female, widow, age 68) "I really don't know because I try to keep very busy, sometimes to my own despair it seems."

(Female, widow, age 66) "You think more about it when not busy. I stay very busy."

The trouble for other respondents who would willingly use leisure time for sex is the lack of opportunity. As one 72-year-old divorcee says, sexual desire doesn't change over the years, but free time can "frustrate you if there is no one there."

With discretionary time you can pursue many interests. Sex is obviously not the only or even the most preferred activity for many older people. Indeed, as one 74-year-old married woman curtly noted: "Why sex? Unless one is so inclined." Everyone has priorities in leisure; sex was not one of hers. But a 71-year-old widow, speaking for a large segment of our respondents, countered this view: "Sex is what I enjoy most about retirement."

In Question 45 we asked: "Does sex change after retirement? How?" The pattern of responses to this more direct question is similar to the previous one. According to 84 percent, sex is the "same" or "better" after retirement (men and women agree—see Table 45). Some 24 percent believe retirement allows for more relaxed lovemaking and heightened enjoyment.

(Male, married, age 68) "Yes. For the better. Never experienced anything better."
(Male, married, age 65) "Yes. I'm home now more than before."
(Male, married, age 66) "More time to it, as sex needs more energy."
(Male, widower, age 68) "I'm not yet retired. For a couple, it could be a chance for more sex. The man is not tired from work."
(Male, widower, age 81) "The urge becomes stronger."
(Female, widow, age 64) "Yes. Don't worry about pregnancy. Not too busy for sex."
(Male, married, age 72) "Yes. I'm enjoying it more."
(Female, divorced, age 66) "More passionate."
(Female, single, age 65) "Yes. More time for romance."
(Male, divorced, age 61) "Don't know. I'm not retired. Looking forward to more sex when I do retire. Won't have to forego sex by going to work."
(Male, married, age 70) "Better. More time to spend building up to pleasure."

Of these, some focus on the quality of relaxation, the lack of pressure and the flexibility of an uncommitted schedule:

(Male, married, age 67) "Some added benefits: less pressures, more relaxed approach, no need to watch the clock, no sleep need be robbed."

(Female, married, age 63) "More relaxed. Afternoons are a good time for sex."

(Female, married, age 61) "More relaxed, more opportunities."

(Female, married, age 60) "Probably. People should be more relaxed, not having to rush off: not be concerned with work."

(Male, married, age 66) "We do it when we get the urge."

(Female, widow, age 74) "More incidental and spontaneous."

(Female, married, age 65) "Yes. Have more time to relax and enjoy it any time of the day or night."

(Female, widow, age 68) "It gets better. One is relaxed, not nervous, not worried. No children are around."

(Male, widower, age 67) "More time and energy for it."

(Female, married, age 66) "If more time is spent together, sex is more frequent."

(Male, married, age 69) "I think it improves. More time."

(Female, divorced, age 65) "Better due to reduced mental pressure."

(Female, married, age 60) "Yes. Actually got better because we weren't so uptight or tired and were still young enough. We retired in our late 50s."

(Male, married, age 64) "More satisfying when worries of the rat race of the business world are eliminated."

(Female, divorced, age 63) "More time for romance! Let's help men stay alive and well longer. Educate for open-mindedness and empathy."

(Female, married, age 74) "Maybe for the better. More leisure, no hassle with job and personnel."

(Male, married, age 76) "No. Might even increase, more matinees."

(Female, widow, age 79) "It didn't for us. Why should it?"

(Male, married, age 68) "Yes because you have more leisure to indulge in sex."

(Male, married, age 70) "Improves because of less anxiety and tension."

(Female, widow, age 66) "It becomes better. More time, no pressure of job, children, etc."

(Female, widow, age 74) "It should become better. No rush to go to business."

(Female, widow, age 82) "A little more frequent because not so tired from business or profession. More relaxed."

(Female, married, age 62) "No, except that there's more time during the day. Nice!!"

(Male, married, age 66) "Yes. Less intense, can take longer. Can have sex at more times during the day."

(Female, widow, age 67) "Yes. It gets better because there is no artificial time barrier. One can make love at any time."

(Male, single, age 66) "Yes. More relaxed and therefore a keener interest in sex."

(Female, married, age 60) "Even better. After my husband's retirement, we have even more time and leisure to enjoy ourselves sexually."

One 68-year-old man confides that he and his wife love to have sex in the morning when they both feel most energetic and aroused; earlier in their marriage, with children around and a heavy work schedule, that was not possible. On a slightly different note, a 71-year-old woman mentions that she and her husband love to be in the nude at home, again something they felt they couldn't do when younger. With time available, sex can follow preferred inclinations rather than externally imposed limits.

For many in our sample (60 percent) the change from a work-centered life to one of leisure has had little or no effect on their sex lives. For this group sexual activity has always been good and it continues that way:

(Male, married, age 73) "My case just the same. Beautiful."

(Female, widow, age 60) "Why should it change if the relationship was desirable all along?"

(Female, widow, age 66) "Not for me. Sex changes after loss of spouse, illness, etc. Not retirement *per se*."

(Female, married, age 62) "No, it doesn't. My husband is as good as ever. I think if I wanted to have sex every day, he would."

(Female, divorced, age 82) "Retirement wouldn't make any difference. One is no different because one retires."

(Female, widow, age 68) "I don't see why it should, unless poor health is present to deter its feasibility. Some vitamins and minerals are great aids. I have read so and am inclined to believe that they are."

(Male, widower, age 67) "I don't think it changes at all. It depends on the sex life before retirement. Active people stay active."

(Female, widow, age 66) "Not at all. Time has nothing to do with it. Sex is an urge, a need to love and be loved."

(Female, married, age 81) "I haven't retired yet so can't say. My husband is 87 and is retired, has a passion for gardening and is happy—I don't think retirement changed our sexual patterns."

(Male, married, age 69) "No change if relations were good and you keep busy."

(Female, married, age 64) "No, unless other functions change."

(Female, widow, age 78) "Retirement doesn't change sex if both parties are capable."

(Male, married, age 68) "No. Sex has nothing to do with retirement."

(Female, married, age 62) "Some older people had time on their hands when they were young, too. It's an individual matter."

(Male, married, age 75) "No. It's the same as before."

(Female, married, age 69) "None. If they are able, they will perform regardless of time."

We should like to point out that many of our respondents have discovered for themselves what professional researchers such as Kinsey, Masters and Johnson, and others took many years to learn—that sex remains pretty much the same unless some outside event intrudes, such as a health problem, the loss of a spouse, impotence, or boredom.

Some who are not yet retired projected their feelings into the future. One married woman of sixty-one asks: "Why should it?" Another, a 60-year-old divorced male says: "Don't know. Hope not. I'm not yet retired." These respondents obviously value their sexuality and look forward to active sex lives.

On the other hand, a small group (17 percent) reports a decrease in sex after retirement:

(Male, widower, age 68) "Yes. Not as often."

(Female, married, age 66) "Less sex. We see more of each other."

(Male, married, age 69) "Gradually diminished."

(Female, widow, age 75) "Slows up."

(Female, widow, age 87) "Yes. Pep and strength not so strong."

(Male, married, age 65) "Frequency only."

(Male, widower, age 71) "You can't perform as often as you like to—it's all in the mind."

(Female, widow, age 65) "I have less need for it. There is no reason for it to change, except in intensity and perhaps frequency."

(Male, married, age 87) "Only in frequency."

(Female, widow, age 64) "Feelings for sex, maybe not as often."

(Female, married, age 73) "Yes. Man changes. I am several years older than spouse."

(Female, widow, age 65) "Slows down."

(Male, widower, age 63) "Less."

(Female, widow, age 66) "Yes. An older person is not as agile and is not in much need for sex. The body must be in pretty good shape to really enjoy a good sexual bout."

Have these respondents fallen victim to the stereotype? Has their desire lessened, or are they fulfilling society's prophecy about the later years? We can't say for sure, but we do know that many others share neither their experiences nor their attitudes.

It is undeniable that sexual fulfillment is tied to satisfaction in life—and vice versa. The effects of retirement on the general well-being, as well as the sexuality, of a person are therefore highly significant. While the merits of early versus later retirement is a much debated issue, the decision is often influenced by many factors. Primary to this is the nature of your work, your attachment to it and, perhaps most important, the options you have created for yourself outside of work. If you live to work and work to live, a common syndrome in our society, retirement will set off a personal crisis. Conversely, if leisure time is a quality of experience which you find deeply rewarding and which adds richness to your life, problems centering around retirement should be minimal.

Perhaps preparation for retirement means clinging to that natural quality we all came into the world with—curiosity. Who has ever seen a bored baby, unless something happened to stifle it? Who has ever witnessed a child unwilling to play, unless its playful spirit was squashed? Curiosity, creativity, the willingness to explore inner and outer worlds can be a lifetime process. It need not be dampened with age. It is the continuing use of our creative selves which is perhaps the best measure of success in life. As Thoreau said, "We have lived not in proportion to the number of years we have spent on this earth, but in proportion to the number we have enjoyed."

The healthy, mature person can now look forward to many post-retirement years. People are living longer today, and may live even longer tomorrow. Gerontologists believe that the human longevity potential is currently 110 to 115 years, given good nutrition and the absence of degenerative disease.

In *Prolongevity*, science writer Albert Rosenfeld reviews the exciting biological research which promises to eventually extend human life far beyond its present limits. Written like an exciting whodunnit, the book infectiously suggests that a super scientific sleuth will soon arrive on the scene with a dramatic and unsuspected solution for doing away with the villain—death—forever. If Rosenfeld's conviction is correct, we will have to totally redesign our concept of the later years. But how will we redefine old age? The problem will be upon us even if the only advances we make are in the conquest of degenerative diseases such as heart ailments and cancer, thereby significantly extending the life span of many people.

It is possible that before the twenty-first century the hundred-year life span will become commonplace. Ten full decades of life will offer the individual a wide screen upon which to play out many themes, fantasies, dreams, and goals. The sequence of this extended life may include several careers and several retirements. In this scheme of things the years before 60 may be a sort of adolescence in preparation for the most productive segments of one's life. A new life of adventure may soon be available to those who are not willing to resign from creative activity, whether that be continuing in the work force beyond 60, 70, or 80, or pursuing more personal activities.

In the new order of things, perhaps the term "retirement" itself will be discarded. When we go from high school to college and from college into the job market we talk of moving on, not of retiring. Other transitions from youth to adulthood are viewed as progression rather than regression or stagnation. Only in the later years do transitions take on the negative cast of retirement. Yet so many older adults—even today—leave one role to move *ahead*, not backward.

There is great truth to the saying "Tomorrow is the first day of the rest of your life." Each day can be a renewal, a new beginning. No one need ever retire—if living a full life is the job.

The Future of Sex

Young people look to the later years with fear, thinking of all the potential negatives and none of the positives. The possible loss of sexual capacity looms large as the later years move closer. But our respondents paint a different picture of the possibilities and the realities. Sex goes on, and for many it is as good or better than before.

If young people fear loss of sexual power with advancing age, how do older people feel about their own sexual future? We asked Question 48, "How do you think your sexual feelings, attitudes, and behavior will change as you get older? Explain."

Most noticeable in the responses is the lack of anxiety or fear and the feeling of 66 percent (60 percent of males and 69 percent of females—Table 48) that their sex lives will remain pretty much the same:

> (Male, married, age 68) "It is the same and will continue to be the maximum in lovemaking."
> (Female, married, age 71) "I am older, and I don't think much has changed."
> (Female, widow, age 68) "I don't think there will be any more changes."
> (Female, widow, age 82) "I am older. Sexual feelings are subdued, sometimes activated by dreams."
> (Male, married, age 68) "Do not think they will change. No, probably will have somewhat of a lessening in sex interest."
> (Male, married, age 62) "I feel and hope I can enjoy it all my life."

(Male, married, age 73) "No change. It comes at a good time since I have acquired more knowledge."

(Female, widow, age 73) "I am already old and the changes are slow."

(Female, married, age 63) "I haven't experienced any changes and I hope I do not in the future."

(Female, divorced, age 64) "Even when half-dead (had been ill), still had sexual drive. Wonder sometimes if it will ever stop!"

(Female, divorced, age 63) "I don't expect it to get any way but better. I think we will continue to look at new ways to please each other and ourselves."

(Male, married, age 69) "I don't expect it to change. I look forward to it and enjoy it."

(Male, married, age 62) "I doubt if I will feel less sexy. I might be more tired, but I haven't gotten there yet."

(Male, married, age 73) "It did change. Slower, but raring to go."

(Female, married, age 73) "I am older and my feelings, attitudes and behavior have not changed."

(Male, married, age 72) "Will not change."

These respondents clearly have a positive attitude about their sexual futures. Their sex drives and interest are very much alive. Some are emphatically sure that sex "will not change." And the power of sex in the later years is perhaps best expressed by the 64-year-old female who still had sexual drive, "even when half-dead."

If changes are expected, there is often the expression of acceptance or resignation: "I suppose as I age my body will deteriorate, sexual desires will diminish—that's life," said a married man, aged 74. One 68-year-old widow, perhaps speaking for many older women without partners, says about her sexual desires, "Without a husband I hope they will lessen." Far from being disconnected from her sexual feelings, this woman, reflecting the traditional attitudes of so many older women, feels her sexuality strongly, but cannot accept the idea of sexual experiences outside of relations with a spouse. From that vantage point, the prospects to her look dim, indeed.

Some see their sexual futures tied to the presence of a compatible partner. This is almost exclusively true for women, since older men have far more choices and options for partners throughout the later years:

> (Female, divorced, age 63) "They may be suppressed if I don't find a good partner. They may get better if I do and there is mutual love."
> (Female, widow, age 67) "As long as I keep the same partner, I will feel the same."
> (Female, married, age 60) "As long as I have an active sexual partner I don't expect to change. My attitude, I feel, is agreeable and don't expect to change."
> (Female, married, age 70) "Unless I get a lover, I doubt it. My sex life will remain zilch."
> (Female, married, age 73) "Should remain the same if my husband remains capable."
> (Female, widow, age 64) "I hope that I can meet someone that I can love and can love me before I really become a frigid old lady."
> (Female, divorced, age 61) "My attitude may not change, but who knows whether opportunity or desire will. I hope not. I still feel very much alive and desirable. I think being sexually active is part of the reason."
> (Female, widow, age 88) "I don't think I would ever change if I had a mate right now."

For those (22 percent) who do expect sexuality to decline, the realization is not always disturbing. Some seem to have grasped on their own the real principle of sex forever—that if you don't set any specific performance requirements, there is no real decline. A 75-year-old married man comfortably observes: "Will phase out slowly and will be replaced by common enjoyment of other things." And a 60-year-old married woman comments: "I think desire for sexual intercourse will diminish, but desire for touching, cuddling, and affection will remain the same."

Finally, there is the statement by the 80-year-old widower that wisely puts sex in perspective: "Sex is not the end of all things. Sure it is necessary, or else we could not carry on." It is a mistake, then, to project middle-aged anxieties onto the later years. Because adults in their 30s, 40s, and 50s fear the loss of sexual potency, we assume that these anxieties continue, or are even more pronounced after 60. The results of our survey do not bear this out.

Fear of aging is, rather, a preoccupation of young and middle-aged adults. This is not a totally new finding. To survive in the later years it is necessary to adapt to the aging process. Ultimately, we must focus on the positive rather than the negative, if we are to continue to grow and develop. Perhaps those who cannot accomplish this simply die earlier. Psychologists, in fact, believe that coping ability and attitude may be important contributors to a long life. This is certainly true of many of our respondents. For most of them, fears and worries have greatly diminished, and they are able to concentrate their energy on doing and being, the essentials of life.

11

Sex Forever: A Guide to Improving Your Sexuality

"I would like sex daily, though I now have it about once a week," writes a 68-year-old man, who goes on to say that he believes "sex stimulates the body hormones that make life more enjoyable." A 70-year-old woman enthusiastically expressing her feelings about sex says, "There are always new surprises." In contrast, a 65-year-old married woman concludes, "At my age, sex is dead."

Why are some older adults vibrant, sexually active, and fulfilled in the later years and others not? Why can't everyone have sex forever? What factors make for joyful sexual functioning throughout the life cycle?

In the course of our discussions, which gave us the opportunity to meet with and question older adults from all over the United States, we learned a great deal that has helped us put together suggestions for improving sexual functioning in the later years. The points should be helpful to younger as well as older adults. For someone wanting to explore these suggestions more fully, there are many well-written manuals available that provide step-by-step exercises for developing sexuality.

While some of our own respondents awakened to sex fairly late in life, most have always experienced a reasonable level of satisfaction, and many a high level. It is clear that the best time to start developing sexual potential is when you are young. It sets the pace for the future. In fact, as our data show, most sexually active older adults were sexually active early in their lives, and then maintained frequent and regular sexual activity throughout the mature years. As with most interests and preferences in life, the trend is one of continuity. More recent reports, such as those by Masters and Johnson, have even indicated—and our data support the finding—that continuous sexual functioning during adulthood helps maintain such youthful physiological mechanisms as vaginal lubrication.

Certainly people can change and develop at any age, if they know what they want and are willing to take risks. Changing long-standing patterns of behavior and relationships is not easy, but it can be done. The key is motivation. You can change if you want to. Older people have the same capacity for change as younger people. The unmotivated younger person is no different than the unmotivated older person: both stay glued to their mold; both are different from the motivated younger or older person who uses flexibility and curiosity to try something a little different.

The saying "You can't teach an old dog new tricks" is the supreme put-down of older people. The more we learn about the later years, the more we realize that older people can change. For example, studies show that intelligence can increase even into the eighth decade of life, especially for those who expose themselves to such growth experiences as travel, reading, and other cultural activities. It is motivation and experience, not age, that determine the degree of personal growth. If you believe in yourself and the possibility of further development, you will seek out experiences that enhance self-improvement. If you don't, then you will pull back and make that negative prophecy a reality.

Freud believed that people over the age of 40 could not be effectively analyzed. But psychotherapists and counselors who are beginning to treat older people find that they often make better progress than younger patients. And why shouldn't they? They have more time to work on change, and have a clearer idea of who and what they are. As one 72-year-old woman said in a group therapy session, "The older I get, the more I can't help being me. It's so good there's so much of me around." Another 69-year-old female patient said, "I've been doing the same thing in my marriage and it hasn't gotten me anywhere. I complain about him and wait for him to change. Now I'm going to take the responsibility. I'm here because now I want to change."

Along with knowing who they are, older people are sometimes more willing to shed the shackles of what other people think. As many have said to us, "What do I have to lose?" With their identities formed, they are less likely to be swayed by outside forces and the opinions of others.

As an older person you can, if you choose, be what society expects you to be—someone on the sidelines of life, allowed and often encouraged to be sick, to complain, and to do mostly for others. But you can also flip the coin and see what's on the other side. You can be a participant in life, healthy in the holistic sense, masterful when possible, and doing for yourself as well as for others. In fact, this is the new emerging image of the older adult. Many of our respondents speak for the "new old," in that they have made the possible a reality. Refusing to let age make them bystanders, they have remained enthusiastic participants, enjoying life with their total selves. Sex for these people is an important confirmation of their awareness of life itself. They seem to have taken the advice of Dr. Alex Comfort: "The first step in preserving your sexuality, which for many people is deeply important in preserving personhood, is to realize that if cultivated, sexuality can be, and normally is, lifelong for both sexes."

In order to develop your sexual potential, it is necessary to overcome the belief that sex is purely a natural function. It is a mistake to overestimate the romance of sex and think that working on sexual technique is mechanical or artificial. The possession of a powerful sex drive or the capacity for pleasure do not guarantee that your early experience and training will teach you how best to use your biological equipment. For those who were thwarted in their sexual development and curiosity, there is all the more reason to consciously develop new modes of sexual behavior and response. With knowledge, awareness, and a commitment to change, everyone can reach a heightened level of sexuality and experience sex forever.

Eighty percent of our respondents believe that sex is a healthy activity that makes you feel better, as illustrated by these typical responses to Question 7, "How do you think sex affects the health of older people?":

(Female, widow, age 78) "It is a must both for physical and emotional fitness."
(Female, married, age 66) "Great for emotional and physical health."

(Male, widower, age 74) "It improves it."

(Male, married, age 67) "Good sex relations for older people is a blessing. Unfortunately too many 'close shop' too soon."

(Female, widow, age 65) "Healthy —makes you feel young and vital, desired and makes me feel like I'm still a woman."

(Male, married, age 69) "Makes me feel great all over. It's good for general health."

(Female, divorced, age 79) "Improves health—there is less need for pills and medical care. Better circulation, less arthritis, etc."

(Male, divorced, age 69) "I think it enhances health. Older people don't play enough. Sex is healthy, emotional, physical and mental exercise."

Experts agree. Dr. Alex Comfort calls sex a "highly undangerous activity." For many people, withdrawing from sex can result in anxiety and depression which is more stressful than sexual activity. For this reason physicians encourage heart patients to resume sexual functioning when they are well enough. In some instances less stressful positions for sexual intercourse, such as the woman on top of the man, are recommended.

Dr. Robert Butler and Myrna Lewis say that, "If you can walk briskly for three blocks without distress in the chest, pain, palpitations, or shortness of breath, you are usually well enough for sex." After reviewing the data on sex and heart attacks Dr. Richard Milsten concludes: "In summary, death during intercourse is unusual and should not be feared by heart patients. . . . The vast majority of heart patients should be able to resume normal sexual activity after an appropriate period of convalescence."

If you have any concern about the relationship between sexual activity and a particular medical or health problem, by all means consult your physician. Concerned physicians are generally supportive in this matter, and you may find your anxiety promptly alleviated.

Eliminating the "Musts"

One of the great obstacles to effective sexual functioning, especially in the later years, is the expectation that you *must* achieve a particular goal in your sexual experiences. Underlying the must is the belief that you are a failure, not a "real" man or woman if the goal is not achieved. In sexual activity, the musts that prevent enjoyment of the experience and which often make people withdraw entirely from sexual activity are: I *must* have an erection; I *must* have a sustained erection; I *must* have an orgasm during intercourse; we *must* come together; I *must* have a beautiful, young-looking body or I can't engage in sex. The musts that people invent can go on endlessly, and are usually related to a lifelong pattern of placing irrational demands on oneself.

Dr. Albert Ellis. founder of Rational Emotive Therapy (RET), coined the term "MUSTabatory activities" to describe the self-destructive actions and beliefs that distance people from the pleasures they so desperately seek. Ellis insists, and he has impressive clinical evidence to support his view, that you can get rid of the musts by substituting positive beliefs about yourself. In doing so you can transform your behavior from destructive to creative forms. In keeping with this philosophy, one of Ellis's goals is to teach his patients to eliminate the words "must" and "have to" from their vocabularies.

Sex therapists have applied Ellis's philosophy by training patients with sexual problems—impotence, orgasmic dysfunction and premature ejaculation—to focus initially on feelings and sensations, and to avoid goals. Most sex therapy programs initially discourage patients from ejaculating or having orgasm. They teach patients, whether individuals or couples, to interrupt whatever sexual activities they are engaging in—masturbation, mutual masturbation, intercourse, oral stimulation—at various stages, but always before they reach orgasm. The process of "sensate focus" and stimulation short of orgasm is then repeated. By eliminating the goal of orgasm, particularly in sex with a partner, the couple learns to enjoy sex without the pressure to produce results. In this relaxed atmosphere, couples lose their fear of failure and a new, exciting level of sexual play is achieved. It opens the door to unlimited possibilities for sexual activity and enjoyment.

If we step back, we will see that even the language we use to describe sexual activities imply goals or outcomes. Psychologist and sex therapist Dr. Barry McCarthy stresses this point in stating his preference for the term "pleasuring" instead of "foreplay." Foreplay, he argues. "suggests something that derives its significance from what follows it."

He goes on to add that, "Pleasuring is not goal-oriented like foreplay; it is an activity that is engaged in for its own sake."

How unfortunate that so many older people impose "musts" on themselves. We are reminded of the 68-year-old man who said to us, "If I could get an erection, there are ten women in my condominium who I could have affairs with." But his reality was a no-sex existence because of his belief that he *must* have an erection to have an affair. Both he and one or more of the older women were losing out. In fact, he avoided dating women for fear of being pressured into putting his potency to the test. What a sad and unnecessary loss of possible love, companionship, and sexual pleasure.

Many of our most sexually active and fulfilled respondents seemed to embrace naturally what sex therapists are just finding out. They enjoy sex without demanding or trying to reach specific goals. "If it doesn't work then we hug and cuddle. That feels good, too," says a 73-year-old man. Speaking about her boyfriend of seven years, a 67-year-old widow comments, "If he doesn't get an erection, we have oral sex; he likes it even if he doesn't climax. I feel the same way." "What's the hurry?" says a 76-year-old married man. "We can try again tomorrow or the next day. We like sex." For these and many other older people sex is a means, not an end. The process is the important thing. They love close physical contact and sexual arousal. The completion of the sexual act is the desired dessert, but the meal is also satisfying.

Self-Awareness

Knowing yourself and your needs is a key starting point for developing your sexuality. After all, you cannot begin to seek effective gratification until you know what it is you want and need. That is your responsibility. To accomplish this self-knowledge you need to be open and honest, especially with that person you know best—yourself. Listen to all the messages around you and relate them to your needs. You may not like many things you hear and see, but that's OK. Be selective. The years have taught you to discriminate. Do so.

Practices and styles of life change from decade to decade and generation to generation. Indeed, what's "right" at one time is "wrong" at another. Different styles work for different people at different times. Know your style. It should fit you like an "original," made to order just for you. If you're still looking around for what fits most comfortably and are a little ill at ease in not having found it yet, or if the "outfit" fits but the "jacket" is a bit too constraining, you need to take a second look. Something is not working for you.

Think of what it is you *need*; what it is you *want*; and what it is that you're *getting*. Remember, a need is something you absolutely must have in order to survive. For example, we all need food and some type of shelter. A want is something you would like, such as a particular type of companionship. What you get will determine how satisfied you are. Here is a simple exercise to help you see what your balance sheet looks like.

Exercise 1: Do you Get What You Want?

Examine the following list of sexual "wants." The list includes preferences and activities reported by our sexually active respondents. If you wish, add other wants to the list that are important to you. Indicate which activities you want by checking off either NO or YES for each entry. Next, in the column labeled GET, describe what you actually get of those wants you said YES to in terms of both quantity and quality where relevant.

	WANT		GET
	No	Yes	
Frequent sexual relations			
Experimentation			
Variety			
Open talk			
Oral sex			
Guiltless masturbation			
Live with a lover			
Extended foreplay			
More nudity			
More cuddling and touching			
Orgasm			

If there is a big gap between what you want and what you get, there is a good chance that you are frustrated and feel unfulfilled. The greater the number of gaps, the greater the frustration.

What can you do about these gaps? You've made the first major step in recognizing the problem. Now it's up to you to begin to think of solutions. Some problems are more under your control than others. For example, you can't make a live-in lover materialize at will. But you can change attitudes and hang-ups, even longstanding ones. Similarly, you can develop entirely new patterns of sexual behavior if you acknowledge your desire to do so and commit yourself to the goal.

If you would like to develop the exercise further, ask your spouse, lover, or close friend to fill out the form. Compare and discuss the results.

A simple exercise like this can be the beginning of new self-awareness. Sharing the exercise with another person can open the door to the discovery and creation of new ways of achieving more satisfying sexual relations.

Communication

Communication is vital to improving sexuality and achieving full sexual gratification, especially when there are problems and dissatisfactions. Your partner has to know what you like, what you don't like, and what you would like to try that you have not dared to reveal. Some of the most sexually active and satisfied older adults we surveyed were those who were able to communicate their needs effectively. No darting in and out of verbal corners, their style was direct. Some of these couples had apparently established good communication patterns early in their marriage and continued these patterns into later life.

Yet couples, whether young or old, often fail to develop honest, open communication. Stating what you need implies a strong "I" message. Some people lack the self-esteem necessary to say "I like," "I need," "I want you to do for me." Expressing needs or dissatisfactions may be perceived as criticism of the other person. Telling the truth, for example, may make a woman feel too aggressive or critical of her partner's masculinity—"You are a poor lover." If she considers herself a "nice," accommodating person who needs to be constantly liked and approved by others, expressing needs will be a problem for her. There is also the fear that if "I criticize you, you will criticize me." To avoid this, the couple may have developed an unwritten agreement: "I won't step on your sensitivities or criticize you, if you will agree to do likewise."

Whatever the dynamics underlying poor communication patterns, once they are set they are difficult to break. Some of the older adults we encountered have endured lifetimes of these sad, unsatisfying kinds of communication. In *Games People Play* psychologist Eric Berne describes many such unconscious interactions that skirt around and protect feelings. One woman gave us a good example of this process when she told us that her husband would frequently sit down to dinner and complain angrily, "The soup is too cold." This had been going on for years. Later she realized that he only complained the day after she denied him sex: "It was not, after all, the soup he was talking about."

Some older people in our sample who had remarried or entered into other new relationships told us that they were able to set fresh patterns of communication with their new partners. Novelty seemed to help break old molds. There is no reason why this should not extend to people in longstanding relationships as well. New patterns can be formed *if* the couple is aware of their closed communications and wants to make the effort to change and develop.

In some instances talking about sex and feelings is itself a turn-on. But keep in mind that what works at one time in your life may not work at another. Some of our respondents who were obviously tuned into their sexuality and eager for sex had little or no sex because their spouses were disinterested, "cold," or lacked sexual desire. One 72-year-old woman, typical of this group, said she wished she had married a man who was more physical and sexual. To the question on sex education this same woman described how frightened of sex she was when she was first married. She had received virtually no sex education and what she heard as a teenager scared her. Typical of many of her generation, both she and her husband were virgins when they married, and they did not have intercourse for the first month of marriage. Possibly due to her unrealistic fears of sex, she had selected a man who was not very "sexual" or "physical." Later, when experience eased her fears, she became sexually responsive. But her husband underwent no such growth. Now at age 72, she looks back grudgingly on a lifetime of sexual frustration and disappointment. She thinks of "what could have been." There are undoubtedly numbers of people who married to satisfy one set of needs but then developed new ones later which may have been in conflict with their earlier needs. Unless you are aware of how your needs have altered and, in turn, are willing to communicate them to your partner, the situation is not likely to change.

For example, an older couple may have to change their style of lovemaking in order to maintain the male's erection. The woman might have to become more active in manipulating her partner's genitals. There are older women who have never done this and men who have not communicated the importance of such arousal. Also, the man may be too embarrassed to initiate or discuss novel ways of sexual performance that can help restore full erection. Some older men have reported to us how some simple technique of manual or oral stimulation, often with a new partner, sometimes with a newly educated longstanding one, cured their erection problem.

A 70-year-old man who recently remarried after the death of his first wife of 40 years told us about the striking difference in his new relationship: "We do things I never would have had the nerve to ask my first wife to do—it's terrific!"

If not willing to communicate and tackle sexual problems, an older couple runs the danger of entering into a silent agreement that "sex is over" or that their sexless life is "normal" for an older couple. This is the self-fulfilling prophecy that unnecessarily moves some older people to the sidelines.

Conversely, when there is understanding and communication, "difficult" problems can miraculously disappear. A simple "touch me there" or "keep doing that" or "let's try a new way," can open a whole new realm of experience that turns boredom into excitement and "impotence" into potency.

Breaking the ice is the most difficult part of establishing new lines of communication. But you must start somewhere to make an inroad. At the same time, you need not revolutionize your style of communicating in one step. If you believe you have to do it all at once, the task will be more difficult, if not impossible. Each person has to move at his or her own pace. To get started it is useful to set aside a time for honest communication about sexuality with your partner. Georgia and Benjamin Graber in *Woman's Orgasm* encourage couples to set aside "private time." We agree that this is most critical in developing communication. This simple exercise can help start you off.

Exercise 2: Open and Closed Communications

Both you and your partner divide a piece of paper into two columns. Label the right side *open* and the left side *closed*. On the open side list the sexual experiences, feelings, ideas, impulses, and desires you have shared with your partner. On the closed side, list those you have not shared or kept secret.

Begin your communication by discussing your open sides. Go over them one at a time in turn. Discussing the open side may help you get into the closed side. You may find, for example, that some of your closed items are open items for your partner. The communication process may help both of you bring more items over to the open column.

After you have thoroughly discussed and shared your open columns, each should then present one item from the closed column. After discussing these two items, share your feelings about revealing the closed items. Afterward, decide whether or not you want to share other closed items. Carry the exchange only as far as you both feel comfortable. Remember there are no "musts." You may prefer to do it over a period of days, sharing one closed item each day. Discuss your reactions to this exercise and the meaning it has for both of you.

Touching and Body Awareness

Can you imagine two people being married for many years and never seeing each other completely naked? Surely that was not typical for our respondents. Far from being modest about nudity, most told us that nudity was one of the most enjoyable and natural aspects of their intimate relations. But these were the more sexually active and fulfilled older people. We have also been approached at senior centers after our lectures by people, obviously talking about themselves, who told us about "someone I knew" or "someone I heard about" who never saw their mate totally naked. Sex for these people took place in the dark, with a quick shift of clothing allowing only fleeting exposure of the necessary parts of the body for sexual intercourse.

One 71-year-old man told us candidly about his own experience: "My first wife, who died three years ago, never let me see her naked. She was a prude." He then told us he had had erection problems for the last fifteen years of their forty-six-year marriage. They engaged in little or no foreplay, yet neither the man or his wife related this to the erection problem. They just assumed that was "the way things had to be." Now he is married to a "completely different kind of woman." They both walk around the house nude and have explored a variety of sexual experiences using Alex Comfort's *The Joy of Sex* as a guide. He added that he first picked up the book "out of curiosity—then I could not put it down and read it out of pleasure." His erection problem is gone, along with many of his inhibitions.

How many people, old and young, perform sexually under the most unstimulating, nonerotic, routine conditions and never wonder why the experience is a let-down? It is for this reason that most "guides" to developing better sexual responses, as well as sex manuals and sex therapy programs, encourage people to explore their own bodies and the bodies of their partners.

One woman of 70 in a new marital relationship told us that having her husband dry her after the bath reminded her of the tender mothering she had had as a child. She said she had not been touched so tenderly in over thirty years. Similarly, a story told to us by a social worker from the Northwest vividly demonstrates the continuing need for touch and contact. On one floor of the nursing home where she worked, there was a group of men in their 80s. The group appeared depressed and listless. They were careless about dressing and apathetic about the world around them. The staff described them as "unmotivated." One day the whole tone of the floor changed. The men had dressed with care, they seemed alert and interested in their environment, and more important, they had suddenly become sociable. The staff could not explain the transformation. Finally, someone discovered the source. A new young female aide had been hired for the night shift. She was moonlighting. Her regular daytime job was in a massage parlor. While putting the men to bed one night, she was observed giving them a lot of touching and physical contact—something they rarely if ever got anymore. The message here is an important one: There is a human craving for physical contact and stimulation, without which people become depressed, psychologically and physically. The sad finale to the story is that the aide was made to stop whatever she was doing. Strange, when we consider the millions spent on research to cure depression. How readily we turn away from answers we don't like or don't wish to hear.

Some older people know very little about how their partner's or even their own body works. It is sometimes a revelation for both partners to locate the different parts of the clitoris and vagina in the woman and the sensitive parts of the penis and testicles in the man. An 80-year-old man told us after one of our meetings that some years ago after his wife had read a sex book she asked him if he knew where the clitoris was. He told her, "It must be a new restaurant in town, because I never heard of it."

If you want to improve your sexuality you may consult some excellent books available such as *Man's Body: An Owner's Manual* and *Woman's Body: An Owner's Manual.* Those who explore their own and their partner's body for the first time may experience them like two good friends who were there all the time but somehow went unnoticed.

For developing your own sense of body awareness, try this next simple exercise.

Exercise 3: Sensing Your Body

For this exercise you will need a few small pieces of cloth of different textures: for example, velvet, silk, chamois, linen, burlap, and wool. You will also need a quiet place where you can be left undisturbed for 20 to 30 minutes.

Lie down in a relaxed position and clear your mind of all thoughts. Concentrate on feeling your body sensations. Listen to your own rhythmic breathing.

When you are fully relaxed, take one of the pieces of cloth and, beginning with your toes, touch yourself in different places. Moving upwards, go from toes, to legs, to thighs, to outer genitals, to belly and breasts until you reach your face and head. Then use the other textures.

While still in a relaxed state, think back on the experience. Were you aware of the different textures? Did you experience your body in a different way? What did you discover about the possibilities for bodily sensations?

This exercise can be carried to another level by having your partner also carry out the procedure—either in the same room or in a different room. You can then share the experience and learn about each other's unique responses.

If you feel comfortable with the idea, you can then carry out the exercise on each other, each in turn lying passively and receiving while the other slowly explores all parts of the body with the different textures. This type of mutual exploration can lead to better understanding of your partner's body and point to ways of enhancing your lovemaking.

Sometimes we perform acts without experiencing them fully. Like the couple who never saw each other in the nude, some people have intercourse but do not feel the sensations of their bodies. Even foreplay can be mechanical and anaesthetic. The simple exercise above can make you aware of how much—or how little—you are in tune with your own body, and show you some of the possibilities for exploring uncharted areas of sexual pleasure with your partner.

Masturbation

Over 80 percent of our respondents say masturbation is an acceptable outlet for sexual needs. But only 46 percent admit actually masturbating. Clearly, many of these people are imprisoned by irrational principles that they do not endorse.

Dr. Robert Butler and Myrna Lewis in *Love and Sex After Sixty* are unhedging in their approval of masturbation for older people: "Self-stimulation or masturbation is a common and healthy practice in later life . . . It is a source of pleasure to be learned and enjoyed for its own sake. It resolves sexual tensions, helps preserve sexual functioning in both men and women who have no other outlets." They further say that abstinence from sex can cause impotence in men and reduced lubrication levels and vaginal changes in women. They even go so far as to suggest to older people the use of a vibrator for masturbation.

Masturbation is universal. It is practiced by the young, old, males, females, married, and single people. Many use masturbation in addition to intercourse for sexual release. Indeed, even many older married people masturbate at times, some regularly.

Masturbation is not only a substitute form of release, but sometimes a preferred one. The importance of masturbation in sexuality is best indicated by the fact that it is a key element in every sex therapy program for developing sexual response.

Proud statements like "I haven't masturbated since I was 16," "I hold out for the real thing," and "If I can't find a man I might have to masturbate on a rare occasion" all display an attitude that masturbation is basically undesirable or associated with adolescence and childhood. For some, masturbation may represent a painful admission of the inability to attract a partner. These attitudes ignore the fact that each sexual activity can have value in itself. But more to the point, such beliefs deny many older people a ready source of pleasure and sexual release.

The Hite Report underlined the new sexual independence of women by boldly stating that orgasm achieved through masturbation was as good and pleasurable as orgasm through intercourse or any other means. The same statement applies to older people as well. Surely most people find sexual release more pleasurable in the context of a relationship. But when a relationship is not available, other possibilities should not be ignored. Masturbation can offer you control over your sexuality, and free you from the trap of life circumstances that makes sexuality solely dependent on another person.

For those who feel bored with sex or think they are "impotent," masturbation and exploration of the sensations of the body can lead to a new awakening. Sex manuals report that "impotent" men can often have erections and ejaculations through masturbation. This can give them confidence that they are not, after all, impotent. It is interesting that many male respondents in our survey who report impotence do not masturbate or try to masturbate. This is also true of "frustrated" women without partners who, seeing no way out of their dilemma, ignore masturbation as a source of gratification and bodily awareness. Even for many in our survey who currently do masturbate, the experience is often only a quick move of the hand in an effort to achieve release as soon as possible. Guilt ridden, they are at war with the impulses of their own bodies, and they see the experience as shameful rather than joyful, as it might be.

The inability to touch yourself for pleasure most likely stems from the teachings of early childhood. It's as if the "no" is still there, like a large danger sign.

Exercise 4: Masturbation:
Turning Yourself On

To feel comfortable with masturbation, it is necessary to rid yourself of irrational beliefs about this source of sexual gratification. Can you accept the idea that it is OK to derive pleasure from your body? Do you feel comfortable with the idea that there are no good and bad bodily pleasures, only different ones? If you can answer an honest "yes" to both of these questions, you are ready to move ahead.

The purpose of this eleven-day exercise is to explore bodily sensations in a free and relaxed manner, preliminary to actual masturbation to orgasm. You should luxuriate in these sensations. First, repeat Exercise 3, "Sensing Your Body" by yourself. Then for the next ten days set aside two separate half-hour periods for pleasuring yourself. Each day repeat the body exploration in Exercise 3, but using your hands instead of the swatches of material.

At the beginning of each session explore your entire body from feet to head using slow, gentle, and varied caresses. Concentrate on the sensations of your body and discover the areas and strokes you like best. For the second part of each session, concentrate your self-arousal on the areas you like best. Do not actually masturbate to orgasm during the exercise periods; that will defeat the purpose of leisurely exploring the sensations. After the second session of the day you can masturbate if you choose.

At the end of the eleven-day program evaluate your reactions. Which strokes and locations do you like best? Have you discovered anything new about your body? Do you feel comfortable exploring your body and pleasuring yourself? If you do not feel fully at ease with the exercise, repeat it for another week. Keep doing additional one-week programs until you do feel comfortable.

If you wish to explore additional techniques of masturbation, there are some good references. Dr. Barry McCarthy in *What You Still Don't Know about Male Sexuality* describes four masturbation exercises for men and *Sex Therapy at Home* by David Kass and Fred Strauss has imaginative exercises for both sexes on masturbation and mutual masturbation.

Exercise 5: The Pleasuring Game

The aim of this exercise is to experience sexual pleasure without having intercourse or orgasm. Even if you think you are impotent you can play this sexual game. If by chance you should have an erection during the game do not use it for intercourse. To make the exercise most effective you should agree in advance with your partner to practice the exercise every day for a period of time, say a week, two weeks, a month—the decision is yours, but the longer the better.

Set aside an hour each day for the exercise. Divide the hour into four fifteen-minute segments. Alternate segments, with you first pleasuring your partner for fifteen minutes and then he or she pleasuring you for fifteen minutes. For the first segment each should explore and caress the other person's body thoroughly. In the second segment each should guide the partner to concentrate on those areas that are most exciting. If you feel yourself approaching orgasm, stop the activity briefly, then start again. After the first few days you may want to consult books or manuals for other stimulating ideas for pleasuring each other. On the other hand, your own imaginations and instincts may be as good or better.

At the end of the exercise each day, if there is a feeling of orgasmic urgency, each can masturbate but intercourse is not allowed. Similarly, if the "impotent" man feels an erection coming on in the course of the exercise he should resist attempts at intercourse. Often men with erection problems will make an anxious effort at entry as soon as anything resembling an erection is sensed. Their anxiousness to per-form quickly in these moments almost always dooms them to failure—the semi-erection goes down.

The point of this exercise is sexual pleasure as an end in itself—there is no performance goal. If you can allow yourself the pleasure of this exercise, you will see the path to a renewed sexuality.

Other Sexual Problems

The most common sexual problems are impotence and premature ejaculation for the male, and difficulty in achieving orgasm (orgasmic inadequacy) for the female. All of these conditions have been successfully treated over relatively short periods of time in therapy based on the pioneering techniques described by Masters and Johnson in *Human Sexual Inadequacy* (1970). Since then there has been an explosion of clinics and individual practitioners specializing in sexual problems. The methods introduced by Masters and Johnson have worked successfully with patients of all ages.

Many of our respondents who complained about their partner's withdrawal from sexual activity seemed to be describing inhibition of sexual desire (ISD), a term coined by well-known sex therapist Dr. Helen Kaplan in her recent book, *Disorders of Sexual Desires*. Dr. Kaplan said that men and women of all ages suffering from loss of sexual desire may say that they just don't have sexual feelings and do not get aroused by sexual stimulation; some report they do not masturbate or have any sexual fantasies. Because of the deeper psychological conflicts associated with ISD, more extended psychotherapy is required.

Some of the techniques used by sex therapists are quite simple, even though the problems they address may be psychologically painful and of longstanding duration. For example, the squeeze technique has been known to be a help with premature ejaculation. This method involves the man indicating to his partner that he is approaching orgasm. At that point, he withdraws his penis and the woman firmly squeezes the frenulum, the area just below the glans. This stops the ejaculatory urge. By repeated practice of this starting and stopping method, the man gains confidence and ultimately can achieve ejaculatory control. But like all successful techniques, it requires openness, cooperation, and honest communication.

Women who have difficulty achieving orgasm have been helped by some of the techniques we have outlined in our exercises on body awareness, exploring sensations, and masturbation.

It may be possible for you to work on a sexual problem with your partner using one of the books clearly designed for home use. For example, Georgia and Benjamin Graber in *Women's Orgasm* have two well-written and sequentially designed programs for the nonorgasmic woman. The first is an eleven-step program for achieving orgasm through masturbation for women who have never had an orgasm. This is followed by a ten-step program for reaching orgasm during intercourse. In *Treat Yourself to a Better Sex Life,* Harvey Gochros and Joel Fischer describe many well-designed exercises for alleviating problems and improving sexuality.

If your problem is a serious one that you feel you cannot work on alone or with your partner, it is best to seek professional help. If your physician does not know about sex therapy programs in your community, contact your local or state mental health association, medical society, or psychological association.

Experimentation

Boredom, according to sex researchers, is one of the major sexual problems of couples. Everyone tends to get into a groove or pattern that can become routine and mindless. Therefore, sex therapists recommend novelty to rejuvenate sexual relationships. When today's older adults first married, open communication and experimentation in sex were not in style. Now, many years later, you may be interested in but embarrassed to try something you have heard or fantasized about. Most people have fantasies about what they would like to do or have done to them. Fantasies are so personalized that what drives one person to a frenzy may be totally meaningless or even nonsexual to another person. A man may dream about his lover undressing him and displaying provocative clothing such as see-through panties or long black stockings. His partner may have a secret desire to have her hair stroked and lurid descriptions of sexual acts whispered to her during lovemaking. Both, however, may be too embarrassed to share their fantasies, feeling perhaps that their secret desires are strange or abnormal. In fact, they are probably quite normal and common.

You may wonder how your partner would respond to your desires, and he or she may be wondering the same about you. If you take the risk, you might find your partner more willing than you think. Some older people we spoke to have become quite daring in their later years. Many of our most "turned-on" responses came from people who were open to trying new sexual experiences. They were willing to take risks.

Once the topic of experimentation is opened up, there are a number of directions in which you can go. First, you may decide to share fantasies with your partner. You might even agree to keep it at the talk level so there is no pressure to perform, just a sharing of thoughts and feelings. Another approach is to look for ideas in books describing different techniques and variations, many of which are sensitively written. Some books, like Gay Gaer Luce's *Your Second Life*, are addressed especially to older people. Or, you can just go to a bookstore and browse. Find books that suit your own individual tastes and sensitivities. Just looking at these books and talking about them with your partner can be liberating.

We were surprised to find so many references to practices which are thought to be the exclusive domain of the young. For example, many of our respondents spoke of their enthusiasm for oral sex. This was particularly striking since the term "oral sex" does not appear in any of our questions; the respondents had to supply it themselves. Clearly oral sex is not only frequent in the sexual repertoire of older people, but for many it is the most exciting form of sexual experience. It is especially desired by women when the man has an erection problem. Men also say they get a better erection when oral sex is performed. Contrary to the findings of Kinsey and others, women seem to enjoy and desire it as much as men. Most impressive was their lack of discomfort or embarrassment about oral sex. They apparently accept it as a natural act, even if some are reluctant to try it themselves. The fact that older people see oral sex as neither deviant nor unique may embolden others to follow their instincts.

Exercise 6: Trying Something New

The aim of this exercise is to break routine molds and to explore what may really turn you and your partner on. Try to add some new element to your lovemaking each week. Keep in mind that new does not necessarily mean techniques that are bizarre or gymnastic. New and exciting can mean something as simple as a new open attitude and a sense of freedom about sex. It may be bathing together, massaging each other, or having sex at a different time of the day.

With this exercise in particular it is important to move at your own pace. Changing negative feelings can require much discussion and many trials. But remember, you don't have to do anything and you certainly don't have to accomplish your goal all at once. You are in control. Do only what makes you feel good.

Perhaps you have a secret fantasy of something that would really excite you that you have not shared with your partner; perhaps it is something from your "closed" column in Exercise 2. If you still haven't communicated your closed column this might be a good time to repeat that exercise.

Have you ever thought about oral sex? Read some of the descriptions of oral techniques and look at the illustrations. Share feelings about oral sex. Many older people (and younger ones) are initially revolted by oral sex because they have been taught that the genitals are dirty. But they report enjoying oral sex immensely once they overcome their initial negative reaction and actually try it.

As already mentioned, one safe way to explore new possibilities is to look through books with your partner. Alex Comfort's *Joy of Sex* and *More Joy of Sex* are useful for this purpose. In fact, a number of older people told us that these two books have enhanced their sexuality. Discuss with your partner your reactions to the sexual techniques and variations described in the books. You may hit on something you would both like to try. But don't feel obligated to perform—that should be understood by both of you in advance. At first, you may be content to look, discuss, and share feelings. That alone can be exciting and pump up your levels of arousal in lovemaking.

The techniques presented in this chapter can only be effective in enhancing your sexuality if you believe in the unlimited possibilities for personal growth at any age. That age is no barrier to sexuality was perhaps best expressed by a 65-year-old woman who said to us: "Old age is in the mind. If a person is healthy and stable in mind, sex is—forever."

Self-Help

How can older people get professional help and counseling for sexual and social problems? As we have seen, many professional "gatekeepers" stopped us from conducting our survey, implicitly denying the sexuality of older people. Individual consultations with physicians often produce similar negative reactions. This is not surprising when we consider a study of the attitudes of fourth-year medical students toward masturbation done in 1961. More than 50 percent of the students expressed primitive and erroneous ideas on the subject, including the belief that masturbating caused insanity. These students are today's middle-aged physicians who treat large numbers of older patients. Even those who are more enlightened are not trained in or necessarily willing to deal with personal and emotional problems. How can they, then, be expected to give sound help with sexual problems? Only very recently have medical schools introduced courses in human sexuality and geriatrics.

One 85-year-old man came up to us sheepishly at a senior center health fair and asked: "Is it possible to have too much sex at 85?" He was obviously concerned. We reassured him that as long as he wasn't trying to break any records and felt good about his sexual experiences there was no general standard of "too" much. He seemed relieved and then added: "I asked my doctor if it was possible to have too much sex at my age. My doctor said don't do it too much." The doctor did not explain what he meant by too much, nor did he inquire about any specifics in the man's sexual activity. This kind of response is typical in regard to the queries. There's a hidden message. A mocking smile or a simple comment like, "At your age you still think about sex?" can put an end to discussion. We heard many such stories.

But more and more people are learning that the best way to change and develop is to help yourself, that is, to take primary responsibility for your own destiny. This is not to say that others can't help you, as well, in the process. But you must provide the lead. Only when you are aware of your needs, communicate them effectively, and become assertive in getting what you want can others help you. For example, many older people are embarrassed about talking to professionals about their sexual problems and concerns. No wonder, when the response is often one of condescension, amusement, or a not-so-subtle put down.

Surely there are professionals who are tuned in to the concerns of older people. To find them, be assertive in asking questions like, "What is your training and experience with older people? What do you think are the needs and problems of people over 60? What are your views on sexuality in the later years?" One good way to get what you want is to act as a group. Organize a number of older people who are as concerned as you with good professional treatment. Appoint a committee from your group to interview a prospective counselor, physician, agency director, etc. When the stakes are 5, 10, 20 or more possible clients you will find that you suddenly have real clout and don't have to feel defensive. Get your senior center, community center, or local office on aging to obtain information on post-graduate courses in geriatric medicine and human sexuality. Many hospitals now offer such courses for practicing physicians. Give the information to your physician and local health center.

Similarly, be assertive in demanding the kinds of programs at your community centers that you want. Here, too, organized numbers can have impact. Don't allow the gatekeepers to protect you or treat you like a fragile and vulnerable child. If you want programs on sex and sexual problems, ask for them. Insist on them. If everyone isn't interested in the topic, start off with a small discussion group. Once started, the interest, as we found with our talks around the country, spreads rapidly. When others in the cities and communities where we gave our talks on love, intimacy, and sexuality heard about them, we were inundated with requests to come to their centers as well.

In all fairness, we must point out that many reluctant professionals are responding to the masks of denial that older people often project. So many older people take on the stereotyped "old act," and conform to the role they have been brainwashed to adopt. These "acts" or roles are so convincing that professionals and others are lured into believing that there is no other person behind the disguise. If you have fallen into acting a role, it's up to you to lift the veil. When professionals observed the enthusiastic response to our talks, they saw a different side of their older constituents. They promptly changed their attitude and their program planning to include more real and upbeat themes. We got the message across. Project a different image and you get a different response.

If you want to be a *whole* person, not an old person, but a person with the full range of needs, feelings, and behaviors that are part of our human heritage, if you want to be a sexual person, then *you* must get the message across.

12

The Revolution of the Old

It's the year 2010 and you've just turned 60. You and your generation witnessed dazzling scientific progress that transformed the physical environment and even brought outer space into our daily orbit. But in spite of this progress, many human concerns remain the same. Whether you ride a horse and buggy or a space shuttle you still need love, intimacy, companionship, fulfillment of basic biological needs, and actualization of creative potential. How do you satisfy your needs in 2010? What is your lifestyle like? What sexual options do you choose?

If you are a woman chances are you live alone—most older women do. If you are a man it is more likely that you are married or live with a woman. Whether you are male or female you have probably been working for over thirty years—in your generation most women worked, and more than half the married women worked outside the home even when they had small children. Now you are looking forward to retirement. How will you spend your time? What will your life be like?

Each generation brings forward different values, expectations, and styles of problem-solving to bear on the crises of life. People born in 1950, the baby boom generation, grew up in the turbulent times of the sexual revolution and the "Woodstock era," a period characterized by a widening range of sexual and emotional lifestyle options. Yours was a generation that rejected traditional morality, adopted new social forms, questioned longstanding institutions, and reached for new ways of adapting to a changing world. Values embraced so passionately in the early and mid-years are not likely to be easily cast aside. The Starr-Weiner Report showed that the parents and grandparents of this generation moved light years away from their upbringing in relating to the sexual and social problems of their later years. Will the

233

2010 generation of elderly, and those in-between, evolve even more far-reaching solutions?

There are many factors that will influence the way in which you live as you enter the sixth decade of life. Your status as an older person will be tied not only to your personal standards and preferences but also to broader economic, political, and social forces.

The later years pose many potential hazards: loss of friends and relatives, loneliness, disenfranchisement, economic vulnerability, just to name a few. All of these reflect on one's sense of personal worth and power. Sex and power, as we have noted, are intertwined so that sexuality will be influenced by the overall status of older people. The number of aged people in society, and thus their relative influence, will be a critical factor. As Richard Easterlin observes in *Birth and Fortune*: "for those fortunate enough to be members of a small generation, life is—as a general matter—disproportionately good; the opposite is true for those who are members of a large generation."

First we must realize that there will be more people over 60 than ever before representing a larger percentage of the population. Minimal estimates say that 20 percent of the population will be over 60 by the beginning of the next century. That figure could increase significantly depending on the birth rate. Everyone who will be 60 in the year 2010 is alive today. The question is how long will they live and how many new births there will be? The ratio of young to old will, for example, determine the feasibility of society delivering on its promise to support older people via social security and pensions. As we have seen from the responses to our survey, leisure and sexuality can go together. But true leisure requires freedom from external worries and concerns. The very reason often cited by those respondents who said sex was better after retirement was the lack of economic pressures and freedom from the strain of work.

The birth rate is closely tied to attitudes toward marriage, childbearing, and the family. The explosion of the single lifestyle, the advent of the two-paycheck marriage, and the fact that women are increasingly involved in careers have an important influence on childbearing, creating a situation of voluntary childlessness or delayed childbearing. Sometimes childbearing is postponed so long that it becomes too much of an economic sacrifice and an intrusion into the couple's firmly established lifestyle, so that the choice is for no children. Also the high divorce rate, particularly in the early years of marriage, has an impact on family planning. A less obvious influence on family size is the status of support systems such as publicly financed preschool and day care programs. As Betty Friedan reminds us: "Fewer than 7 percent of Americans are now living in the kind of family arrangement to which politicians are always paying lip service—daddy-the-breadwinner, mother-the-housewife, two children plus a dog and a cat . . ." (*New York Times*, November 18, 1979). Should public policy continue to be punitive to the real and emerging modern family built on flexibility and nonsexist roles, the birth rate may decline further.

A sizable increase in the percentage of elderly will place many pressures on society which could fuel a generational conflict, however. One critical issue will be whether a shrinking young population will be willing to support a growing army of retired elderly.

The social security system and pension plans are based on a Catch 22 principle that has backfired. The longevity tables on which these programs were developed in the 1930s predicted that few people would actually collect and that those who did would certainly not collect for long. But advances in medicine and nutrition, as well as our adapting generally healthier lifestyles have turned the tables on the social planners. As a result, these programs face the possibility of bankruptcy in the near future; some are reported to be already near bankruptcy. And what bankruptcy doesn't destroy, inflation will. How will the elderly react to the reneging of a lifetime promise that was made to them?

As we become further removed from the Protestant work ethic, work will no longer reflect on one's moral character or sense of self-worth; it will have to stand on its own as a contributor to personal fulfillment. We may already have broken the rigid conception of work life as a straight line from apprenticeship to the gold watch. More and more we hear about the mid-life career changes and multiple careers of those in search of more meaning and relevance in work.

When we take a close look at the actual nature of most jobs—their boredom, drudgery, and oppressiveness—we must conclude that some people hang on not for love of the job but economic necessity and perhaps, more importantly, a crisis in the use of leisure time. As professionals, politicians, and business executives fight to remove mandatory retirement restrictions, we are led to believe that everyone wants to work as long as they are physically able. But there is also an opposing trend that upholds early retirement, a trend that fits well with the growing emphasis on leisure-time activities, and the increasingly accepted notion that play may indeed be as fulfilling and meaningful as work. This point is driven home by the recent report that 1800 out of 2200 executives at Sears Roebuck elected early retirement when an incentive was offered (only one-third were expected to elect this option). These mostly lower-level executives with a minimum of 20 years of service, who are at least 55 years of age, are not likely to find comparable executive positions after retirement—they apparently really want to retire (*New York Times,* November 15, 1980).

Social scientists are beginning to reflect on the attitudes expressed so vividly by blue-collar and white-collar workers who speak out in Studs Terkel's book *Working*: "For the many, there is a hardly concealed discontent. The blue-collar blues is not more bitterly sung than the white-collar moan. 'I'm a machine,' says the spot welder, 'I'm caged,' says the bank teller and echoes the hotel clerk. 'I'm a mule,' says the steelworker. 'A monkey can do what I do,' says the receptionist. 'I'm less than a farm implement,' says the migrant worker. 'I'm an object,' says the high-fashion model. Blue collar and white call upon the identical phrase: 'I'm a robot.'"

But the future will very likely bring change. Surely, the "Woodstock generation" has different attitudes toward work than their parents. In the 1960s there was the fear that work was going out of style, that young people would kick the habit. Economic pressures may have brought them back into the fold, but not with the mentality that places work on a pedestal. The year-2010 generation of elderly may turn to other alternatives for survival when the personal and economic rewards of working diminish. In any event, the very nature of work may change and allow for a smoother flow between work and play, which may be particularly appealing to older people. The "electronic cottage" described by Alan Toffler in *The Third Wave* opens the possibility of people working at home while hooked up to a vast network of computers.

Recognizing the economic problems that will develop as a result of

the expanding elderly population and the diminishing younger population, some gerontologists have suggested that in the future the elderly
will have to continue working well beyond the current retirement age.
This, they say, will be necessary not only for their own economic
survival but also because their skills will be needed by society.

But will the old choose to work? And if not, can they be forced to,
even if it does serve the needs of society? The mid-life crisis so well
described by Gail Sheehy in *Passages* leads many people to reassess
their life goals and to alter their time perspective. As people come to
grips with their unfulfilled dreams and the sense that time is running
out, they often begin a frantic period of readjustment. Those who
successfully surmount the crisis turn to other goals and values. In the
past this crisis has been primarily associated with men, but as more and
more women enter the work and professional world in their youth
rather than in their middle years, the mid-life crisis will become similar
for both sexes.

The new-old are not likely to submit to the dictates of society unless
there is something in it for them which relates to their life perspective.
Even economic necessity may have little power of persuasion on the
old in the year 2010, as Nancy Meyer's view of work in *The Male
Mid-life Crisis* suggests:

> Trained for a world that no longer exists, they discover at mid-life
> that the values they believed in have either disappeared or been
> discredited. Job security is a thing of the past; climbing up the ladder
> becomes impossible after forty; and hard work gets you nowhere
> today. Worse still, in the middle years excessively hard work produ-
> ces anxiety, depression, ulcers, alcoholism and heart attacks.

If the old listen to their inner voices rather than the voice of society,
the "Hell no we won't go" of the 1960s may become the "We won't
go to work" of the generation at maturity. Instead alternative lifestyles
for survival, such as communal living to reduce economic burdens and
expand socialization, may surface as appealing alternatives. If the
Woodstock generation was not too thrilled with the prospect of irrelevant work in the 1960s, they are not likely to embrace it in their later
years when personal values take on even greater importance in their
lives.

Will the elderly return to the extended family to solve their economic and social problems? First, the extended family already doesn't exist for the most part, and that will become increasingly the case. Furthermore, it is doubtful that either young or old really want the extended family. It suits neither of their lifestyles. It intrudes on the privacy and freedom of both. It is well known, for example, that the sexuality of older widows is often squelched by their adult children. Alan Rabuka and Bruce Jacobs in *Old Folks at Home* report that, in 1940, 35 percent of all elderly lived with an adult child or relative. By 1970 the figure had shrunk to 13 percent. The trend is unmistakably toward greater independence and separation.

The extended family has often been overly romanticized. This becomes clear when we take a closer look at the facts. In its heyday when even more than 35 percent of the elderly who survived lived with children and relatives—life expectancy at the turn of the century was 48 for men and 51 for women—they were usually assigned service roles that hardly call for nostalgia: cooking, cleaning, babysitting, house watching, and a multitude of other chores. Their personal lives were severely restricted. The common rationalization for this treatment of the elderly was in the true tradition of the plantation owners during slavery: "That's what they like to do; it makes them happy."

The independent and upbeat spirit of the new elderly will not submit to the oppressiveness of the extended family. Just as young adults seeking their identity leave home to explore their individuality more fully, so will the elderly, lest they return to a child-like role in which their individuality, freedom, and sexuality are threatened and curtailed. As one 64-year-old woman said about her middle-aged daughter, "I have to keep reminding her that I'm not fragile. She treats me like a helpless child." The point is further punctuated by a recent study at the Philadelphia Geriatric Center by Miriam Moss and Powell Lawton. They found that older people living alone or with spouse socialize more with friends than older people living with younger relatives.

Intergenerational households of young and old people who have selected each other for communal living seem to work better, at least based on the informal reports we have heard from older people living in such settings. But these arrangements and the participants are not typical. Perhaps in some idyllic future, acceptance of the individual will transcend age stereotypes. A new liaison between people of all ages might then be possible, one that would promote an intergenerational society in which everyone profits. In the near future, however, older people will have to band together to buttress themselves against the agism of society.

Commentators bemoan the loss of intergenerational communities and the exodus of the elderly to retirement communities. But older people opt for these communities because they offer them what they want. Among those who remain behind are many who do so for lack of the financial resources to relocate rather than for love of their present life situation. The fact is, there is no floodtide of elderly returning to the crime-ridden, high-cost-of-living cities with their poor, and unsafe transportation systems, and their restricted opportunities for socialization, particularly after dark.

Finally, those who criticize the types of popular leisure activities offered in many retirement communities should question the basis for their judgment. Many of the activities are the very same ones the elderly pursued before retirement, but with less opportunity, less frequency, and less enjoyment. One should also keep in mind that each successive generation that occupies retirement homes or creates communes will fashion them after their own needs. If desired, bingo halls can easily be converted into theaters, shuffleboard courts into gardens or greenhouses, and recreation halls into meditation centers.

Our imaginations have been fired recently by the exciting reports of longevity research. Stories of chemicals that reverse aging and extend life flood the press and titillate our dreams of a modern-day fountain of youth. Indeed, the long sought-after goal may even be close at hand. But will we let it happen? Can society deal with increased longevity when it is already groaning under even less dramatic degrees of extended life? As the generational tensions intensify, we might find longevity research curtailed, as a kind of modern day form of euthanasia to preserve an economic and social system that has not anticipated and cannot absorb extended life. What direction this issue takes, as well as other issues that have an impact on the future lifestyles of older people, will no doubt be influenced by whether the young or the old control governmental policy. On that score we have to look to trends in political organization and the voting patterns of the elderly.

Older people are organizing. They are forming groups and networks in formal social and political organizations. This is happening in senior centers, retirement communities, widow and widower groups, associations of retired people, political activist groups such as the Gray Panthers, and a host of church and community associations. Groups like the American Association of Retired Persons (AARP) and the Gray Panthers have local chapters and national organizations. Older people are no longer isolated from each other, and their affiliation with a group or center will increase. In addition TV programs like "Over Easy" and "Prime of Life" are addressed to older audiences, and there is a mushrooming of magazines for older people, like *Modern Maturity* and *Fifty Plus,* which along with their upbeat tones keep older people informed about issues related to their interests and welfare. The trend toward this type of media presentation will increase as we move toward the next century.

The organization of Gray America differs from other minority movements which, at least in their beginnings, had to turn to other groups to lend expertise and provide leadership. The elderly have the establishment already in their ranks—retired lawyers, judges, business executives, politicians, administrators, and other professionals. These people know from a lifetime of experience how to achieve a given goal. They have only to continue using the skills acquired over their working lives. Of no insignificance is the fact that they also have the sympathies of middle-aged and older legislators who see their own destinies in the elder lobbyists who pound at their doors.

Gerontologist and public policy expert Stanley Brody has been flashing warning signs for many years when he talks about the "demographic imperative." Speaking to a group of social workers at a Veterans Administration conference on aging in Philadelphia he playfully but seriously pointed his finger at the audience: "I'll be 65 in a few years and I'm a veteran. You're not going to keep me waiting two hours for a prescription. I know the system and know how to press the right buttons. So do others right behind me," referring to the more than 11 million World War Two veterans who are approaching an average age of 60. Each upcoming generation of elderly, he reminded the audience, will be better educated and will come from the system.

Developmental psychologist Bernice Neugarten talks about the "younging" of the old, a phenomenon that will change the very nature and concept of the later years. Sociologist Ethel Shanas who has also been monitoring the revolution of the old warns that the elderly will have to organize for self-defense. And we should listen to Maggie Kuhn, founder of the Gray Panthers, who calls for political activism and advocacy to change the image of "sweet old people who play shuffleboard and bingo."

What is undoubtedly emerging is the possibility of a finely tuned political machine with great power. With the educational levels of each successive generation of older people increasing, the political potential of the machine will grow. But how much it will actually be activated in the future will again depend on the economic and social climate for the future elderly. If economic support systems (social security and pensions) collapse and an attempt is made to impose dreary lifestyles on the elderly, then the sleeping giant will awaken.

At some point, too, the phenomenon of the organized elderly will not go unnoticed by younger adults. In an economically harsh world, the fight for limited resources may also drive younger people to organize better to counter the march of the old.

Political scientists/gerontologists Robert Hudson and Robert Binstock report that political interest remains high during the later years. Of greater importance is their observation that voting participation continues at the same level as earlier years, when such extraneous factors as relocation are controlled for.

We tend to think of the elderly as conservative. This conclusion may be somewhat deceptive when we consider that the radical positions of one era may be the conservative positions of a later one. But in the case of the Woodstock generation it is not the particular issues of their generation that are as significant as their activist orientation. Activism applied to current issues could transform conservativism into new radicalism.

Political activism, dropping out, experimentation with maverick lifestyles, and an oppositional stance toward government and society—long the benchmark of the young—may well be the banners of the old by the next century. The radical-conservative stereotypes would then be reversed, with the young perhaps even chastising the old for their defiant, nonconformist iconoclasm. A fiercely competitive technological society with a shrinking and overburdened young population in developed countries could very well encourage their conservativism making the old take on a more nonconformist or a loyal opposition stance.

As we move toward the next century older people will be much more aware of their sexuality, and this will in turn feed on their sense of self-esteem and power. It is not accidental that the political muscle of older adults is emerging at the same time as is their sexuality. The two go together because they derive from the same source. To suppress one is to suppress the other. By the year 2010 their folk songs may be dated and their burning issues a bit charred, but the sexual freedom and the lesson of personal and group power that they learned back in the 1960s will continue to be an integral part of their being. If pushed into second-class citizenship in the later years, they will reach into their generational heritage for the inspiration needed to tackle the existential problems of aging in unique ways.

One of the very real problems of the later years is the greater number of women compared to men. This ratio is not likely to change. There is some speculation that women will catch up to men in mortality statistics because of stress-related illnesses that will increase as they enter the professional and work world in greater numbers. But for the moment, the gap in longevity between men and women is widening rather than diminishing. Women are likely to continue to outlive men and therefore, as previously mentioned, live their lives without partners.

By the year 2010 the ranks of women who are alone will also swell from other sources. As we enter the 1980s the divorce rate continues to zoom—more than 40 percent of marriages now end in divorce. In some states the divorce rate exceeds the marriage rate; and divorces after twenty and twenty-five years of marriage, a small number in previous decades, are also becoming commonplace. There seems to be no abatement to this trend, and many young people are choosing not to marry at all, opting for a single lifestyle with or without a live-in lover on a temporary, longterm, or permanent basis.

The potpourri of new lifestyles that shocked our traditional sensitivities in the 1960s are now only casually noted. While the new lifestyles, especially serial relationships, may be preferable and enhance the early adult years, they could lead to social problems in the later years. But at the same time, experience with different modes of living in the earlier years could turn out to be a valuable training ground for developing flexibility. One of the problems of many unhappy older people today is their limited and rigid conception of acceptable ways of living. For example, while in our survey 91 percent endorse the principle of living together outside of marriage, it is doubtful that many would actually do so themselves. In the future that will not be the case.

When we consider specific alternatives for sexual gratification, no doubt changes will take place. Surely masturbation, the most readily available sexual outlet, will be turned to more easily by future generations of older people. While the majority of our sample endorsed this form of sexual release in principle, many could not overcome the taboo of their childhoods and actually do it. Certainly the next century's generation of older people will feel no such inhibition. On the contrary, they are likely to feel free to explore all available sources of sexuality.

Still, in spite of convincing pronouncements that an orgasm is an orgasm, most people prefer sex in a relationship with a partner. Masturbation may relieve some frustration for women alone, but at the same time it can actually accentuate the desire for intimacy with another person. Will future generations be able to cope more effectively with limited sexual options than the present generation of people over 60?

Some writers commenting on the predicament of older women without partners suggest that the solution may lie in older women taking younger lovers. On the surface this would seem to make sense. Our survey shows that older women would certainly welcome this solution. It is also in line with the biological program that calls for men to peak sexually much earlier than women.

As desirable as this option may be, however, it is not likely to present itself as a solution for many women. Although we hear of the occasional 65-year-old woman and her 45-year-old lover, such cases are far from epidemic. In fact, they are rare enough to attract our attention and, not infrequently, raise our eyebrows. Some women are beginning to take more aggressive action on this front. The *New York Daily News* (Oct. 16, 1980) reported on a new organization, The Sea Gull Society, established by concert pianist Jessica Krane to help older women and younger men meet socially. This development will bear watching. But to date, there is no indication that young men seek out older women on any wide scale. On the contrary, all evidence shows that both men and women are generally drawn to their own generation. When men do choose women outside their generation, they tend to select younger, not older, women. This has been true throughout history, and there does not appear to be any sign of imminent change. If the pattern of partner choices were to change, it would probably have to happen in the earlier years; that is, young adult women would have to start cultivating men a number of years younger than themselves.

We must also pay attention to the finding of our survey that older women fantasize an ideal lover close to their own age. Since fantasies, by definition, give one the chance to depart from reality, we can only assume that this wish, although a real one, is not based on practical considerations. Surprisingly, too, most older men, who as we know have wider options, also choose an ideal lover close to their own age.

The responses to our "ideal lover" question point up the fact that sex is more than a physical experience. Our respondents are telling us that they want relationships with partners with whom they can share common experiences. As one 60-year-old woman said to us: "So I'll go to bed with a 30-year-old man. Say sex is great. Then what? We'll have to talk, right? But what will we talk about? His world won't be mine and mine won't be his. What will we do then? More sex? Good, but that can't last forever. Even good steak becomes a bore if it's the only diet."

In the year 2010 will some women choose polygamy as a way of dealing with the uneven ratio between the sexes? While some women in our present sample made this suggestion, it was not a popular solution. Polygamy is not likely to be a widespread choice in the future for a number of reasons. First, if sex is the main objective of the arrangement, it is doubtful that older men could adequately service the sexual needs of many women. Even if the male erectile potential becomes enhanced by surgical implants (penile prosthesis is currently used successfully with erection problems) or other advances in biological engineering occur, polygamy would still not hold much appeal for most women, for it would violate the independent spirit of the year 2010. Remember, these women came through the feminist movement and, therefore, are not likely to subordinate themselves within a polygamous relationship.

For pure physical sex older women may be more inclined toward male prostitutes. In the 1970s we saw the emergence of explicit female-oriented sex magazines—the equal-rights answer to *Playboy* and *Penthouse*. Carrying that sentiment further we can foresee the open acceptance of male prostitution for women alone. Our respondents certainly show a receptivity to this idea (Question 23); it may take future generations to put it into practice.

What would be more fitting for the social and personal outlook of the "Woodstock generation" of elderly is a loosely defined social setting in which sexuality would be one part of a shared communal environment. In fact, in the year 2010 communal ways of sharing men will probably evolve as one of the more viable alternatives. The theme of communal living will be familiar to the elderly in the year 2010. In the late 1960s it was a familiar experimental lifestyle. Those who didn't experience it personally had a friend or a relative or acquaintance who did. At that time young people were also looking for solutions. They were looking for ways to live more peacefully with their fellow humans and to escape the rape of the earth and the stress of a society searching for a new identity. Communes provided companionship and intimacy while offering a simple self-sufficient lifestyle that escaped the economic rat race.

In the year 2010 communes in different forms may again be turned to for many of the same reasons. Economic hardships are likely to be as oppressive in the year 2010 as today. If two can live as cheaply as one, it is simplistic to observe that four, ten, fifty, or a hundred can live even more inexpensively. This may have a great appeal to a generation that feels comfortable with the concept of communal living, especially when it can also offer companionship, friendship, intimacy, sexuality, and a supportive social environment. At the present time communes can offer the same advantages to today's elderly. Why don't they opt for them then? The explanation points up the impact of generational differences. Today's older people have a staunch ethic of individuality and independence. The idea of communal living is alien and abrasive to their outlook. We have heard of many frustrating attempts by well-intentioned social workers and other professionals to start up commu-

nal types of housing arrangements for the elderly. While this type of
housing would have solved many problems for the older people whom
they tried to convince, they could not get the idea off the ground. But
the proposal will not fall on deaf ears in the year 2010. On the contrary,
it will secm natural.

For a small number of elderly the idea of sharing is beginning to take
hold even today. At every meeting of associations of older people we
have attended recently, there is always at least one presentation on
communal-type living: a 70-year-old woman describing the mechan-
ics of setting up a communal apartment in a city; an elderly minister
telling about his experience with a communal house where the resi-
dents built a greenhouse to have inexpensive vegetables year round;
and so on. The audiences of older people listened attentively, some
taking notes.

What about homosexuality as an answer for the vast majority of
women who have no partners? For the present population of older
people, homosexuality has little appeal as a personal lifestyle. To
Question 43, "Homosexuality seems much more open these days.
How do you feel about it?" an impressive 64 percent say that homosexuality is all right for those who choose it. Apparently the visibility
of the gay community, their demand that society accept their lifestyle,
has filtered down to our respondents, even though few endorse homosexuality for themselves. In response to a number of other questions
there are a few suggestions of lesbian relationships as an alternative for
women without partners. On the question addressed to sexual experimentation, just a few respondents admit a desire to try a homosexual
experience. These findings are readily understandable. If masturbation
is still taboo for many of our respondents, then homosexuality is even
further beyond personal consideration.

But what about the future? The generation of elderly in the year
2010 and beyond will have lived through the gay rights movement.
They will also have seen the American Psychiatric Association
remove homosexuality from its list of pathologies. Many young people in the 1960s and 70s tried homosexual experiences in the spirit of
sexual experimentation of the times. Bisexuality also became a popular
topic for discussion and experimentation. Neither totally accepting nor
rejecting homosexuality, there was a desire to explore what was natural

to the human being. Those who rejected homosexuality for themselves tended to do so objectively, rather than subjectively or as a response to the "homophobia" tendencies of earlier generations.

While arguments favoring homosexuality and bisexuality may be rejected for married people or those with heterosexual partners, we may find a growing interest in them among older women who find themselves without partners in the later years. Much more open and uninhibited about sexual practices from an early date, the year-2010 generation of older women will have few hesitations about exploring whatever workable lifestyles are available. Doers as well as *copers,* they will not sit back and accept their lot, abandoning their sexuality. This has not been their style in the past, and there is no reason to expect it to be their style in the future.

The attraction of the homosexual solution for older women will be further enhanced by the even greater openness toward homosexuality that will likely be prevalent in the future. Of even greater significance is that most women by the year 2010 will have had some homosexual experience. Even Kinsey, interviewing people in the 1930s and 40s, found a surprisingly high incidence of homosexual experience among the women in his sample: by age 40, 19 percent of the women in his sample had a conscious homosexual experience in which one or both of the participants were actively seeking erotic arousal—a finding that for unexplained reasons has not been widely reported. If women born around the turn of the century pursued some homosexual experiences, it does not take much of a leap of the imagination to speculate that an even larger percentage of those who witnessed or were part of the Woodstock generation will move toward homosexuality in their later years when the possibilities for heterosexual relationships narrow.

It is well known in psychology that we all have a masculine as well as a feminine component, one of which is usually dominant and guides the development of our sexual identity. Societal prohibitions and restrictions may inhibit us from experiencing the other self, but we know that under conditions of isolation, such as imprisonment, the other self often emerges. Homosexuality is rampant in prisons, even among those who were formerly exclusively heterosexual. Given the dramatic changes in the social and sexual mores that will be firmly established in the future, will women imprisoned by the circumstances of life move toward the other self? The conclusion seems obvious and compelling.

The hints suggesting a path for the future are already there in the answers of a few of our respondents. A 72-year-old woman, a highly sexual person who "would like to have sex every day," writes in response to the question of what is a good sexual experience: "In this order: heterosexual; homosexual; masturbation." Although she clearly prefers heterosexual relations—homosexual relations are "not all that satisfying"—she indicates that she moved toward bisexuality in the later years when she found herself alone. How many older women in the future will find the same path the most viable? Will they turn away from choices that are available even if not their favorite, and for which they have no severe moral prohibitions?

In *The Bisexual Option* psychiatrist Dr. Fred Klein presents some persuasive arguments on the changing conception of what is "normal" in sexual relations. His depiction of healthy and neurotic bisexuality as well as healthy and neurotic heterosexuality focuses on the capacity for intimacy and relationships rather than sexual orientation and prefer-ence *per se*. Gender identity—that is, the sense of being male or female—is established very early in life, by about eighteen months of age. But sexual identity, Klein insists, "has little to do with attraction for the same or opposite sex.... A bisexual male, for example, having a deep relationship with a woman who lets him know in words and action that she loves the man he is, can in turn feel his inner maleness with another man who is turned on, so to speak, by the same qualities the woman found exciting." His clinical case histories illustrate that a bisexual can have a well-balanced personality and function effectively in work, play, and love.

Klein estimates that there are more bisexuals than has previously been suspected. Using Kinsey's scale of 0-6 for measuring sexuality from exclusively heterosexual to exclusively homosexual, he estimates that 30 to 40 percent of Kinsey's male population and 15 to 35 percent of his female population were bisexual. This estimate is even more impressive because it excludes those who were completely homosex-ual. In Kinsey's time, men had greater freedom and opportunity in sexual practices than women, probably accounting for the lower fig-ures for female bisexuality. But, in general, the greater options for men at all stages of life would encourage them to determine a sexual lifestyle earlier in life than women—let's say by about age 35—which they will carry with them into the later years. Many women, on the other hand, will be prompted toward the homosexual or bisexual option in later life because of their changed social situation and the limited choices available to them.

In fact, as society moves toward greater consciousness of the social dilemmas of older women, younger women may opt for the bisexual choice sooner as a means of preparing for the future. Bisexuality may, in short, be an important feminist issue of the 1980s.

We have always believed that older people are conservative by nature. But in the future we may see a reversal of this view as older people make maverick choices of lifestyles that set the direction for younger people; in particular, homosexuality among older women may sanction it for younger women.

Unlike the present generation of elderly who are largely copers and adapters, future generations are likely to be doers and shapers. Rather than molding their own behavior and needs to conform to a given reality, they will be more likely to alter the environment to fit their needs. Freed of the stereotypes of what an old person should be, dedicated to personal fulfillment and convinced of the power of people to unite in shaping their world, they will *act*, not react. They will come up with solutions and alternatives that will change the face of the later years.

The more we focus in on the characteristics of the coming generations of elderly over the next decades, the more compelling is the conclusion that we can expect dramatic social changes. It may be that the prediction of a dynamic social revolution made back in the 1960s was not wrong. Only the timing and the source of the revolution were off. It will come a little later than expected, but more surprising it will be initiated not by the young but by the old. The new spirit that points the way to the future is perhaps best expressed by the comment of a 68-year-old respondent: "We should have kicked the taboos that society lays on old people long ago. We are the society. We are the people."

Appendix

The numbers on the tables in the appendix correspond to the numbers of the questions. For questions that have two parts the second part is identified by the question number plus the decimal .5. For example, Question 15 asks, "Do you masturbate? How often?" Table 15 gives the statistics on the first part—"Do you masturbate?" The statistics for "How often?" are in Table 15.5. Tables that give variations or sub-analyses of the main questions are represented by letters following the numbers of the questions. For example, the statistics for the question, "How important is orgasm or climax in your sexual experiences?" is presented in Table 9. The same question analyzed according to age groups (60–69, 70–79, over-80) appear in Table 9A.

The scores on each question are reported for the total population of 800 and then separately for the 518 females and 282 males. The absolute number as well as the percentage is given for each scored category. Percentages appear in parentheses. The "adjusted" columns report the percentages for those who actually responded to each question (the total minus the "No Response" and "Not Applicable" categories). "Not Applicable" is a form of no response in which the respondent feels the question doesn't apply. For example, if a respondent answers "No" to "Do you masturbate?" then the question "How often do you masturbate" is "Not applicable." On other questions it is not always as clear why the item is considered not applicable, but we wanted to differentiate the "Not applicable" category from the more general "No Response" category.

Additional dimensions which are analyzed for some of the questions are: sexually active vs. sexually inactive, married vs. unmarried, and age groups (60–69, 70–79, and over-80). On these tables only the adjusted figures are reported.

251

We did not score Questions 3, 8, and 47, but rather used the responses to these questions qualitatively and impressionistically to cast light on the older person's concept of sex. The responses to these questions were very varied and individual, not easily falling into scoreable categories.

Statistics giving the descriptive characteristics of our population of 800 older adults are presented in Tables 51–60.

TABLE 1. WHAT IS A GOOD SEXUAL EXPERIENCE?

CATEGORY	TOTALS		MALES		FEMALES	
	All Subjects	Adjusted*	All Subjects	Adjusted	All Subjects	Adjusted
Orgasm	520 (64.9%)	(70.1%)	187 (66.3%)	(71.4%)	333 (64.3%)	(69.4%)
Intercourse	115 (14.4)	(15.5)	32 (11.3)	(12.2)	83 (16.0)	(17.3)
Oral Sex	7 (0.9)	(0.9)	3 (1.1)	(1.1)	4 (0.8)	(0.8)
Love	52 (6.5)	(7.0)	19 (6.7)	(7.3)	33 (6.4)	(6.9)
Other	48 (6.0)	(6.5)	21 (7.5)	(8.0)	27 (5.2)	(5.6)
Not Applicable	6 (0.7)		0		6 (1.2)	
No Response	52 (6.6)		20 (7.1)		32 (6.2)	
Total Responses	800		282		518	

*Percentages adjusted for those who actually responded to each question.

TABLE 2. HOW DOES SEX FEEL NOW COMPARED WITH WHEN YOU WERE YOUNGER?

CATEGORY	TOTALS		MALES		FEMALES	
	All Subjects	Adjusted	All Subjects	Adjusted	All Subjects	Adjusted
Better	255 (31.9%)	(35.7%)	74 (26.2%)	(27.1%)	181 (35.0%)	(41.0%)
Same	277 (34.6)	(38.8)	102 (36.2)	(37.4)	175 (33.8)	(39.7)
Worse	182 (22.7)	(25.5)	97 (34.4)	(35.5)	85 (16.4)	(19.3)
Not Applicable	39 (4.9)		3 (1.1)		36 (6.9)	
No Response	47 (5.9)		6 (2.1)		41 (7.9)	
Total Responses	800		282		518	

QUESTION 3. "WHAT DO YOU THINK IS AN IDEAL SEX LIFE FOR OLDER PEOPLE?"

Note: Not scored. Material used qualitatively.

TABLE 4. WHAT IN THE SEX ACT IS MOST IMPORTANT TO YOU?

CATEGORY	TOTALS		MALES		FEMALES	
	All Subjects	Adjusted	All Subjects	Adjusted	All Subjects	Adjusted
Orgasm	322 (40.2%)	(43.6%)	133 (47.2%)	(49.6%)	189 (36.5%)	(40.1%)
Foreplay	196 (24.5)	(26.5)	62 (22.0)	(23.1)	134 (25.7)	(28.5)
Love	121 (15.1)	(16.4)	30 (10.6)	(11.2)	91 (17.6)	(19.3)
Intercourse	63 (7.9)	(8.5)	26 (9.2)	(9.7)	37 (7.2)	(7.9)
Satisfying Partner	37 (4.6)	(5.0)	17 (6.0)	(6.3)	20 (3.9)	(4.2)
Not Applicable	7 (0.9)		0		7 (1.4)	
No Response	54 (6.7)		14 (5.0)		40 (7.7)	
Total Responses	800		282		518	

TABLE 5. DO YOU LIKE SEX?

CATEGORY	TOTALS		MALES		FEMALES	
	All Subjects	Adjusted	All Subjects	Adjusted	All Subjects	Adjusted
Yes	765 (95.6%)	(97.1%)	275 (97.5%)	(99.3%)	490 (94.6%)	(95.9%)
No	23 (2.9)	(2.9)	2 (0.7)	(0.7)	21 (4.0)	(4.1)
No Response	12 (1.5)		5 (1.8)		7 (1.4)	
Total Responses	800		282		518	

TABLE 5A. DO YOU LIKE SEX?
(ADJUSTED FREQUENCIES FOR AGE GROUPS)

CATEGORY	60-69			70-79			80-91		
	Total	Male	Female	Total	Male	Female	Total	Male	Female
Yes	443 (97.4%)	154 (99.4%)	289 (96.3%)	265 (97.4%)	97 (100%)	168 (96.0%)	57 (93.4%)	24 (96.0%)	33 (91.7%)
No	12 (2.6)	1 (0.6)	11 (3.7)	7 (2.6)	0 (0)	7 (4.0)	4 (6.6)	1 (4.0)	3 (8.3)
Total Responses	455	155	300	272	97	175	61	25	36

TABLE 6. HOW OFTEN WOULD YOU LIKE TO HAVE SEXUAL RELATIONS IF YOU COULD WHENEVER YOU WANTED TO?

CATEGORY	TOTALS		MALES		FEMALES	
	All Subjects	Adjusted	All Subjects	Adjusted	All Subjects	Adjusted
When in the Mood	99 (12.4%)	(13.3%)	24 (8.5%)	(8.8%)	75 (14.5%)	(15.9%)
Three Times a Week or More	194 (24.2)	(26.1)	101 (35.8)	(36.8)	93 (17.9)	(19.8)
Twice a Week	164 (20.5)	(22.0)	64 (22.7)	(23.4)	100 (19.3)	(21.3)
Once a Week	171 (21.4)	57 (23.0)	114 (20.2)	(20.8)	(22.0)	(24.3)
Three Times a Month	5 (0.6)	(0.7)	2 (0.7)	(0.7)	3 (0.6)	(0.6)
Twice a Month	36 (4.5)	(4.8)	14 (5.0)	(5.1)	22 (4.2)	(4.7)
Once a Month	37 (4.6)	(5.0)	6 (2.1)	(2.2)	31 (6.0)	(6.6)
Less than Once a Month	31 (3.9)	(4.2)	5 (1.8)	(1.8)	26 (5.0)	(5.5)
Never	7 (0.9)	(0.9)	1 (0.4)	(0.4)	6 (1.2)	(1.3)
No Response	56 (7.0)		8 (2.8)		48 (9.3)	
Total Responses	800		282		518	

Note: Average frequency per week: 1.83 (total population)
2.04 (males)
1.69 (females)
(See Table 21 for method of computation.)

TABLE 6A. HOW OFTEN WOULD YOU LIKE TO HAVE SEXUAL RELATIONS IF YOU COULD WHENEVER YOU WANTED TO? (ADJUSTED FREQUENCIES FOR SEXUALLY ACTIVE AND INACTIVE)

CATEGORY	SEXUALLY ACTIVE			SEXUALLY INACTIVE		
	All Subjects	Male	Female	All Subjects	Male	Female
When in the Mood	64 (11.8%)	20 (8.3%)	44 (14.5%)	23 (18.9%)	1 (5.3%)	22 (21.4%)
Three Times a Week or More	160 (29.5)	92 (38.3)	68 (22.4)	15 (12.3)	3 (15.8)	12 (11.7)
Twice a Week	127 (23.4)	57 (23.8)	70 (23.1)	22 (18.0)	4 (21.1)	18 (17.5)
Once a Week	118 (21.7)	47 (19.6)	71 (23.4)	33 (27.0)	7 (36.8)	26 (25.2)
Three Times a Month	4 (0.7)	2 (0.8)	2 (0.7)	1 (0.8)	0 (0.0)	1 (1.0)
Twice a Month	24 (4.4)	12 (5.0)	12 (4.0)	7 (5.7)	2 (10.5)	5 (4.8)
Once a Month	24 (4.4)	4 (1.7)	20 (6.6)	8 (6.6)	2 (10.5)	6 (5.8)
Less than Once a Month	21 (3.9)	5 (2.1)	16 (5.3)	8 (6.6)	0 (0.0)	8 (7.8)
Never	1 (0.2)	1 (0.4)	0 (0.0)	5 (4.1)	0 (0.0)	5 (4.8)
Total Responses	543	240	303	122	19	103

Note: Average frequency per week for sexually active:
    1.91 (total population)
    2.07 (males)
    1.76 (females)
Average frequency per week for sexually inactive:
    1.49 (total population)
    1.44 (males)
    1.51 (females)
(See Table 21 for method of computation)

TABLE 6B. HOW OFTEN WOULD YOU LIKE TO HAVE SEXUAL RELATIONS IF YOU COULD WHENEVER YOU WANTED TO? (ADJUSTED FREQUENCIES FOR AGE GROUP)

CATEGORY	60-69			70-79			80-91		
	Total	Male	Female	Total	Male	Female	Total	Male	Female
When in the Mood	57 (13.0%)	16 (10.3%)	41 (14.5%)	35 (14.0%)	7 (7.2%)	28 (18.3%)	7 (13.2%)	1 (4.5%)	6 (19.3%)
Three Times a Week or More	127 (29.0)	66 (42.6)	61 (21.6)	59 (23.6)	30 (30.9)	29 (19.0)	7 (13.2)	5 (22.7)	2 (6.5)
Twice a Week	102 (23.3)	38 (24.5)	64 (22.6)	54 (21.6)	22 (22.7)	32 (20.9)	7 (13.2)	4 (18.2)	3 (9.7)
Once a Week	93 (21.3)	25 (16.1)	68 (24.0)	61 (24.4)	25 (25.8)	36 (23.5)	17 (32.1)	7 (31.8)	10 (32.2)
Three Times a Month	1 (0.2)	1 (0.6)	0	4 (1.6)	1 (1.0)	3 (2.0)	0	0	0
Twice a Month	19 (4.3)	5 (3.2)	14 (4.9)	12 (4.8)	6 (6.2)	6 (3.9)	4 (7.5)	3 (13.6)	1 (3.2)
Once a Month	18 (4.1)	2 (1.3)	16 (5.7)	12 (4.8)	2 (2.1)	10 (6.5)	7 (13.2)	2 (9.1)	5 (16.1)
Less than Once a Month	17 (3.9)	1 (0.6)	16 (5.7)	12 (4.8)	4 (4.1)	8 (5.2)	2 (3.8)	0	2 (6.5)
Never	4 (0.9)	1 (0.6)	3 (1.1)	1 (0.4)	0 (0.0)	1 (0.7)	2 (3.8)	0	2 (6.5)
Total Responses	438	155	283	250	97	153	53	22	31

TABLE 7. (EVALUATION OF) HOW DO YOU THINK SEX AFFECTS THE HEALTH OF OLDER PEOPLE?

CATEGORY	TOTALS		MALES		FEMALES	
	All Subjects	Adjusted	All Subjects	Adjusted	All Subjects	Adjusted
Positive	610 (76.3%)	(80.3%)	210 (74.5%)	(77.8%)	400 (77.2%)	(81.6%)
Negative	28 (3.5)	(3.7)	12 (4.25)	(4.4)	16 (3.1)	(3.3)
No Effect	122 (15.2)	(16.0)	48 (17.0)	(17.8)	74 (14.3)	(15.1)
Not Applicable	4 (0.5)		0		4 (0.8)	
No Response	36 (4.5)		12 (4.25)		24 (4.6)	
Total Responses	800		282		518	

QUESTION 8. "WHAT DOES IT MEAN TO BE A SEXY PERSON?"

Note: Not scored. Material used qualitatively.

TABLE 9. HOW IMPORTANT IS ORGASM OR CLIMAX IN YOUR SEXUAL EXPERIENCES?

CATEGORY	TOTALS		MALES		FEMALES	
	All Subjects	Adjusted	All Subjects	Adjusted	All Subjects	Adjusted
Very Important	510 (63.8%)	(66.5%)	198 (70.2%)	(72.5%)	312 (60.2%)	(63.2%)
Somewhat Important	209 (26.1)	(27.2)	65 (23.0)	(23.8)	144 (27.8)	(29.1)
Not Important	48 (6.0)	(6.3)	10 (3.5)	(3.7)	38 (7.3)	(7.7)
Not Applicable	4 (0.5)		1 (0.4)		3 (0.6)	
No Response	29 (3.6)		8 (2.8)		21 (4.1)	
Total Responses	800		282		518	

TABLE 10. HOW IMPORTANT IS TOUCHING AND CUDDLING IN YOUR SEXUAL EXPERIENCES?

CATEGORY	TOTALS		MALES		FEMALES	
	All Subjects	Adjusted	All Subjects	Adjusted	All Subjects	Adjusted
Very Important	642 (80.2%)	(84.0%)	232 (82.3%)	(84.1%)	410 (79.2%)	(84.0%)
Somewhat Important	105 (13.1)	(13.8)	40 (14.2)	(14.5)	65 (12.5)	(13.3)
Not Important	17 (2.1)	(2.2)	4 (1.4)	(1.4)	13 (2.5)	(2.7)
Not Applicable	3 (0.4)		0		3 (0.6)	
No Response	33 (4.1)		6 (2.1)		27 (5.2)	
Total Responses	800		282		518	

TABLE 10.5. HAS THIS CHANGED OVER THE YEARS? (TOUCHING AND CUDDLING)

CATEGORY	TOTALS		MALES		FEMALES	
	All Subjects	Adjusted	All Subjects	Adjusted	All Subjects	Adjusted
More Important	150 (18.8%)	(20.8%)	52 (18.4%)	(19.8%)	98 (18.9%)	(21.4%)
Same	526 (65.7)	(73.0)	191 (67.7)	(72.6)	335 (64.7)	(73.1)
Less Important	45 (5.6)	(6.2)	20 (7.1)	(7.6)	25 (4.8)	(5.5)
Not Applicable	6 (0.7)		1 (0.4)		5 (1.0)	
No Response	73 (9.1)		18 (6.4)		55 (10.6)	
Total Responses	800		282		518	

TABLE 11. WHAT KIND OF PRE-INTERCOURSE FOREPLAY (KISSING, TOUCHING, ETC.) DO YOU LIKE BEST?

CATEGORY	TOTALS		MALES		FEMALES	
	All Subjects	Adjusted	All Subjects	Adjusted	All Subjects	Adjusted
Kissing/Touching	415 (51.9%)	(54.5%)	139 (49.3%)	(50.0%)	275 (53.1%)	(57.1%)
Everything	161 (20.1)	(21.2)	70 (24.8)	(25.2)	91 (17.5)	(18.8)
Genital/Erogenous	138 (17.3)	(18.1)	57 (20.2)	(20.5)	81 (15.6)	(16.8)
Body Contact	27 (3.4)	(3.5)	7 (2.5)	(2.5)	20 (3.9)	(4.2)
Other	10 (1.2)	(1.3)	2 (0.7)	(0.7)	8 (1.5)	(1.7)
None	10 (1.2)	(1.3)	3 (1.1)	(1.1)	7 (1.4)	(1.4)
Not Applicable	4 (0.5)		0		4 (0.8)	
No Response	35 (4.4)		4 (1.4)		32 (6.2)	
Total Responses	800		282		518	

TABLE 12. DO YOU GET EXCITED LOOKING AT
SEXY PICTURES, BOOKS, OR MOVIES?

CATEGORY	TOTALS		MALES		FEMALES	
	All Subjects	Adjusted	All Subjects	Adjusted	All Subjects	Adjusted
Yes	485 (60.6%)	(62.2%)	210 (74.5%)	(75.0%)	275 (53.1%)	(55.0%)
No	295 (36.9)	(37.8)	70 (24.8)	(25.0)	225 (43.4)	(45.0)
Not Applicable	2 (0.2)		0		2 (0.4)	
No Response	18 (2.2)		2 (0.7)		16 (3.1)	
Total Responses	800		282		518	

TABLE 13. WHAT PART SHOULD SEX PLAY WHEN A COUPLE
GETS MARRIED OR REMARRIED IN LATER LIFE?

CATEGORY	TOTALS		MALES		FEMALES	
	All Subjects	Adjusted	All Subjects	Adjusted	All Subjects	Adjusted
Large Part	320 (40.0%)	(51.6%)	128 (45.4%)	(55.7%)	192 (37.1%)	(49.2%)
Some Part	291 (36.4)	(46.9)	98 (34.8)	(42.6)	193 (37.3)	(49.5)
No Part	9 (1.1)	(1.5)	4 (1.4)	(1.7)	5 (1.0)	(1.3)
Not Applicable	57 (7.1)		21 (7.4)		36 (6.9)	
No Response	123 (15.4)		31 (11.0)		92 (17.7)	
Total Responses	800		282		518	

TABLE 13.5 HOW DOES SEX DIFFER FROM AN EARLIER MARRIAGE?

CATEGORY	TOTALS		MALES		FEMALES	
	All Subjects	Adjusted	All Subjects	Adjusted	All Subjects	Adjusted
Better	166 (20.7%)	(30.9%)	58 (20.6%)	(30.0%)	108 (20.8%)	(31.3%)
Same	303 (37.9)	(56.3)	109 (38.7)	(56.5)	194 (37.5)	(56.2)
Worse	69 (8.6)	(12.8)	26 (9.2)	(13.5)	43 (8.3)	(12.5)
Not Applicable	87 (10.9)		32 (11.3)		55 (10.6)	
No Response	175 (21.9)		57 (20.2)	(22.8)	118	
Total Responses	800		282		518	

TABLE 14. MANY OLDER PEOPLE MASTURBATE TO RELIEVE SEXUAL TENSIONS. WHAT DO YOU THINK ABOUT THIS?

CATEGORY	TOTALS		MALES		FEMALES	
	All Subjects	Adjusted	All Subjects	Adjusted	All Subjects	Adjusted
Accept	606 (75.8%)	(81.9%)	200 (70.9%)	(76.3%)	406 (78.4%)	(84.9%)
Reject	134 (16.8)	(18.1)	62 (22.0)	(23.7)	72 (13.9)	(15.1)
Not Applicable	6 (0.7)		2 (0.7)		4 (0.8)	
No Response	54 (6.7)		18 (6.4)		36 (6.9)	
Total Responses	800		282		518	

TABLE 15. DO YOU MASTURBATE?

CATEGORY	TOTALS		MALES		FEMALES	
	All Subjects	Adjusted	All Subjects	Adjusted	All Subjects	Adjusted
Yes	345 (43.1%)	(45.9%)	119 (42.2%)	(43.6%)	226 (43.6%)	(47.0%)
No	407 (50.9)	(54.1)	152 (53.9)	(56.1)	255 (49.2)	(53.0)
No Response	48 (6.0)		11 (3.9)		37 (7.2)	
Total Responses	800		282		518	

TABLE 15.5. HOW OFTEN? (DO YOU MASTURBATE?)

CATEGORY	TOTALS		MALES		FEMALES	
	All Subjects	Adjusted	All Subjects	Adjusted	All Subjects	Adjusted
When in the Mood	64 (8.0%)	(19.7%)	20 (7.1%)	(17.8%)	44 (8.5%)	(20.6%)
Three Times a Week or More	14 (1.8)	(4.3)	10 (13.5)	(8.9)	4 (0.8)	(1.9)
Twice a Week	28 (3.5)	(8.6)	14 (4.6)	(12.6)	14 (2.7)	(6.6)
Once a Week	30 (3.8)	(9.2)	8 (2.8)	(7.1)	22 (4.2)	(10.3)
Three Times a Month	5 (0.6)	(1.5)	1 (0.4)	(0.9)	4 (0.8)	(1.9)
Twice a Month	33 (4.1)	(10.2)	15 (5.3)	(13.4)	18 (3.5)	(8.5)
Once a Month	66 (8.2)	(20.3)	18 (6.4)	(16.1)	48 (9.2)	(22.5)
Less than Once a Month	85 (10.6)	(26.2)	26 (9.2)	(23.2)	59 (11.4)	(27.7)
Not Applicable	371 (46.4)		137 (48.6)		234 (45.2)	
No Response	104 (13.0)		33 (53.6)		71 (13.7)	
Total Responses	800		282		518	

TABLE 15A. DO YOU MASTURBATE?
(ADJUSTED FREQUENCIES BY MARITAL STATUS)

CATEGORY	MARRIED			WIDOWED		
	Total	Male	Female	Total	Male	Female
Yes	141 (39.4%)	69 (40.1%)	72 (38.7%)	127 (46.5%)	25 (43.9%)	102 (47.2%)
No	217 (60.6)	103 (59.9)	114 (61.3)	146 (53.5)	32 (56.1)	114 (52.8)
Total Responses	358	172	186	273	57	216

CATEGORY	DIVORCED			SINGLE		
	Total	Male	Female	Total	Male	Female
Yes	55 (63.2%)	16 (57.1%)	39 (66.1%)	22 (75.9%)	9 (69.2%)	13 (81.2%)
No	32 (36.8)	12 (42.9)	20 (33.9)	7 (24.1)	4 (30.8)	3 (18.8)
Total Responses	87	28	59	29	13	16

TABLE 15B. DO YOU MASTURBATE?
(ADJUSTED FREQUENCIES FOR AGE GROUPS)

CATEGORY	60-69			70-79			80-91		
	Total	Male	Female	Total	Male	Female	Total	Male	Female
Yes	217 (49.0%)	80 (52.6%)	137 (47.1%)	107 (41.8%)	28 (29.5%)	79 (49.1%)	21 (39.6%)	11 (45.8%)	10 (34.5%)
No	226 (51.0)	72 (47.4)	154 (52.9)	149 (58.2)	67 (70.5)	82 (50.9)	32 (60.4)	13 (54.2)	19 (65.5)
Total Responses	443	152	291	256	95	161	53	24	29

TABLE 16. WHAT MAKES YOU FEEL MOST EXCITED DURING LOVEMAKING?

CATEGORY	TOTALS		MALES		FEMALES	
	All Subjects	Adjusted	All Subjects	Adjusted	All Subjects	Adjusted
Foreplay	351 (43.9%)	(49.4%)	131 (46.5%)	(49.8%)	220 (42.5%)	(49.1%)
Intercourse	64 (8.0)	(9.0)	27 (9.6)	(10.3)	37 (7.1)	(8.3)
Orgasm	99 (12.4)	(13.9)	41 (14.5)	(15.6)	58 (11.2)	(12.9)
Everything	80 (10.0)	(11.3)	30 (10.6)	(11.4)	50 (9.7)	(11.2)
Caring/Love	63 (7.9)	(8.9)	15 (5.3)	(5.7)	48 (9.3)	(10.7)
Oral Sex	28 (3.5)	(3.9)	12 (4.3)	(4.6)	16 (3.1)	(3.6)
Nothing	12 (1.5)	(1.7)	3 (1.1)	(1.1)	9 (1.7)	(2.0)
Other	14 (1.7)	(2.0)	4 (1.4)	(1.5)	10 (1.9)	(2.2)
Not Applicable	9 (1.1)		2 (0.7)		7 (1.3)	
No Response	80 (10.0)		17 (6.0)		63 (12.2)	
Total Responses	800		282		518	

TABLE 17. WHAT ABOUT SEX EMBARRASSES YOU THE MOST?

CATEGORY	TOTALS		MALES		FEMALES	
	All Subjects	Adjusted	All Subjects	Adjusted	All Subjects	Adjusted
Nothing	405 (50.6%)	(57.2%)	147 (52.2%)	(57.0%)	258 (49.8%)	(57.3%)
Nudity/Body	61 (7.6)	(8.6)	10 (3.5)	(3.9)	51 (9.8)	(11.3)
Erection Problem	44 (5.5)	(6.2)	38 (13.5)	(14.7)	6 (1.2)	(1.3)
Unconventional	40 (5.0)	(5.7)	7 (2.5)	(2.7)	33 (6.4)	(7.4)
Messy/Smell	22 (2.7)	(3.1)	10 (3.5)	(3.9)	12 (2.3)	(2.7)
Other	136 (17.0)	(19.2)	46 (16.3)	(17.8)	90 (17.4)	(20.0)
Not Applicable	2 (0.3)		0		2 (0.4)	
No Response	90 (11.3)		24 (8.5)		66 (12.7)	
Total Responses	800		282		518	

TABLE 18. SOME PEOPLE SAY THAT INTERCOURSE IS NOT THE MOST IMPORTANT PART OF SEX. HOW DO YOU FEEL ABOUT THIS?

CATEGORY	TOTALS		MALES		FEMALES	
	All Subjects	Adjusted	All Subjects	Adjusted	All Subjects	Adjusted
Disagree	391 (48.9%)	(51.6%)	165 (58.5%)	(61.1%)	226 (43.6%)	(46.4%)
Agree	311 (38.9)	(41.1)	90 (31.9)	(33.3)	221 (42.7)	(45.4)
Intercourse Plus	55 (6.9)	(7.3)	15 (5.3)	(5.6)	40 (7.7)	(8.2)
Not Applicable	6 (0.7)		3 (1.1)		3 (0.6)	
No Response	37 (4.6)		9 (3.2)		28 (5.4)	
Total Responses	800		282		518	

TABLE 19. HOW HAS SEX CHANGED SINCE THE MENOPAUSE (CHANGE OF LIFE)?

CATEGORY	TOTALS		MALES		FEMALES	
	All Subjects	Adjusted	All Subjects	Adjusted	All Subjects	Adjusted
Better	249 (31.1%)	(38.9%)	48 (17.0%)	(29.6%)	201 (38.8%)	(42.1%)
No Change	282 (35.3)	(44.1)	68 (24.1)	(42.0)	214 (41.3)	(44.7)
Worse	109 (13.6)	(17.0)	46 (16.3)	(28.4)	63 (12.2)	(13.2)
Not Applicable	70 (8.7)		63 (22.3)		7 (1.3)	
No Response	90 (11.2)		57 (20.2)		33 (6.4)	
Total Responses	800		282		518	

TABLE 20. DO SEXUAL EXPERIENCES LEAVE YOU SATISFIED?

CATEGORY	TOTALS		MALES		FEMALES	
	All Subjects	Adjusted	All Subjects	Adjusted	All Subjects	Adjusted
Yes	526 (65.7%)	(71.7%)	217 (77.0%)	(81.6%)	309 (59.7%)	(66.0%)
Sometimes	168 (21.0)	(22.9)	40 (14.2)	(15.0)	128 (24.7)	(27.4)
No	40 (5.0)	(5.4)	9 (3.2)	(3.4)	31 (6.0)	(6.6)
Not Applicable	8 (1.0)		1 (0.4)		7 (1.3)	
No Response	58 (7.3)		15 (5.2)		43 (8.3)	
Total Responses	800		282		518	

TABLE 20.5. WHAT DO YOU DO WHEN YOU ARE NOT SATISFIED?

CATEGORY	TOTALS		MALES		FEMALES	
	All Subjects	Adjusted	All Subjects	Adjusted	All Subjects	Adjusted
Nothing	191 (23.9%)	(39.9%)	52 (18.4%)	(31.7%)	139 (26.8%)	(44.3%)
Masturbate	95 (11.9)	(19.9)	27 (9.6)	(16.5)	68 (13.1)	(21.6)
Frustration/Anger	85 (10.6)	(17.8)	27 (9.6)	(16.5)	58 (11.2)	(18.5)
Seduce/Continue Trying	85 (10.6)	(17.8)	53 (18.8)	(32.3)	32 (6.2)	(10.2)
Diversionary Activity	22 (2.8)	(4.6)	5 (1.8)	(3.0)	17 (3.3)	(5.4)
Not Applicable	160 (20.0)		65 (23.0)		95 (18.3)	
No Response	162 (20.2)		53 (18.8)		109 (21.1)	
Total Responses	800		282		518	

TABLE 21. HOW OFTEN DO YOU HAVE SEXUAL RELATIONS?

CATEGORY	TOTALS		MALES		FEMALES	
	All Subjects	Adjusted	All Subjects	Adjusted	All Subjects	Adjusted
When in the Mood	43 (5.4%)	(6.1%)	17 (6.0%)	(6.5%)	26 (5.0%)	(5.9%)
Three Times a Week or More	85 (10.6)	(12.1)	39 (13.8)	(14.9)	46 (8.9)	(10.4)
Twice a Week	93 (11.6)	(13.2)	43 (15.2)	(16.5)	50 (9.6)	(11.3)
Once a Week	129 (16.1)	18.3	61 (21.6)	(23.4)	68 (13.1)	(15.4)
Three Times a Month	7 (0.9)	(1.0)	3 (1.1)	(1.1)	4 (0.8)	(0.9)
Twice a Month	57 (7.1)	(8.1)	23 (8.2)	(8.8)	34 (6.6)	(7.7)
Once a Month	69 (8.6)	(9.8)	29 (10.3)	(11.1)	40 (7.8)	(9.0)
Less than Once a Month	70 (8.8)	(10.0)	27 (9.6)	(10.3)	43 (8.3)	(9.7)
Not Active	150 (18.8)	(21.3)	19 (6.7)	(7.3)	131 (25.2)	(29.6)
No Response	97 (12.1)		21 (7.5)		76 (14.7)	
Total Responses	800		282		518	

Note: Computation of average frequency of intercourse for total group that reported a specific frequency.

A Times per Week	B Number of Respondents	C A x B
3X week	85	255
2X week	93	186
1X week	129	129
3X month (.75X week)	7	5.25
2X month (.5X week)	57	28.50
1X month (.25X week)	69	17.25
	440	621.00

Average frequency per week: $621/440 = 1.40$ (total population)
1.44 (males)
$(1.39$ (females)

TABLE 21A. HOW OFTEN DO YOU HAVE SEXUAL RELATIONS? (ADJUSTED FREQUENCIES FOR AGE GROUPS)

CATEGORY	60-69			70-79			80-91		
	Total	Male	Female	Total	Male	Female	Total	Male	Female
When in the Mood	26 (6.2%)	9 (5.8%)	17 (6.5%)	15 (6.2%)	7 (7.6%)	8 (5.4%)	2 (4.0%)	1 (5.0%)	1 (3.3%)
Three Times a Week or More	57 (13.7)	27 (17.5)	30 (11.4)	24 (10.0)	10 (10.9)	14 (9.4)	4 (8.0)	2 (10.0)	2 (6.7)
Twice a Week	65 (15.6)	28 (18.2)	37 (14.1)	28 (11.6)	15 (16.3)	13 (8.7)	0	0	0
Once a Week	85 (20.4)	36 (23.4)	49 (18.6)	36 (14.9)	20 (21.7)	16 (10.7)	8 (16.0)	5 (25.0)	3 (10.0)
Three Times a Month	6 (1.4)	3 (1.9)	3 (1.1)	1 (0.4)	0	1 (0.7)	0	0	0
Twice a Month	30 (7.2)	10 (6.5)	20 (7.6)	23 (9.55)	10 (10.9)	13 (8.7)	4 (8.0)	3 (15.0)	1 (3.3)
Once a Month	40 (9.6)	20 (13.0)	20 (7.6)	25 (10.4)	8 (8.7)	17 (11.4)	4 (8.0)	1 (5.0)	3 (10.0)
Less than Once a Month	39 (9.4)	10 (6.5)	29 (11.2)	23 (9.55)	12 (13.0)	11 (7.4)	8 (16.0)	5 (25.0)	3 (10.0)
Not Active	69 (16.5)	11 (7.2)	58 (22.1)	66 (27.4)	10 (10.9)	56 (37.6)	20 (40.0)	3 (15.0)	17 (56.7)
Total Responses	417	154	263	241	92	149	50	20	30

TABLE 22. DOES SEXUAL INTERCOURSE GIVE YOU ANY PAIN OR DISCOMFORT?

CATEGORY	TOTALS		MALES		FEMALES	
	All Subjects	Adjusted	All Subjects	Adjusted	All Subjects	Adjusted
No	642 (80.3%)	(86.4%)	243 (86.2%)	(91.4%)	399 (77.0%)	(83.6%)
Yes	68 (8.5)	(9.2)	15 (5.3)	(5.6)	53 (10.2)	(11.1)
Sometimes	33 (4.1)	(4.4)	8 (2.8)	(3.0)	25 (4.8)	(5.3)
Not Applicable	8 (1.0)		2 (0.7)		6 (1.2)	
No Response	49 (6.1)		14 (5.0)		35 (6.8)	
Total Responses	800		282		518	

TABLE 23. HOW DO YOU FEEL ABOUT OLDER MEN AND WOMEN WITHOUT PARTNERS GOING TO PROSTITUTES TO RELIEVE SEXUAL NEEDS?

CATEGORY	TOTALS		MALES		FEMALES	
	All Subjects	Adjusted	All Subjects	Adjusted	All Subjects	Adjusted
Approve	504 (63.0%)	(67.8%)	196 (69.5%)	(74.0%)	308 (59.5%)	(64.4%)
Disapprove	239 (29.9)	(32.2)	69 (24.5)	(26.0)	170 (32.8)	(35.6)
No Response	57 (7.1)		17 (6.0)		40 (7.7)	
Total Responses	800		282		518	

TABLE 24. HOW LONG DOES THE SEX ACT USUALLY LAST?

CATEGORY	TOTALS		MALES		FEMALES	
	All Subjects	Adjusted	All Subjects	Adjusted	All Subjects	Adjusted
2 Minutes or Less	36 (4.5%)	(7.0%)	21 (7.4%)	(9.7%)	15 (2.9%)	(5.0%)
3-15 Minutes	161 (20.1)	(31.1)	72 (25.5)	(33.2)	89 (17.2)	(29.7)
16-30 Minutes	143 (17.9)	(27.7)	56 (19.9)	(25.8)	87 (16.8)	(29.0)
More than 30 Minutes	107 (13.4)	(20.7)	44 (15.6)	(20.3)	63 (12.2)	(21.0)
Varies	70 (8.7)	(13.5)	24 (8.5)	(11.1)	46 (8.9)	(15.3)
Not Applicable	15 (1.9)		1 (0.4)		14 (2.7)	
No Response	268 (33.5)		64 (22.7)		204 (39.3)	
Total Responses	800		282		518	

TABLE 24.5 HOW DOES THIS [DURATION] COMPARE WITH WHEN YOU WERE YOUNGER?

CATEGORY	TOTALS		MALES		FEMALES	
	All Subjects	Adjusted	All Subjects	Adjusted	All Subjects	Adjusted
Same	220 (27.5%)	(39.0%)	75 (26.6%)	(34.9%)	145 (28.0%)	(41.5%)
Longer	219 (27.4)	(38.8)	97 (34.4)	(45.1)	122 (23.6)	(35.0)
Shorter	125 (15.6)	(22.2)	43 (15.2)	(20.0)	82 (15.8)	(23.5)
Not Applicable	21 (2.6)		3 (1.1)		18 (3.5)	
No Response	215 (26.9)		64 (22.7)		151 (29.1)	
Total Responses	800		282		518	

TABLE 25. HOW DOES YOUR PARTNER KNOW WHAT YOU LIKE IN SEX?

CATEGORY	TOTALS		MALES		FEMALES	
	All Subjects	Adjusted	All Subjects	Adjusted	All Subjects	Adjusted
Talk	323 (40.4%)	(49.8%)	122 (43.2%)	(51.9%)	201 (38.8%)	(48.7%)
Assumes	206 (25.7)	(31.8)	81 (28.7)	(34.5)	125 (24.1)	(30.3)
Show	64 (8.0)	(9.9)	16 (5.7)	(6.8)	48 (9.3)	(11.6)
Doesn't Know	55 (6.9)	(8.5)	16 (5.7)	(6.8)	39 (7.5)	(9.4)
Not Applicable	22 (2.7)		5 (1.8)		17 (3.3)	
No Response	130 (16.3)		42 (14.9)		88 (17.0)	
Total Responses	800		282		518	

TABLE 26. DESCRIBE THE IDEAL LOVER OF YOUR FANTASY.

CATEGORY	TOTALS		MALES		FEMALES	
	All Subjects	Adjusted	All Subjects	Adjusted	All Subjects	Adjusted
60 Plus	223 (27.9%)	(32.2%)	46 (16.3%)	(19.0%)	177 (34.2%)	(39.3%)
Middle Aged (45-59)	90 (11.2)	(13.0)	28 (9.9)	(11.6)	62 (12.0)	(13.8)
30-44	36 (4.5)	(5.2)	20 (7.1)	(8.3)	16 (3.1)	(3.6)
20-29	13 (1.6)	(1.9)	9 (3.2)	(3.7)	4 (0.8)	(0.9)
Teenager	3 (0.4)	(0.4)	3 (1.1)	(1.2)	0 (0.0)	(0.0)
Young Person	30 (3.7)	(4.3)	20 (7.1)	(8.3)	10 (1.9)	(2.2)
No Age Named/ Ageless	218 (27.3)	(31.5)	92 (32.6)	(38.0)	126 (24.3)	(28.0)
Celebrity	23 (2.9)	(3.3)	4 (1.4)	(1.6)	19 (3.7)	(4.2)
No Fantasy	56 (7.0)	(8.1)	20 (7.1)	(8.3)	36 (6.9)	(8.0)
No Response	108 (13.5)		40 (14.2)		68 (13.1)	
Total Responses	800		282		518	

TABLE 27. WHY DO YOU THINK THAT SOME OLDER PEOPLE DO NOT HAVE SEXUAL RELATIONS AS OFTEN AS THEY WOULD LIKE TO?

CATEGORY	TOTALS		MALES		FEMALES	
	All Subjects	Adjusted	All Subjects	Adjusted	All Subjects	Adjusted
No Partner Available	194 (24.3%)	(28.1%)	52 (18.4%)	(21.3%)	142 (27.4%)	(31.8%)
Poor Health	172 (21.5)	(25.0)	64 (22.7)	(26.2)	108 (20.9)	(24.2)
Impotence	41 (5.1)	(5.9)	19 (6.7)	(7.8)	22 (4.3)	(4.9)
No Desire	92 (11.5)	(13.3)	38 (13.5)	(15.6)	54 (10.4)	(12.1)
Sex Inappropriate for Older People	151 (18.9)	(21.8)	57 (20.2)	(23.4)	94 (18.1)	(21.0)
Other	41 (5.1)	(5.9)	14 (5.0)	(5.7)	27 (5.2)	(6.0)
No Response	109 (13.6)		38 (13.5)		71 (13.7)	
Total Responses	800		282		518	

TABLE 28. WHO DO YOU THINK IS MORE INTERESTED IN SEX, THE OLDER MAN OR THE OLDER WOMAN?

CATEGORY	TOTALS		MALES		FEMALES	
	All Subjects	Adjusted	All Subjects	Adjusted	All Subjects	Adjusted
Older Man	336 (42.0%)	(47.0%)	111 (39.4%)	(43.5%)	225 (43.4%)	(48.9%)
Older Woman	149 (18.6)	(20.8)	56 (19.9)	(22.0)	93 (18.0)	(20.2)
Both/No Difference	230 (28.8)	(32.2)	88 (31.2)	(34.5)	142 (27.4)	(30.9)
No Response	85 (10.6)		27 (9.6)		58 (11.2)	
Total Responses	800		282		518	

TABLE 29. HOW DO YOU FEEL ABOUT OLDER PEOPLE WHO ARE NOT MARRIED HAVING SEXUAL RELATIONS OR LIVING TOGETHER?

CATEGORY	TOTALS		MALES		FEMALES	
	All Subjects	Adjusted	All Subjects	Adjusted	All Subjects	Adjusted
Approve	700 (87.5%)	(91.1%)	255 (90.4%)	(95.1%)	445 (85.9%)	(89.0%)
Disapprove	68 (8.5)	(8.9)	13 (4.6)	(4.9)	55 (10.6)	(11.0)
No Response	32 (4.0)		14 (5.0)		18 (3.5)	
Total Responses	800		282		518	

TABLE 30. IT IS SAID THAT OLDER PEOPLE HAVE MORE TIME ON THEIR HANDS. HOW DOES THIS AFFECT SEX?

CATEGORY	TOTALS		MALES		FEMALES	
	All Subjects	Adjusted	All Subjects	Adjusted	All Subjects	Adjusted
Positive Effect	292 (36.5%)	(45.5%)	105 (37.2%)	(44.7%)	187 (36.1%)	(45.9%)
No Effect	292 (36.5)	(45.5)	109 (38.7)	(46.4)	183 (35.3)	(45.0)
Negative Effect	58 (7.3)	(9.0)	21 (7.4)	(8.9)	37 (7.1)	(9.1)
Not Applicable	25 (3.1)		9 (3.2)		16 (3.1)	
No Response	133 (16.6)		38 (13.5)		95 (18.4)	
Total Responses	800		282		518	

TABLE 31. IN THE LATER YEARS THERE ARE MORE WOMEN THAN MEN. HOW CAN OLDER WOMEN DEAL WITH THIS?

CATEGORY	TOTALS		MALES		FEMALES	
	All Subjects	Adjusted	All Subjects	Adjusted	All Subjects	Adjusted
Diversionary Activities	235 (29.4%)	(35.9%)	45 (16.0%)	(20.8%)	190 (36.7%)	(43.3%)
Find Partner	167 (20.9)	(25.5)	82 (29.1)	(38.0)	85 (16.4)	(19.3)
Nothing	74 (9.3)	(11.3)	19 (6.7)	(8.8)	55 (10.6)	(12.5)
Masturbate	68 (8.5)	(10.4)	20 (7.1)	(9.3)	48 (9.3)	(10.9)
Maverick Arrangements	65 (8.1)	(9.9)	30 (10.6)	(13.9)	35 (6.7)	(8.0)
Get Younger Lover	22 (2.7)	(3.4)	11 (3.9)	(5.1)	11 (2.1)	(2.5)
Friend/Companion	24 (3.0)	(3.6)	3 (1.1)	(1.4)	15 (2.9)	(3.5)
No Response	145 (18.1)		66 (23.4)		79 (15.3)	
Total Responses	800		282		518	

TABLE 32. HOW CAN OLDER PEOPLE DEAL WITH THEIR SEXUAL FEELINGS IF THEY ARE NOT MARRIED OR IF THEY DO NOT HAVE PARTNERS?

CATEGORY	TOTALS		MALES		FEMALES	
	All Subjects	Adjusted	All Subjects	Adjusted	All Subjects	Adjusted
Diversionary Activities	238 (29.7%)	(35.9%)	48 (17.0%)	(20.7%)	190 (36.7%)	(44.1%)
Find Partner	173 (21.6)	(26.0)	94 (33.4)	(40.5)	79 (15.2)	(18.2)
Masturbate	171 (21.4)	(25.8)	57 (20.2)	(24.6)	114 (22.0)	(26.5)
Nothing	52 (6.5)	(7.8)	17 (6.0)	(7.3)	35 (6.7)	(8.1)
Maverick Arrangements	26 (3.3)	(3.9)	15 (5.3)	(6.5)	11 (2.1)	(2.5)
Get Younger Lover	4 (0.5)	(0.6)	1 (0.4)	(0.4)	3 (0.6)	(0.7)
Not Applicable	13 (1.6)		4 (1.4)		9 (1.7)	
No Response	123 (15.4)		46 (16.3)		77 (14.9)	
Total Responses	800		282		518	

TABLE 33. WHAT ABOUT SEX DO YOU LIKE THE LEAST?

CATEGORY	TOTALS		MALES		FEMALES	
	All Subjects	Adjusted	All Subjects	Adjusted	All Subjects	Adjusted
Nothing	245 (30.6%)	(38.5%)	110 (39.0%)	(45.8%)	135 (26.1%)	(34.1%)
Insensitive Lover	115 (14.4)	(18.1)	31 (11.0)	(12.9)	84 (16.2)	(21.2)
Mess	100 (12.5)	(15.7)	35 (12.4)	(14.6)	65 (12.5)	(16.4)
Unconventional Acts	35 (4.4)	(5.5)	8 (2.8)	(3.3)	27 (5.2)	(6.8)
Other	141 (17.6)	(22.2)	56 (19.9)	(23.3)	85 (16.4)	(21.5)
Not Applicable	6 (0.8)		1 (0.4)		5 (1.0)	
No Response	158 (19.7)		41 (14.5)		117 (22.6)	
Total Responses	800		282		518	

TABLE 34. WHAT DO YOU THINK OF WHILE YOU ARE MAKING LOVE?

CATEGORY	TOTALS		MALES		FEMALES	
	All Subjects	Adjusted	All Subjects	Adjusted	All Subjects	Adjusted
Doing It/Sensations	399 (49.9%)	(56.5%)	129 (45.7%)	(49.4%)	270 (52.1%)	(60.7%)
Person I'm With	153 (19.1)	(21.7)	74 (26.2)	(28.4)	79 (15.3)	(17.8)
Fantasy	72 (9.0)	(10.2)	27 (9.6)	(10.3)	45 (8.7)	(10.1)
Nothing	48 (6.0)	(6.8)	23 (8.2)	(8.8)	25 (4.8)	(5.6)
Abstract Diversionary	34 (4.2)	(4.8)	8 (2.8)	(3.1)	26 (5.0)	(5.8)
Not Applicable	7 (0.9)		0		7 (1.4)	
No Response	87 (10.9)		21 (7.4)		66 (12.7)	
Total Responses	800		282		518	

TABLE 35. WHO USUALLY BEGINS THE LOVEMAKING, YOU OR YOUR PARTNER?

CATEGORY	TOTALS		MALES		FEMALES	
	All Subjects	Adjusted	All Subjects	Adjusted	All Subjects	Adjusted
Man Does	434 (54.2%)	(59.2%)	159 (56.4%)	(59.5%)	275 (53.1%)	(59.0%)
Woman Does	63 (7.9)	(8.6)	28 (9.9)	(10.5)	35 (6.8)	(7.5)
Either or	236 (29.5)	(32.2)	80 (28.4)	(30.0)	156 (30.1)	(33.5)
Not Applicable	13 (1.6)		3 (1.1)		10 (1.9)	
No Response	54 (6.7)		12 (4.3)		42 (8.1)	
Total Responses	800		282		518	

TABLE 36. WHAT HAPPENS WHEN YOU ARE IN THE MOOD AND YOUR PARTNER IS NOT?

CATEGORY	TOTALS		MALES		FEMALES	
	All Subjects	Adjusted	All Subjects	Adjusted	All Subjects	Adjusted
Never Happens	126 (15.8%)	(17.8%)	35 (12.4%)	(13.4%)	91 (17.6%)	(20.4%)
Nothing/Sleep	326 (40.8)	(46.1)	143 (50.7)	(54.6)	183 (35.3)	(41.1)
Seduce	182 (22.7)	(25.7)	50 (17.7)	(19.1)	132 (25.5)	(29.7)
Quarrel/Anger/ Fight	38 (4.7)	(5.4)	20 (7.1)	(7.6)	18 (3.5)	(4.1)
Masturbate	19 (2.4)	(2.7)	11 (3.9)	(4.2)	8 (1.5)	(1.8)
Diversionary Activity	16 (2.0)	(2.3)	3 (1.1)	(1.1)	13 (2.5)	(2.9)
Not Applicable	15 (1.9)		1 (0.4)		14 (2.7)	
No Response	78 (9.7)		19 (6.7)		59 (11.4)	
Total Responses	800		282		518	

TABLE 37. HOW OFTEN DO YOU REACH CLIMAX OR ORGASM WHEN MAKING LOVE?

CATEGORY	TOTALS		MALES		FEMALES	
	All Subjects	Adjusted	All Subjects	Adjusted	All Subjects	Adjusted
Always	288 (36.0%)	(43.8%)	135 (47.9%)	(53.8%)	153 (29.5%)	(37.7%)
Most of the Time	214 (26.8)	(32.6)	76 (27.0)	(30.3)	138 (26.7)	(34.0)
Sometimes	144 (18.0)	(21.9)	35 (12.4)	(13.9)	109 (21.0)	(26.8)
Never	11 (1.4)	(1.7)	5 (1.8)	(2.0)	6 (1.2)	(1.5)
Not Applicable	18 (2.2)		4 (1.4)		14 (2.7)	
No Response	125 (15.6)		27 (9.6)		98 (18.9)	
Total Responses	800		282		518	

TABLE 37A. HOW OFTEN DO YOU REACH ORGASM IN YOUR SEXUAL EXPERIENCES? (ADJUSTED FREQUENCIES BY AGE GROUPS)

CATEGORY	60-69			70-79			80-91		
	Total	Male	Female	Total	Male	Female	Total	Male	Female
Always	169 (42.4%)	84 (57.5%)	85 (33.7%)	105 (48.4%)	42 (49.4%)	63 (47.7%)	14 (33.3%)	9 (45.0%)	5 (22.7%)
Most of the Time	133 (33.4)	43 (29.5)	90 (35.7)	65 (30.0)	27 (31.8)	38 (28.8)	16 (38.1)	6 (30.0)	10 (45.5)
Sometimes	91 (22.9)	18 (12.3)	73 (29.0)	42 (19.3)	13 (15.3)	29 (22.0)	11 (26.2)	4 (20.0)	7 (31.8)
Never	5 (1.3)	1 (0.7)	4 (1.6)	5 (2.3)	3 (3.5)	2 (1.5)	1 (2.4)	1 (5.0)	0 (0)
Total Responses	398	146	252	217	85	132	42	20	22

TABLE 37B. HOW OFTEN DO YOU REACH ORGASM IN YOUR SEXUAL EXPERIENCES? (ADJUSTED FREQUENCIES FOR SEXUALLY ACTIVE AND INACTIVE)

	ACTIVE			INACTIVE		
	Total	Male	Female	Total	Male	Female
Always	240 (47.0%)	126 (56.0%)	114 (39.9%)	24 (26.4%)	2 (15.4%)	22 (28.2%)
Most	165 (32.3)	68 (30.2)	97 (33.9)	31 (34.0)	6 (46.2)	25 (32.0)
Sometimes	99 (19.4)	28 (12.4)	71 (24.8)	32 (35.2)	3 (23.1)	29 (37.2)
Never	7 (1.3)	3 (1.3)	4 (1.4)	4 (4.4)	2 (15.4)	2 (2.6)
Total Responses	511	225	286	91	13	78

TABLE 37.5. HOW DOES THIS COMPARE
WITH WHEN YOU WERE YOUNGER?

CATEGORY	TOTALS		MALES		FEMALES	
	All Subjects	Adjusted	All Subjects	Adjusted	All Subjects	Adjusted
Better	96 (12.0%)	(15.1%)	17 (6.0%)	(7.0%)	79 (15.3%)	(20.0%)
Same	434 (54.2)	(68.0)	175 (62.1)	(72.0)	259 (50.0)	(65.6)
Worse	108 (13.5)	(16.9)	51 (18.1)	(21.0)	57 (11.0)	(14.4)
Not Applicable	18 (2.3)		3 (1.1)		15 (2.9)	
No Response	144 (18.0)		36 (12.8)		108 (21.8)	
Total Responses	800		282		518	

TABLE 38. DO YOU TALK ABOUT SEX WITH YOUR PARTNER?

CATEGORY	TOTALS		MALES		FEMALES	
	All Subjects	Adjusted	All Subjects	Adjusted	All Subjects	Adjusted
Yes	459 (57.4%)	(68.2%)	176 (62.4%)	(70.1%)	283 (54.7%)	(67.0%)
No	214 (26.7)	(31.8)	75 (26.6)	(29.9)	139 (26.8)	(33.0)
Not Applicable	15 (1.9)		6 (2.1)		9 (1.7)	
No Response	112 (14.0)		25 (8.9)		87 (16.8)	
Total Responses	800		282		518	

Note: Responses to the second part of the question "What part of the sexual experience do you discuss?" were general and not scored. More specific responses on communication were eclicited in answers to other questions.

TABLE 39. HOW DO YOU FEEL ABOUT BEING NUDE WITH YOUR PARTNER?

CATEGORY	TOTALS		MALES		FEMALES	
	All Subjects	Adjusted	All Subjects	Adjusted	All Subjects	Adjusted
Like/Positive	579 (72.4%)	(80.9%)	226 (80.1%)	(87.3%)	353 (68.1%)	(77.2%)
Don't Like/Negative	137 (17.1)	(19.1)	33 (11.7)	(12.7)	104 (20.1)	(22.8)
Not Applicable	6 (0.7)		2 (0.7)		4 (0.8)	
No Response	78 (9.8)		21 (7.4)		57 (11.0)	
Total Responses	800		282		518	

TABLE 39.5. HAS THIS (ATTITUDE TOWARDS NUDITY) CHANGED OVER THE YEARS?

CATEGORY	TOTALS		MALES		FEMALES	
	All Subjects	Adjusted	All Subjects	Adjusted	All Subjects	Adjusted
Yes	150 (18.8%)	(21.7%)	39 (13.8%)	(15.1%)	111 (21.4%)	(25.8%)
No	540 (67.5)	(78.3)	220 (78.0)	(84.9)	320 (61.8)	(74.2)
Not Applicable	12 (1.5)		4 (1.4)		8 (1.5)	
No Response	98 (12.3)		19 (6.7)		79 (15.3)	
Total Responses	800		282		518	

TABLE 39A. HOW DO YOU FEEL ABOUT BEING NUDE WITH YOUR PARTNER?
(ADJUSTED FREQUENCIES FOR MARRIED AND UNMARRIED)

	MARRIED			UNMARRIED		
CATEGORY	TOTAL	MALE	FEMALE	TOTAL	MALE	FEMALE
Like/Positive	290 (82.6%)	147 (89.1%)	143 (76.9%)	289 (79%)	79 (84.0%)	210 (77.2%)
Don't Like/Negative	61 (17.4)	18 (10.9)	43 (23.1)	77 (21.0)	15 (16.0)	62 (22.8)
Total Responses	351	165	186	366	94	272

TABLE 40. IT IS SAID THAT OLDER MEN HAVE DIFFICULTY GETTING AN ERECTION. IS THIS TRUE IN YOUR EXPERIENCE?

CATEGORY	TOTALS		MALES		FEMALES	
	All Subjects	Adjusted	All Subjects	Adjusted	All Subjects	Adjusted
Yes	409 (51.1%)	(58.8%)	164 (58.2%)	(60.1%)	245 (47.3%)	(57.9%)
No	287 (35.9)	(41.2)	109 (38.7)	(39.9)	178 (34.4)	(42.1)
Not Applicable	13 (1.6)		0		13 (2.5)	
No Response	91 (11.4)		9 (3.2)		82 (15.8)	
Total Responses	800		282		518	

TABLE 40A. IT IS SAID THAT OLDER MEN HAVE DIFFICULTY GETTING AN ERECTION. IS THIS TRUE IN YOUR EXPERIENCE?
(ADJUSTED FREQUENCIES FOR AGE GROUPS)

CATEGORY	60-69			70-79			80-91		
	Total	Male	Female	Total	Male	Female	Total	Male	Female
Yes	232 (56.4%)	85 (55.9%)	147 (56.8%)	142 (60.4%)	61 (63.5%)	81 (58.3%)	35 (70.0%)	18 (72.0%)	17 (68.0%)
No	179 (43.6)	67 (44.1)	112 (43.2)	93 (39.6)	35 (36.5)	58 (41.7)	15 (30.0)	7 (28.0)	8 (32.0)
Total Responses	411	152	259	235	96	139	50	25	25

TABLE 41. HOW AND WHAT WERE YOU TAUGHT ABOUT SEX AS A CHILD?

CATEGORY	TOTALS		MALES		FEMALES	
	All Subjects	Adjusted	All Subjects	Adjusted	All Subjects	Adjusted
Positive	85 (10.6%)	(11.6%)	25 (8.9%)	(9.7%)	60 (11.6%)	(12.6%)
Negative	648 (81.0)	(88.4)	232 (82.3)	(90.3)	416 (80.3)	(87.4)
No Response	67 (8.3)		25 (8.9)		42 (8.1)	
Total Responses	800		282		518	

Note: These responses were scored enlightened, informative teachings (positive) and no teachings or frightening and distorted communications (negative).

TABLE 41.5. HOW AND WHAT DID YOU TEACH YOUR CHILDREN?

CATEGORY	TOTALS		MALES		FEMALES	
	All Subjects	Adjusted	All Subjects	Adjusted	All Subjects	Adjusted
Positive	356 (44.5%)	(54.2%)	107 (37.9%)	(47.6%)	249 (48.1%)	(57.6%)
Negative	223 (27.9)	(33.9)	92 (32.6)	(40.9)	131 (25.3)	(30.3)
No Children	78 (9.7)	(11.9)	26 (9.2)	(11.6)	52 (10.0)	(12.1)
No Response	143 (17.9)		57 (20.2)		86 (16.6)	
Total Responses	800		282		518	

TABLE 42. HOMOSEXUALITY SEEMS MUCH MORE OPEN THESE DAYS. HOW DO YOU FEEL ABOUT IT?

CATEGORY	TOTALS		MALES		FEMALES	
	All Subjects	Adjusted	All Subjects	Adjusted	All Subjects	Adjusted
Accept	471 (58.9%)	(63.8%)	153 (54.3%)	(58.6%)	318 (61.4%)	(66.7%)
Reject	267 (33.4)	(36.2)	108 (38.3)	(41.4)	159 (30.7)	(33.3)
No Response	62 (7.7)		21 (7.4)		41 (7.9)	
Total Responses	800		282		518	

TABLE 43. WHAT CAN A COUPLE DO WHEN THE MAN IS UNABLE TO HAVE AN ERECTION?

CATEGORY	TOTALS		MALES		FEMALES	
	All Subjects	Adjusted	All Subjects	Adjusted	All Subjects	Adjusted
Other Stimulation	315 (39.4%)	(47.7%)	117 (41.5%)	(48.0%)	198 (38.2%)	(47.6%)
Nothing	155 (19.4)	(23.5)	57 (20.2)	(23.4)	98 (18.9)	(23.6)
Professional Help	117 (14.6)	(17.7)	32 (11.3)	(13.1)	85 (16.4)	(20.4)
Oral Sex	73 (9.1)	(11.1)	38 (13.5)	(15.6)	35 (6.8)	(8.4)
Not Applicable	13 (1.6)		4 (1.4)		9 (1.7)	
No Response	127 (15.9)		34 (12.1)		93 (18.0)	
Total Responses	800		282		518	

TABLE 44. HOW DO YOU FEEL ABOUT OLDER MEN HAVING YOUNGER LOVERS?

CATEGORY	TOTALS		MALES		FEMALES	
	All Subjects	Adjusted	All Subjects	Adjusted	All Subjects	Adjusted
Approve	642 (80.2%)	(86.4%)	235 (83.3%)	(90.0%)	407 (78.6%)	(84.4%)
Disapprove	101 (12.6)	(13.6)	26 (9.2)	(10.0)	75 (14.5)	(15.6)
No Response	57 (7.1)		21 (7.4)		36 (6.9)	
Total Responses	800		282		518	

TABLE 44.5 HOW DO YOU FEEL ABOUT OLDER WOMEN HAVING YOUNGER LOVERS?

CATEGORY	TOTALS		MALES		FEMALES	
	All Subjects	Adjusted	All Subjects	Adjusted	All Subjects	Adjusted
Approve	611 (76.4%)	(82.6%)	198 (70.2%)	(77.0%)	413 (79.7%)	(85.5%)
Disapprove	129 (16.1)	(17.4)	59 (20.9)	(23.0)	70 (13.5)	(14.5)
No Response	60 (7.5)		25 (8.9)		35 (6.8)	
Total Responses	800		282		518	

TABLE 45. DOES SEX CHANGE AFTER RETIREMENT? HOW?

CATEGORY	TOTALS		MALES		FEMALES	
	All Subjects	Adjusted	All Subjects	Adjusted	All Subjects	Adjusted
Same	384 (48.0%)	(59.6%)	138 (49.0%)	(58.2%)	246 (47.5%)	(60.5%)
Better	154 (19.2)	(23.9)	55 (19.5)	(23.2)	99 (19.1)	(24.3)
Worse	106 (13.2)	(16.5)	44 (15.6)	(18.6)	62 (12.0)	(15.2)
Not Applicable	50 (6.3)		14 (5.0)		36 (6.9)	
No Response	106 (13.3)		31 (11.0)		75 (14.5)	
Total Responses	800		282		518	

TABLE 46. WOULD YOU LIKE TO TRY NEW SEXUAL EXPERIENCES THAT YOU HAVE HEARD ABOUT, READ ABOUT, OR THOUGHT ABOUT?

CATEGORY	TOTALS		MALES		FEMALES	
	All Subjects	Adjusted	All Subjects	Adjusted	All Subjects	Adjusted
Yes	281 (35.1%)	(38.7%)	132 (46.8%)	(51.2%)	149 (28.7%)	(31.8%)
No	387 (48.3)	(53.3)	103 (36.5)	(39.8)	284 (54.8)	(60.7)
No, Did Everything	58 (7.2)	(8.0)	23 (8.2)	(8.9)	35 (6.8)	(7.5)
No Response	74 (9.2)		24 (8.6)		50 (9.7)	
Total Responses	800		282		518	

TABLE 46.5. EXPLAIN (WHAT SEXUAL EXPERIENCES)

CATEGORY	TOTALS		MALES		FEMALES	
	All Subjects	Adjusted	All Subjects	Adjusted	All Subjects	Adjusted
Variety	165 (20.6%)	(77.8%)	83 (29.4%)	(83.8%)	82 (15.8%)	(72.6%)
More Freedom and Openness	32 (4.0)	(15.1)	10 (3.5)	(10.1)	22 (4.3)	(19.4)
More Partners	15 (1.9)	(7.1)	6 (2.2)	(6.1)	9 (1.7)	(8.0)
Not Applicable	391 (48.9)		113 (40.1)		278 (53.7)	
No Response	197 (24.6)		70 (24.8)		127 (24.5)	
Total Responses	800		282		518	

QUESTION 47. "WHEN IN YOUR LIFE WAS SEX BEST? WHY?"

Note: Not scored. Material used qualitatively. This question often produced responses not directly related to sex. Rather, respondents seemed to reflect upon life experiences in a more general way.

TABLE 48. HOW DO YOU THINK YOUR SEXUAL FEELINGS, ATTITUDES AND BEHAVIOR WILL CHANGE AS YOU GET OLDER?

CATEGORY	TOTALS		MALES		FEMALES	
	All Subjects	Adjusted	All Subjects	Adjusted	All Subjects	Adjusted
Same	458 (57.2%)	(66.4%)	151 (53.5%)	(60.9%)	307 (59.2%)	(69.4%)
Better	82 (10.2)	(11.9)	26 (9.2)	(10.5)	56 (10.8)	(12.7)
Worse	150 (18.8)	(21.7)	71 (25.2)	(28.6)	79 (15.3)	(17.9)
No Response	110 (13.8)		34 (12.1)		76 (14.7)	
Total Responses	800		282		518	

TABLE 49. LOOKING OVER YOUR SEX LIFE, PAST AND PRESENT, WHAT WOULD YOU WANT TO CHANGE?

CATEGORY	TOTALS		MALES		FEMALES	
	All Subjects	Adjusted	All Subjects	Adjusted	All Subjects	Adjusted
Nothing	363 (45.4%)	(49.9%)	132 (46.8%)	(51.4%)	231 (44.6%)	(49.2%)
Freer/More Experiences	232 (29.0)	(31.9)	88 (31.2)	(34.2)	144 (27.8)	(30.6)
Different Partner	65 (8.1)	(8.9)	20 (7.1)	(7.8)	45 (8.7)	(9.6)
Other	67 (8.4)	(9.2)	17 (6.0)	(6.6)	50 (9.6)	(10.6)
No Response	73 (9.1)		25 (8.9)		48 (9.3)	
Total Responses	800		282		518	

QUESTION 50. "IS THERE ANYTHING ABOUT SEX AND OLDER PEOPLE THAT WAS NOT COVERED IN THIS QUESTIONNAIRE? PLEASE FEEL FREE TO ADD OR COMMENT."

Note: Responses to this question were not scored. They were used to develop the final questionnaire by identifying the important areas of sexuality to investigate.

TABLE 51. AGE BREAKDOWN

	60-69			70-79			80-91	
Total	Male	Female	Total	Male	Female	Total	Male	Female
462	157 (34%)	305 (66%)	277	100 (36%)	177 (64%)	61	25 (41%)	36 (59%)

Note: Of the total population of 800, 462 = 57.8%, 277 = 34.6% and 61 = 7.6%.

TABLE 52. EDUCATION

	TOTAL	MALE	FEMALE
Elementary School	101 (12.6%)	40 (14.2%)	61 (11.8%)
Some High School	116 (14.5)	37 (13.1)	79 (15.3)
High School Graduate	152 (19.0)	44 (15.6)	108 (20.8)
Some College	196 (24.5)	70 (24.8)	126 (24.3)
College Graduate	134 (16.8)	43 (15.2)	91 (17.6)
Advanced Degree	98 (12.2)	47 (16.7)	51 (9.8)
No Response	3 (0.4)	1 (0.4)	2 (0.4)
Total Responses	800	282	518

TABLE 53. RELIGION

	TOTAL
Catholic	159 (19.9%)
Protestant	380 (47.5)
Jewish	208 (26.0)
Other	53 (6.6)
Total Responses	800

TABLE 54. HOW RELIGIOUS?

	TOTAL
Very Religious	87 (10.9%)
Moderately Religious	330 (41.3)
Somewhat Religious	189 (23.6)
Not Religious	194 (24.2)
Total Responses	800

TABLE 55. MARITAL STATUS

CATEGORY	TOTAL	MALE	FEMALE
Married	382 (47.8%)	180 (63.8%)	202 (39.0%)
Widowed	294 (36.7)	57 (20.2)	237 (45.7)
Divorced	91 (11.4)	29 (10.3)	62 (12.0)
Single	33 (4.1)	16 (5.7)	17 (3.3)
Total Responses	800	282	518

TABLE 56. HEALTH

	TOTAL
Excellent	203 (25.4%)
Good	376 (47.0)
Fair	199 (24.9)
Poor	22 (2.7)
Total Responses	800

TABLE 57. LIVING ARRANGEMENTS

	TOTAL
Live Alone	360 (45.0%)
Live with Spouse	373 (46.6)
Live with Children	25 (3.1)
Live with Relative	11 (1.4)
Live with Friend	31 (3.9)
Total Responses	800

TABLE 58. OCCUPATION

	TOTAL
A Profession	202 (25.3%)
Own Business	53 (6.6)
Office	86 (10.7)
Retail or Sales	39 (4.9)
Factory	28 (3.5)
Homemaker	209 (26.1)
Other	115 (14.4)
No Response	68 (8.5)
Total Responses	800

Note: Occupational identification on the face sheet of the questionnaire (see page 32) is loosely defined. Therefore, it is unclear, for example, how different respondents interpreted the term "profession."

TABLE 59. RETIRED? (EXCLUSIVE OF HOMEMAKER)

	TOTAL
Yes	373 (71.1%)
No	151 (28.9)
Total Responses	523

TABLE 60. REGION

	TOTAL
Northeast	377 (47.1%)
West and Northwest	219 (27.4)
Midwest	103 (12.9)
South and Southwest	101 (12.6)
Total Responses	800

References

Brewer, J. S., and Wright, R. W. 1979. *Sex research bibliographies from the Institute for Sex Research.* Phoenix, Arizona: Oryx Press.

Butler, R. N., and Lewis, M. I. 1977. *Love and sex after sixty.* New York: Harper and Row.

Chesler, P. 1979. *With child: a diary of motherhood.* New York: Thomas Y. Crowell.

Comfort, A. 1972. *The joy of sex.* New York: Crown.

——. 1975. *The more joy of sex.* New York: Crown.

Cowart, D. A.. and Pollack, R. H. 1979. "A Gutman Scale of Sexual Experience." *Journal of Sex Education and Therapy* 1:3–6.

Dahl, G. 1971. *Time, work and leisure.* New York: Christian Century Foundation.

Dally, P. 1975. *The fantasy game: how man's and woman's sexual fantasies affect our lives.* New York: Stein and Day.

Diagram Group. 1976. *Man's body: an owner's manual.* London/New York: Paddington Press.

——. 1977. *Woman's body: an owner's manual.* London/New York: Paddington Press.

Dodson, B. 1972. *Liberating masturbation.* Self published and distributed by Betty Dodson.

Easterlin, R. 1980. *Birth and fortune: the impact of numbers on personal welfare.* New York: Basic Books.

Eddy, G. S. 1932. *Sex and youth.* Garden City, New York: Doubleday, Doran and Co., Inc.

Finkle, A. L., et al. 1959. "Sexual potency in aging males. 1. frequency of coitus among clinic patients." *Journal of the American Medical Association* 170:1391–3.

Friedan, B. 1963. *The feminine mystique.* New York: W. W. Norton.
———. *The New York Times.* November 18, 1979.
Gelfand, D. E., and Kutzik, J., eds. 1979. *Ethnicity and aging.* New York: Springer Publishing.
Gochros, H. L., and Fischer, J. 1980. *Treat yourself to a better sex life.* Englewood Cliffs, New Jersey: Prentice-Hall, Inc.
Godbey, G., and Parker, S. 1976. *Leisure studies and services: an overview.* Philadelphia: Holt, Rinehart and Winston, Inc.
Graber, see Kline-Graber.
Greenbank, R. K. 1961. "Are medical students learning psychiatry?" *Pennsylvania Medical Journal* 64:989–992.
Hass, A. 1979. *Teenage Sexuality.* New York: Macmillan.
Heiman, J., LoPiccolo, L., and LoPiccolo, J. 1980. *Becoming orgasmic: a sexual growth program for women.* Englewood Cliffs, New Jersey: Prentice-Hall, Inc.
Hite, S. 1976. *The Hite report.* New York: Macmillan Publishing Co.
Hudson, R. B., and Binstock, R. H. 1976. "Political systems and aging." In R. H. Binstock and E. Shanas, eds. *Handbook of aging in the social sciences.* New York: Van Nostrand Reinhold Co.
Jarvik, L. F., ed. 1978. *Aging into the 21st century: middle agers today.* New York: Gardner Press.
Kaplan, H. S. 1974. *The new sex therapy.* New York: Brunner/Mazel.
———. 1979. *Disorders of sexual desire.* New York: Brunner/Mazel.

Kass, D. J. and Stauss, F. F. 1976. *Sex therapy at home.* New York: Simon & Schuster.
Kassorla, Irene. 1980. *Nice girls do, and now you can too!* Los Angeles: Stratford Press.
Kinsey, A. C., Pomeroy, B., and Martin, E. 1948. *Sexual behavior in the human male.* Philadelphia: W. B. Saunders Company.
———, 1953. *Sexual behavior in the human female.* Philadelphia: W. B. Saunders Company.
Klein, F. 1978. *The bisexual option.* New York: Arbor House.
Klein, R. L. 1972. "Age, sex and task difficulty as predictors of social conformity." *Journal of Gerontology* 27:229–236.
Kline-Graber, G., and Graber, B. 1975. *Women's orgasm: a guide to sexual satisfaction.* New York: Bobbs-Merrill Co., Inc.
Lief, H. I. 1974. "Sexual knowledge, attitudes and behavior of medical

students: implications for medical practice." In D. W. Abse and L. M. R. Louden, eds. *Marital and sexual counseling in medical practice.* New York: Harper and Row.

LoPiccolo, J., and LoPiccolo, L., eds. 1978. *Handbook of sex therapy.* New York: Plenum Press.

Luce, G. G. 1979. *Your second life: vitality and growth in middle and later years.* New York: Delacorte Press.

McCarthy, B. 1977. *What you still don't know about male sexuality.* New York: Thomas Y. Crowell.

Masters, W. H., and Johnson, V. E. 1966. *Human sexual response.* Boston: Little, Brown and Company.

———. 1970. *Human sexual inadequacy.* Boston: Little, Brown and Company.

———. 1970. *The pleasure bond.* Boston: Little, Brown and Company.

Mayer, N. 1978. *The male mid-life crisis.* New York: Doubleday.

Meyerhoff, B. 1968. *Number our days.* New York: E. P. Dutton.

Milsten, R. 1979. *Male sexual function: myth, fantasy and reality.* New York: Avon Books.

Moss, M. S., and Lawton, P. M. "Use of time in different types of households." Unpublished paper presented at the 33rd annual meeting of the American Gerontological Society, San Diego, California, November 1980.

Neugarten, B. L. 1974. "Age groups in American society and the rise of the young-old." *Annals of the American Academy,* Sept. 1974:187–198.

Newman, G. and Nichols, C. R. 1960. "Sexual activities and attitudes in older persons." *Journal of the American Medical Association* 173:33–35.

Nudel, A. 1978. *For the woman over 50: a practical guide for a full and vital life.* New York: Taplinger.

Pfeiffer, E. 1969. "Sexual behavior in old age." In E. W. Busse and E. Pfeiffer, eds. *Behavior and adaptation in late life.* Boston: Little, Brown and Company.

Pfeiffer, E., Verwoerdt, A., and Wang H., 1968. "Sexual behavior in aged men and women. 1. Observations on 254 community volunteers." *Archives of General Psychiatry* 19:753–758.

Pietropinto, A., and Simenauer, J. 1977. *Beyond the male myth.* New York: Times Books.

Plutchik, R., Conte, H., and Weiner, M. B. 1973. "Studies of body image. II. dollar values of body parts." *Journal of Gerontology* 28, 1:89–91.

Pocs, O., Godow, A., Tolone, W. L., and Walsh, R. H. 1977. "Is there sex after 40?" *Psychology Today,* June 1977, p. 54.

Rabushka, A., and Jacobs, B. 1980. *Old folks at home.* New York: Free Press.

Robinson, P. 1976. *The modernization of sex.* New York: Harper and Row.

Rosenbaum, M. 1981. "Vibrators—today's love toy." *Mademoiselle,* January 1981, p. 92.

Rubin, I. 1965. *Sexual life after sixty.* New York: Basic Books.

Seaman, B., and Seaman, G. 1977. *Women and the crisis in sex hormones.* New York: Rawson.

Sedwick, R. 1975. "Myths in human sexuality." *Nursing Clinics of North America* 10:539–550.

Sheehy, G. 1976. *Passages.* New York: E. P. Dutton.

Sherfy, M. J. 1973. *The nature and evolution of female sexuality.* New York: Random House, Vintage Books.

Talese, G. 1980. *Thy neighbor's wife.* New York: Doubleday.

Tavris, C. and Sadd, S. 1977. *The Redbook report on female sexuality.* New York: Delacorte Press.

Terkel, S. 1974. *Working: people talk about what they do and how they feel about what they do.* New York: Pantheon.

U.S. Senate. 1976. *Report of the longterm care subcommittee of the special committee on the aging.* Washington, D.C.: Government Printing Office.

Wagenvoord, J., ed. 1978. *Men: a book for women.* New York: Avon.
———. 1979. *Women: a book for men.* New York: Avon.

Weinberg, M. S., ed. 1976. *Sex research: studies from the Kinsey Institute.* New York: Oxford University Press.

Winkler, B. 1979. "Aging: How to fight it, hide it, cope with it." *Family Circle.* July 17, 1979, p. 88.

Wolfe, L. 1980. "The sexual profile of that Cosmopolitan girl." *Cosmopolitan.* September 1980, p. 254.

Index